At last, a book that uses plain language and good common sense for those of us who have taken a wrong turn on life's rocky road. This author offers us practical solutions from her experience while reminding us of the additional support we find in God's unconditional love.

—BOB AND VALERIE BLOEMINK

This book helped me to understand the baggage I have carried into my eighties from my abusive childhood and how it has affected the life choices I have made. It has given me the tools I need to help me to live a richer life. I will read it over and over to absorb all the wisdom it contains.

—LOU HEFFERNAN

A JOURNEY TO

JOY

A JOURNEY TO

JOY

13 Steps To Heal
Your Self-esteem

VICTORIA O'KANE

Cover design by Lindsay B. Behrens
Interior design by Leah LeFlore

Published in the United States of America

ISBN: 9780692993248
1. Christian Self-Help   2. Self Esteem
07.09.07

DEDICATION

For my daughters, Katie and Laura, who have saved my life in ways they don't even know. For my husband, Mike, who came to me with love like I've never before known and inspired in me love like I've never before felt. For my family, especially Helene and Joe, without whose support and sacrifices my journey would never have begun, and most of all, for God, because of the truth in Romans 8:28.

CONTENTS

FOREWORD

Many people travel through life thinking that no one else really understands the anguished experiences of our private journeys. Their challenge and pain create a backroom of secrets, sucking it up and creating a façade of emotional health because our world chastises emotionally challenged people. We often go into hiding so that no one will really know the private suffering too painful to share, too agonizing to ignore, and too raw to uncover.

Henry David Thoreau wrote, "Most men live lives of quiet desperation and go to the grave with the song still in them." Oh, how blessed the world would be if we would carefully sing every note of the opera developing in us; the dissonance and the consonance, the conflict and resolution.

There is dynamic value in sharing not only the struggle, but also the road to recovery, healing and victory. Victoria O'Kane opens her life's journey for us to see. She has offered a glimpse into the journey of singing her personal life aria. She has skillfully performed her oratories of challenge, pain, and the road to healing for us to consider. Her experiences combined with her wordsmith abilities create a bridge to emotional growth and healing.

She comes alongside of the reader, and in ways only she can, helps the reader know someone has been there before and understands. Someone offers directions for the way out. God has joined her libretto and has truly brought blessing out of pain. Don't just read, sing along!

—REVEREND DR. STEVEN G. REDMOND

There is a phoenix
within us all.
We fear there is no way
to bear this
wave of sorrow.
Though it is so full
and swollen,
and in its rage
its power
knocks us to the ground
and heaps the debris
of grief upon us,
we shall rise up again.
And though our steps
will be slow
and troubled,
we shall walk
from the sea of pain.
We will dry our faces
in the sun.
There shall be
survival.

PROLOGUE

I once read somewhere that most people are aware of their fear of dying, but few are aware of their fear of living. These are people who have hopelessly confused comfort with happiness. They have settled for survival, existence, a life far short of joy. If you are trapped in feelings of mediocrity rather than joy, then you are among those who fear to live. Many of them may believe they have succeeded in life, but they may not have succeeded *at* life, for the true meaning of success is completely independent of the trappings our society associates with success.

Success does not depend on wealth. It is not achieved by a certain career choice or even a high level of power reached within that career. It does not come from anything that can be measured visibly: not money, not beauty, not fashion and not social status.

Success, true success, is simply being happy, deep down in your core happy. This kind of happiness cannot occur if you are not happy, first and foremost, with who you are. Circumstances are constantly changing in life. This is sometimes because of choices you make and sometimes due to things completely out of your control, but who you are and how you feel about who you are, is present at all times. Whether the circumstances are easy or difficult, desired or disastrous, you cannot escape yourself.

If you are happy with yourself it makes the challenges more bearable and leaves you much more capable of remaining happy during the hard times. It helps you to be able to discern between what is actually a crisis and what is merely an inconvenience. Confidence always creates a more accurate perception because those who possess it have the great comfort of knowing they can and will recover from life's difficulties. By the same measure, if you are not happy with who you are, no matter what is going great in your life, you will never be able to truly enjoy it because there are always these underlying feelings of pain and dissatisfaction. To make things worse, when you are unhappy with yourself every inconvenience feels like a crisis because without confidence we believe every setback in life can and will defeat us.

You may be unhappy with yourself because you are not seeing yourself clearly, but with a vision that has been warped by certain people or events in your life. If you could heal that warped vision and learn to see yourself for who you truly are, you would much more easily learn to love yourself and feel good about who you are.

There simply is no greater pain than that of self-loathing. It casts a pall over every single aspect of your life because it is the one thing you can never escape, no matter how you try to bury, hide, mask, or numb the feelings with any variety of distractions. If you feel shame, you will bring that shame with you everywhere. It is the pain of never feeling good enough.

This kind of pain runs through your life like a river. It cuts through the landscape of your life and separates who you are from who you are meant to be. It separates who you truly are from who you think you are.

I am here to help you to build a bridge across that river. You will read a brief synopsis of my life history. I wrote it because it illustrates one example of how life and people, even well intentioned people who love you, can erode your self-esteem and send messages that say you are not good enough, that you are not worthy of love.

I cannot erase a painful history, not mine and certainly not yours. What I can do is show you through the things I learned and applied in my journey to joy how to overcome that past and the pain it brings you even now. I can teach you how to cross that river and change behavior that is saturated with historical repetition and the habits that consistently bring about the same results. Even though they are often painful results, if they are familiar there exists a warped kind of comfort in them that contributes to the vicious cycle you may be locked in.

I can show you how to move yourself into behaving in fresh, new ways that can free you from those ruts and open the doors to tomorrow, allowing you to enter a world filled with hope, opportunity, and joy.

I cannot make you cross this bridge or walk through those open doors, only you can do that. I have tried with many over the past several years. Some have taken a few tentative steps on that journey. Some have taken many. Others have refused to move at all. They remain paralyzed by their fear of the unknown and their doubt that there is any hope for them. They are victims of the inertia that is so completely habitual that they simply cannot conceive of movement and of change. They do not recognize their own power and responsibility to do anything different and purposeful to create a better life for themselves.

This book is not guaranteed to radically change your whole life, but it can change how you feel about yourself, and consequently, how you live your life. It has been written to help you to discover in a personal, real, transforming way that you are worth fighting for and working on, and you are deserving of the life you have dreamed of having.

The changes may seem subtle at first. It will not, of course, give you a college degree for example, but it may help you to recognize your value and abilities, which could give you the courage to go and get that degree. That degree just may open up the door to a career doing something you deeply love, instead of settling for a job you can only tolerate, but keep out of necessity to get your bills paid. This book will not make "Prince Charming" ride up your driveway on a white horse to beg your hand in marriage, but it may help you to attract quality people instead of the losers that people of low self-esteem often attract.

If you already have a great career, it can help you to truly enjoy it by allowing you to feel deserving of the rewards it brings, rather than feeling afraid, incapable, or undeserving. It can help you to move past the fear of failure or the fear that someone will find out you are not really up to snuff.

If you're already fortunate enough to be in a relationship with a great person, it can help you to believe that you deserve that person's love. The healthy self-esteem this book can help you to gain can allow you to relax in a relationship, rather than constantly feeling that you may lose that person, or that you have to prove yourself. It may help you to stop constantly demanding that your partner prove his or her love for you.

This is all about helping you to see yourself as the wonderful, unique, lovable person that you are. It is based mainly on two truths. The first is that *what you choose to look at, determines also what you do not see.* The second is that *if you change your thoughts, you will change your feelings, and if you change your feelings, you will change your behavior, and if you change your behavior, you will change your life.*

I cannot encourage you strongly enough to begin your own journey to joy. Take the first step and begin reading this book with an open mind and a willing heart, and you will learn how to change the way you see yourself and ultimately how to change the way you feel about yourself.

It is an undeniable fact that part of the human condition is that all people need to feel loved and appreciated. When you feel that way about yourself, you receive a steady stream of love; your own love, love that is not dependent upon the moods or availability of anyone else. You are then able to build a life of joy for yourself where "if only" and "I should have" can be transformed into "dreams come true."

My life is living proof. When I was fifteen I dreamed of becoming a writer or a psychologist. When I was thirty I had no hope of ever accomplishing anything worthwhile in my life. Here in my forties I am fulfilling the purpose of both, even without a college degree. So join me on this journey to joy. Dare to become proactive and take responsibility for the quality of your life, because you and only you have the power to change it.

We are all fledgling explorers,
unfettered trail blazers
on the brink of the maiden voyages
of our spiritual expeditions.
We are all lifelong masons,
building our temples
out of the bricks life hands us
and those we choose with care.
We are all passionate revolutionaries
exercising unrehearsed heroics
certain to alter the destiny of our galaxy
or at least one person in it.
We are all God's angels.
We spin sugar dreams
into a cosmic choir.
We rejoice in the heavens
even when our access
appears to be remote,
even when the chorus of our lives
falls into a hush.
We are all sweet lovers, interwoven,
the kindlers of all levels
and manners of love,
the givers and takers
and the moonsingers of love.
We are all singular artists,
perhaps not master craftsmen,
but we sculpt our lives,
color our souls and scribe our futures
across all of our days.
We are all born full
of abundant and unlimited possibilities.
We are all frontiersmen.
We are all students
and we are all teachers.
We are all gifted
and we are all
extraordinary.

PART ONE

chapter one

EARLY CHILDHOOD

I wasn't exactly raised by June and Ward Cleaver, but I bet Wally and the Beav didn't live at your house either. That's not to say my parents were beating or raping me. They were just your average, run of the mill alcoholics. I grew up in the sixties in a classically dysfunctional home. Of course we didn't know it at the time. In fact, I don't believe the term "dysfunctional family" even existed back then, at least not in the familiar way we all recognize it now.

I am the youngest of three girls. We were the third generation of our family to be born in San Francisco. By the time I was born, my oldest sister was seven and had already lived at several different addresses in the city, none of them places you would really want to live in if you had some real options. We didn't.

I'm sure you've heard this story or one just like it from someone you know. God knows it's far too common. My dad drank too much, too often and for too long. He lost jobs on a fairly regular basis. That was one of the few things we could truly seem to count on. So we moved *a lot*. It's hard to pay the rent when you're out of work and it's hard to remain in a place where you're not paying the rent. By the time I left high school I was leaving the ninth school I had attended.

You've probably surmised by now that life in my home (wherever it was at the time) was pretty chaotic. That kind of chaos doesn't leave much time or energy for building the self-esteem of children, nor is it conducive to bonding and developing those close, loving relationships that teach trust, intimacy and the inherent value present in us all.

My sisters and I were fairly bonded in that "us against them" kind of way, but it did little to relieve my overwhelming sense of being isolated.

It's almost as though I could pinpoint
when my life broke down.
It's 1968.
Martini music wafts like a breeze
In the background.
It's Sinatra or Mancini
or Connie Francis.
There are record albums strewn
all about the Hi Fi.
They are drinking again,
maybe Manhattens,
or perhaps what they call high-balls.
We live in a rented
three bedroom tract home
and yet he drinks in a smoking jacket
and she smokes
through an overstated
and lengthy cigarette holder.
It's like a scene in some old movie
designed to depict
the glamour of Hollywood.
We are eight and ten and fifteen
and exiled to the family room
lest we disrupt their martini musings,
their dream drinking,

their perfect little drama
unfolding in the living room
as they each play the role
of a success,
of a couple cradled
in some opulent lap of living,
pretending they are not
always overdrawn,
that they do not
have these three daughters,
that there has not been
countless bars and other women
and lost jobs,
that there has been no jail
ever having penned our father in,
and no entry level job
waiting for our mother
to drag her hangover into tomorrow.
No they sit and nurse their drinks
and discuss trendy subjects,
politics and the space race,
like guests on the tonight show.
They compare the vocal styles
of Perry Como
and Andy Williams
while they float down
their own moon river.
They are so chic in that room,
so elegant, so sophisticated,
creations of their own longings,
willing victims
of their own denial,
while we watch re-runs
on an old black and white
and create our own fantasy,
a world where we
are not laughed at,

and wear
current fashion trends to school,
a world in which we live in a house
where home cooked meals
are eaten promptly at six in the dining room
every evening,
served by a tender mother
while jovial conversation
floats in the lamplight.
Yes, we pretend
we are not waiting for that ever dangling
other shoe to drop,
pretend that we do not wade through
muddy pools of anxiety,
certain of banging into
that next fight,
the one that always comes in
on the heels of one drink too many
and throws us up against the wall,
listening for juicy details
while simultaneously fighting back
the need to urinate,
desperately wanting to avoid
having to parade through
the battle zone
on our way to the bathroom.
We wait
for the volume to go down
on their voices
and up on the music,
trying to time our intrusion
so as to be less intrusive,
not daring to risk the wrath
being redirected at us,
knowing that if we can hold out long enough,
three drinks too many
will send them staggering,

> *oh so elegantly,*
> *to their bedroom*
> *and set us free*
> *to race to the bathroom*
> *and then the safety*
> *of our bedroom*
> *where we can float free*
> *down our own moon river*
> *of sleep,*
> *both as sisters*
> *and as huckleberry friends.*

It's not as though I got no attention. I did get some, but it was mostly because I was sickly and asthmatic and particularly susceptible to pneumonia. Oh, I got attention from kids at school too, but most of it was *not* the kind of attention you want. The attention I suffered from at school was the kind that only proved the willingness and uncanny creative ability that kids have to be cruel.

I was a skinny white girl with freckles and what was often referred to by some of those cruel kids as a "ski slope" nose (it turned up), wavy, yet stringy hair and a prominent, dark unibrow. Believe it or not, when I was really little, I was a pretty cute kid, but from the years of about six to thirteen or fourteen, I was hopelessly gawky. As if that weren't bad enough, I was always out of fashion.

My father's employment instability left little money for luxuries like current fashion trends and to add a little (or a lot of) insult to that injury, having moved out of San Francisco when I was five, I grew up in a succession of neighborhoods that were predominantly Hispanic and white kids were definitely not cool. Long, straight hair and big bustlines, were cool. I of course had been blessed with neither. Come to think of it, I still don't have either.

By the time I was nine, I guess my mother had finally had enough sleepless nights wondering if my father was in jail again or just with another woman, and kicked him out. He was gone for close to a year during which I can only recall having seen him a couple of times. No regular visitation for this divorced dad. Heck, we could never depend on when we'd see him while he did live with us, so it's certainly no surprise that he was undependable out on his own.

When I was ten we moved again and my mother took my father back. She didn't tell us that the reconciliation was only because he was dying of cancer, but then she never told us much of anything. When it came to information, she raised us like mushrooms. She kept us in the dark and fed us manure. Communication required real relationships and she was never really good at those.

Though he'd been in and out of the hospital, we were still not told he was dying, nor were we allowed to visit him when he was in the hospital until his last stay there. Finally, one Friday night we were told to put on something nice because we were going to the hospital to see our dad. I had no idea what to expect, but I can assure you I did not expect to see my father weighing only eighty-seven pounds.

I don't remember whatever awkward small talk took place, but I'll never forget him telling us that he was never coming home. Perhaps if I had been older I would have known immediately that his death was imminent. I might have figured it out even before that visit by picking up on all the signs. Even standing there in the hospital though, in my young mind I managed to glean a small spark of hope contrary to the cold, hard reality of his impending death. I remember asking him if that meant he would be spending the rest of his life there in the hospital. He would in fact be doing just that, but there was no mistaking the fact that I was hoping the rest of his life would be a normal life expectancy, not a life that would end at forty. Ironically that still seemed pretty old to me at the time.

It was explained to us then, really to me I suppose, that he was dying. We were almost immediately ushered out of the room after that, I guess so that we would not upset him with our pesky tears.

That night at home my mother suggested we write "goodbye" letters to him. I'm sure it was a suggestion made by a nurse or someone who thought it would help us cope. It dawned on me about a year ago that it would have been a lot more helpful if he had written "goodbye" letters to us. I don't remember him ever having told me that he loved me. He may have done it, but I don't remember it, so I find it hard to believe it could have been all that frequent or all that meaningful if it ever did happen. Anyway, it sure would have been nice to have had some tangible evidence of his love. It seems to me it would have been a rather prudent time for him to profess his love for us, but it didn't happen.

I was awakened by the ringing of the telephone at about five a.m. the next morning. It was the hospital calling to tell my mother that he had slipped into a coma and didn't have much time. As she was dressing to go to the hospital, I begged her to let me come with her, but she refused. It quickly became a moot point as shortly after that first call, came a second call from the hospital informing her that he had died or "passed away" if you prefer that term. (Personally, I don't see how using a slightly more cryptic term makes the reality of death any less harsh.)

Anyway, again, he was gone, and again I'd been abandoned, this time forever. I cried myself to sleep alone on the living room floor. I was eleven years old.

It was Saturday March 18, 1971. That Monday morning my mother sent me to school. I guess she thought that was what was best for me. Wrong again. It wasn't. It just so happened that there was a field trip scheduled for our sixth grade class that day, an event normally looked forward to by the whole class. My teacher gave me his condolences, although I don't know how he knew. The kids however greeted me with furtive glances and whispers. I soon overheard what they were whispering about. They were gossiping about the field trip being more important to me than my father. I've never forgotten how deeply that hurt me.

It didn't take long before my mother began dating. After all, she was a very beautiful woman. I had always been proud to introduce her because she wasn't old and fat like most of the other moms I knew.

Fortunately when I was only four years old my grandmother had moved in with our family to take care of us kids, so that my mother could be free to work to help provide some income during my father's "down times." This also freed her up to go out after my father died. Before long, my mother remarried. I was twelve years old.

It was about that time that I had become friends with the girl who sat next to me in my seventh grade class. I had been put in the geeky class with all the smart, but nerdy, kids. Looking back, I guess someone knew what they were doing when they made out that roster. I was clearly both.

After spending the previous year trying desperately to fit in with the cool kids in my former class, I just figured I was moved because I was a loser. The teasing and the humiliation and all those fist fights that I had lost because I had been too paralyzed with fear to really fight were proof enough to me of my grand "loserhood."

That class switch turned out to be the best thing that could have happened to me thanks to a seating arrangement that put me next to Julie. She was probably the first person I ever became truly close to, the first person I ever learned I could truly trust. She accepted me completely and allowed me to safely open up without fear of having things I confided get turned into ugly, public gossip that would be used against me.

We made daisy chains
in your backyard.
We learned to fall down
and even fall up
together.
We learned to
French kiss boys
at dark dances
in the same autumn.
We learned
to drive fast
and to fall in love
hard,
in the same summer.
We learned
how rare and precious
friendship like ours is.
But most importantly,

we learned how to trust
way back
when we were
exchanging secrets
in Cherry Grove park
and making daisy chains
in your backyard.
The greatest gift
God gave me
was your friendship.
The greatest gift
you gave me
was that trust.
Of course I love you,
as I have loved many,
but I trust you
as I have trusted
very few.

Within the safety of that precious friendship I began slowly developing a personality, an identity. When we got to junior high school that next fall I had learned to make other friends as well by using this goofy sense of humor that seemed to work for me.

I wore my father's old Levi jacket everyday and had started smoking Marlboro cigarettes as if I were cool. Compared to the nerds I hung out with I probably was. How sad is that?

Though my proficiency test scores in the seventh grade had reflected I could perform at upper high school and college grade levels, my grades sucked. But who cared? I had friends, at least until just after my thirteenth birthday when my mother and new stepfather bought a house in another town and I had to move again.

Goodbye, Julie. Goodbye, friends. Hello isolation. I had to start over, alone, again...

chapter two

EARLY TEENS

Ok, so you're probably not crying great big tears over my sad childhood. Sadder still, you're probably not laughing at this still goofy
sense of humor either. (Maybe it doesn't work for me after all, or
maybe it's just tough material.)

Anyway, life went on. I did make new friends and even began
to land some pretty hot boyfriends. Of course, I never wanted them
long after I discovered that they wanted me. I guess I suffered from
that "I wouldn't want to join a club that would have me as a member"
syndrome.

Julie and I did keep in touch through hours long phone conversations and occasional visits when we could get someone to drive us
to each other's house. Though we only lived fifteen minutes apart
by car, it sure wasn't the same as the few blocks that had separated
us before. We weren't attending the same school and were therefore
living different lives in different circles and to young teenagers their
social circles are the very epicenter of the universe.

As luck, fate, or God would have it, close to the end of my freshman year another freshman girl named Anne moved in next door to
me. Her family life was actually worse than mine was at the time. At
least since my mother had married a good, stable man (even though
he was fourteen years younger than her) things had calmed down in

my house and we were beginning to discover some stability, financially and emotionally. Well, at least as much emotional stability as you can expect in a house where two teenage girls live. My oldest sister, Katrina, had moved out and married her high school sweetheart John the September after my father died. That was just nine months before my mom married my stepfather, Bill. My other sister, Danni (short for Danielle), was only two years my senior and was of course still at home. At last we had our own bedrooms and for the first time in our lives were not sharing one.

Danni and I were as opposite as two girls could be. I was wild and rebellious, and she was kind of prim and proper. To illustrate the differences between us I'll use our taste in music as an example. She would listen to the Carpenters, in her room while I was blasting Led Zeppelin in mine. She had also been seriously involved with a boyfriend for over a year who occupied most of her free time, while I had the romantic attention span of a gnat and was usually single and on the prowl. We had little beyond our genealogy in common and the majority of our conversations were hostile, to put it mildly. So Anne couldn't have come at a better time to fill the void left in my life by having moved away from Julie and having lost Danni to her boyfriend.

My parents occupied a bedroom on the opposite side of the house. It was as far away from the other bedrooms as it could be while still being attached to the same house. My mom would come home from work, and most nights, drink for a while and go to bed. Mostly Danni and I hung out in our respective rooms, as most teenagers will, so there were still no real relationships developing. In fact, I was pretty much left in many ways to raise myself as my mother was fairly self-absorbed and didn't seem to have the energy to truly parent me. I freely admit though that being a very strong willed kid, often referred to as a demanding and spoiled rotten brat, would have required an awful lot of energy and hard work to raise.

Anne had moved in with her father and stepmother who were our neighbors, because she wasn't getting along in the home with her bitter, divorced mother. Anne came from a home where she was one of five girls, all close in age, as well as relationally, into a house where her father was gone a lot as the captain of a fire department. To make matters worse, her stepmother had made it extremely clear to Anne that she did not welcome the intrusion of this teenage daughter who would not only be in the way, but would also be stealing away some of her father's precious attention. So Anne hung out at my house in my room with me most of the time. Thank God!

Now, in my freshman year I had maintained all honor roll grades in college prep classes. I was in the class senate and then I was class president. In fact, as a freshman, I had actually become pretty popular after having barely survived that horrible mid-eighth grade year change of schools. (During those first few months in that new school I had even managed to avoid getting beaten up by that really big girl who had instantly decided I should die.)

Also in my freshman year my braces came off, which back then were not common and were a great source of ammunition for teasing. I had even developed a slender and petite figure that was not all that hard to look at. I had also learned some pretty good make-up tricks and thanks to some diligent plucking I even had two, count em, two, eyebrows. All that combined with a much greater budget for fashion had managed to make me kind of pretty. Who'd have guessed? Wouldn't you think I would have felt good about myself? I didn't.

By this time I had also been given my greatest gift; a talent for writing poetry. Granted, not the most marketable gift by any means, but nonetheless it is my greatest talent and has become an endless source of passionate joy for me. Back in the eighth grade, when I was still thirteen, I had written my first poem. I had been all alone in my new room in my new house after a rough day at my new school. It was a hokey love poem that rhymed (yuck), but it somehow ignited something in me that has never been extinguished.

> If the earth
> should stop revolving,
> If the oceans
> should go dry,
> If the sun

> *should lose the power*
> *to brighten up*
> *the sky,*
> *If we lose*
> *the stars and moon*
> *and if everything*
> *should die,*
> *then maybe*
> *I'll stop loving you,*
> *Maybe…if I try.*

Anne was probably not a great influence on me in many ways. To this day, nearly thirty years later, we still joke about who corrupted who, although in reality, we have both agreed, it was probably a mutual friend of ours who corrupted us both.

Anne and I, in our pursuit of popularity (translation: love, acceptance, and confidence), the holy grail that we (along with millions of other teenagers), constantly chased after, neglected our homework. For that matter, we neglected our classes too. We chose instead to hang out in the smoking area where all the cool guys hung out. Hard to believe a high school in California had a designated smoking area, but back then it did. This was, after all, the seventies, which should also clue you in that there was more than tobacco being smoked in that smoking area.

School was all about socializing and social climbing. Our priorities quickly became drinking, smoking, and getting high as we tried to impress the boys our parents were sure to hate. So much for the honor roll.

But the one thing Anne did do for me was encourage my writing. She loved my hokey poems and eagerly read each one. This probably made the difference between this book, along with over a thousand poems, being in existence or never having seen the light of paper. Oh, occasionally my grandmother would indulge me and read one or listen to me read one to her, but that was it for encouragement from my family as far as my writing was concerned, so I truly do thank God for Anne.

My grandmother had a positive influence on me in many other ways as I was growing up. She tried to undo some of the damage caused by our chaotic upbringing. I had received the lions share of my mothers attention (such as it was) and as mentioned in the last chapter, I had received this not by accomplishment as much as by default, due to being sick often and occasionally seriously so. Being the baby of the family didn't hurt in the competition for my mother's attention either.

I was born with severe asthma and had suffered pneumonia as many as eight or nine times by the time I saw my teens. I missed massive amounts of school and logged several huge stretches of time in oxygen tents in hospitals. Those tents are very cold, damp, and lonely places for a little girl.

So, because of all the illnesses, especially those that had been life threatening, my mother had a hard time denying me much. She also tended to side with me in any argument I had with either of my sisters. All of this certainly helped me, but only to become that demanding, spoiled rotten brat I referred to earlier.

My sisters resented me deeply, understandably so I might add, and often (and accurately) let me know what a brat I was. This was not their opinion alone mind you. I'd had this little fact pointed out to me countless times by the one remaining aunt my mother still spoke to, as well as my grandmother and even my own father.

This label hurt and eventually became my own definition of myself and would remain with me well into my thirties, decades after I had stopped being a brat. My grandmother tried to help me to become better than that brat with her care and consistency. She even helped to keep me from becoming a hypochondriac (like my mother). Since the slightest illness brought my otherwise inattentive mother running, looking for signs of my asthma, abnormally focusing on my health and possible illnesses could have easily become a very seductive practice for me to indulge in. My grandmother never would have stood for it though. She demanded that my mother encourage me, or at least allow me, to go out and play and engage in sports and things like other kids, rather than let me retreat into invalid status as my mother might have had me do.

Ma, not exactly an aristocratic title, but what we called my grandmother, tried to be a calm and stable figure in our house. She actually acted more maternal in many ways than my mother since early on my mother had been forced to take on the role of provider and had become almost more of a paternal figure due to the instability in the father we actually had. Ma baked homemade bread, and cookies, and cinnamon rolls and such for us. She was the one to dry us off after we had walked home in the rain. She cared for us when we were sick, did the laundry, and cooked our meals. She was always careful to feed us before my parents got home back when my dad was around, so they could be free to drink in the evenings without being interrupted by us kids. She was a God-sent bit of constancy and balance amid all the uncertainties in our home.

Ma

I can be standing in the check-out line,
my mind on groceries,
like which ones will be used in
dinner for my family tonight
or getting a jump start on writing the check
in an effort to save
even a few precious seconds,
when I'll spot the lifesavers
in the seductive candy rack
that preys on the impulses of adults
and the persistence of children,
and all at once,
as the wint-o-green rolls catch my eye,
you are spanning decades
and you are back,
being my grandmother, being Ma.

You're pulling that green roll
out of the pocket of your housecoat
with your gnarled hands,
those same hands
that would tirelessly knead bread dough
into the very definition of home,
of warmth, of comfort.
I can smell it baking
while I wait impatiently
to slather a warm slice with butter.
Or perhaps the dough your hands are working
is destined to become
your almost famous cinnamon rolls
that will grace our coffee table
on Christmas morning
or some other special occasion.
There are so many ways you loved us,
so many roles you played,
as though you were somehow intent
on redeeming your own past,
making up for some long ago sin
by caring for us
even better than you did your own children.
Perhaps there were still remnants
of a life you lived
caught in your pack of Pall Malls
or that occasional cocktail you indulged in.
But to me
you were always Ma
and you were walking me and my sisters
downtown to the "dime store"
where you would spend
your few precious dollars
mostly on us.
You were the one putting Nestlé's Quick
in my Malt-O-Meal,
turning mush to magic with chocolate

then making me chase it down
with a tablespoon of honey
mixed with vinegar
to ward off illness in winter.
Yes, I am surrounded by strangers
in the grocery store,
but I am being treated
to those make-shift Popsicles you served
after freezing Kool-aid in the ice cube trays
to ward off the heat in summer.
I am watching with amusement
as you chase the dog with the broom
for some great infraction she committed.
I am not smelling the cologne
on the young man bagging the groceries.
I am smelling home-made cornbread,
then laundry as you hang it out on the line,
and then your breath,
fresh from a wint-o-green lifesaver.
I am seeing you scoop that old goldfish up
to clean its bowl
with nothing but your loving hand.
I am seeing you at the bus stop
because you never learned how to drive.
I am seeing comfort food
like that thick beef stew,
that your mother,
a former cook in fancy people's homes
during the depression,
taught you how to make.
I am seeing those round, pink plastic boxes
of talcum powder,
the kind with the big puffy applicator
that we thought you liked so much
that we gave you a new one
for every birthday.
I didn't know as a child

or even as you loved me into
my own life as a mother
that these things would come
to define you in my head,
how these images would break across
the plains of my mind
at unexpected times
and bring you back,
sailing forth upon the wind of memory,
until you have rushed into full view,
in my heart,
filling me with sudden gusts
of love and warmth,
of nostalgia and angst,
and my childhood,
until it bursts wide open
and the smell of baking bread
and wintergreen
explode inside my head and
overtake the current moment
with missing you.

My sister, Katrina had of course established her own household with her husband, John, and they too had a profoundly positive influence on me. They provided a refuge from our house by always opening their home to both me and Danni. They kept us at their homes often on weekends and several times for long stretches over the summer. They even took us on camping trips with them several times, providing us with the only vacations we had ever known.

John had always been unbelievably attentive and loving to us, even when he was a teenage boy of sixteen. He was surprisingly devoted to trying to help us to overcome the dysfunctional conditions we were growing up in. He took us to amusement parks and on day trips to various places, things our parents had very rarely done with us.

At one point in my teenage years, when my grades were at their worst, they even took me in for a whole semester in an effort to try to help me improve them. My partying had seriously jeopardized my chances of graduating.

I write about these people because I see that though I had certainly lacked the support I needed from my parents, God had made sure to equip me with other people to help fill in the gaps. My life has been, like most peoples lives, a mixture of people and events and influences; some that were good for me, others that were harmful to me. There were people who exerted real effort in trying to affect a positive outcome for me and those who intentionally or, more often unintentionally, inflicted lasting emotional damage on me. In the end though, all the responsibility became mine, for it is my life and ultimately it has been lived based on my choices.

chapter three

TROUBLED TEENS

It is human nature to need to be loved and to need to feel appreciated. Every teenager goes through the depths of emotional angst in their attempt to get those needs met. For the emotionally wounded like I was, this need can become all consuming.

I directed all my energies toward boys and had pretty much given up on any other endeavors or investments in myself or my future. This, of course, applies to my education as well. I see now that I did not recognize any value in myself and was looking outside for my happiness and the validation that everyone needs, especially teenagers.

Being dependent on other people for those basic human needs straps you into a roller coaster ride that never stops. Just as you would desperately want to get off a roller coaster at an amusement park if you'd been stuck on it for ages, I also wanted off my emotional roller coaster after a lifetime of riding it.

I would end up trapped on that ride for decades, but even at fifteen, I somehow realized that I wanted off. I didn't know exactly what it was that I wanted off of, but I knew whatever I was doing was not working for me. I did not feel loved, valuable, or content, though I doubt I could have articulated it at the time. All I knew was that I was happy for only brief periods here and there and they almost always had to do with some guy's attention.

I even tried the "God thing" for a while around that time. My sister, Danni, had brought me to church with her and her new boyfriend to meet one of the guys there that she thought I would hit it off with. I didn't.

Though I had initially gone in hopes of finding romance, I did come to believe in the teachings of the Christian faith. I actually made a stab at religion, but felt judged and rejected at the church my sister attended and soon felt that I was a dismal failure as a Christian and a failure in Gods eyes as well. I smoked and still committed a variety of other "sins" so I was certain God was always disappointed with me. To make matters worse, Danni's boyfriend's family was pretty wealthy and his sister often made critical comments regarding my clothes and such, leaving me feeling, yet again, hopelessly inadequate.

I spent hours in high school
paying penance in my bedroom,
longing to love
the girl who came through the mirror,
came straight at me,
armed with the stark and brutal truth
that lied to me,
that showed to me
only mediocrity,
blatant in its inadequacy.
I sold the soul of my joy
to that mirror,
and bought instead
unrealism, illusion,
an unattainable image
of some divine perfection
created by master make-up artists,
hair stylists
and air brushes,

> *images that accompanied*
> *free samples of perfume*
> *sandwiched between the pages*
> *and free samples of shame*
> *tucked between my envy*
> *and despair.*
> *If you looked at the photographs*
> *of me back then,*
> *you would see a lovely girl,*
> *for you would compare me to no one,*
> *while I saw the root of self-loathing*
> *in those same images,*
> *for I compared myself*
> *to every woman*
> *ever loved by a lens.*

I was never asked out by any of the other boys in the youth group at that church either. I not only figured I was not good enough, but that I also must not be pretty enough. I thought that I could not find love and acceptance even in a church, not even from God. So, I continued along the same road I had been traveling. It may not have been too productive and it may not have brought much joy, but at least it was comfortable because it was familiar.

I'd love to tell you that things changed for me, but they didn't. Actually, my desperate search led to one bad choice after another. At seventeen, after having moved from Katrina's house back in with my parents, I was facing the inevitability of not being able to graduate with my class despite the progress I had made at Katrina's.

I hadn't dropped out though. I planned to finish and graduate even if it would be late. I would be turning eighteen in a couple of months and I would be legally able to write my own notes to excuse myself from class whenever I wished rather than just cutting the class. This was pretty ironic because by then I actually wanted to go to class so that I could at least earn my diploma.

Always in need of money, I took a job in a retail store. It was my third or fourth job. There I became friends with an older girl named Debbie. She lived on her own in an apartment. We had gone out together several times; drinking, dancing, and doing drugs. (Not exactly good old fashioned, wholesome fun for the whole family, kind of stuff.) She was twenty-one and though I was legally under the drinking age, I had a fake I.D. that got me into bars with little or no resistance.

Bars and discos were a common source of entertainment for us. Again, it was the seventies. For me it was all about that unending hope, that in every bar "Mr. Wonderful-ready to make all my dreams come true" could be right there waiting for me; "Ms. Right-the answer to all his prayers" to walk in.

On one such Saturday night I was sound asleep on the couch in her living room, having gotten to bed rather late. I awoke with a knife at my throat. My first thought was that it was a friend of Debbie's and that this was a joke. I simply could not grasp the situation. He had asked me where my wallet was and I guess I told him. I still could not wrap my mind around the possibility that I had been awakened to be robbed. I hadn't.

He told me that he had a gun and that as long as I did what he told me to, I would not be hurt. I guess he had watched his share of old "B" movies to have come up with such an original line. He asked me who else was in the apartment and I told him that Debbie and her boyfriend were in the bedroom. This was not a clever rouse from me in an attempt to scare him into believing there was a man in the apartment. It was true.

He pulled me up and with the knife still pressed against my throat, he made me lead him into the bedroom. Once inside he immediately tied up Debbie's boyfriend having caught him by surprise as he had caught me, and then proceeded to tie up Debbie and me. We were also blindfolded and gagged, and for the next four or five hours we were both repeatedly and brutally raped. I remember praying that this would not be the way I was to spend my last hours on earth, as I was fairly certain I would not come through this horror alive.

At last he left and Debbie's boyfriend freed himself, then Debbie, and then me. He had to go to the manager's office to call the police as the phone line had been cut by our attacker.

If only I hadn't been so naïve and had known this wasn't a robbery when he first woke me up, but that a rape was about to take place, and if only I had been educated in rape prevention, perhaps I might have screamed and summoned help, instead of us having to endure that night. Though I know that he may have just as easily followed through on his threat to kill me if I had screamed, that "if only" thought still haunts me to this day if I let it.

The police turned out to be nearly as humiliating as the rape itself, as they all competed for the assignment of taking our statements. I just wanted to go home and do whatever I could to blot the whole ordeal from my mind. I did not want to file a report, for I was terrified of what this would do to my mother if she found out. I knew she could never handle this. It was her worst nightmare come true.

They forced me to cooperate, however, by threatening to take me into protective custody if I didn't, since I was still a minor. Finally I agreed, but I still could not bring myself to call my mother, so I turned to the person that I usually turned to when I was absolutely forced to ask for any kind of help and called Katrina.

She said she'd call Mom for me and break it to her as gently as she could. There was no way to avoid it since they were taking me to the county hospital so that they could "gather evidence" and they would need my mom to sign the paperwork because of my age.

As if to prove things could still get less dignified, they took me to the hospital in the back of a squad car.

I had put on my bravest act since the moment the ordeal began and probably needed nothing more than to be able to fall into the arms of my mother where I could finally break down, fall apart and cry until I was comforted by the love and the security of family. Of course, that was not an option. I knew if I let her see me upset she would become hysterical. I was not being noble. It was a decision based purely on self-defense. I could never have stood causing her that much pain, nor could I have handled her hysteria. I had seen how she flipped out when I had asthma attacks and I knew this situation could induce hysteria that would surpass those outbursts exponentially.

It just so happened we were having a rare family barbeque that day and were expecting my aunt and her family over as well as some of Katrina's in-laws. I guess I welcomed the distraction because I insisted that it go on as scheduled.

All the practice I'd had at burying painful and unbearable feelings came in very handy that day. I just killed off a little more of myself and carried on. That is what happens when you bury feelings rather than deal honestly with them. In effect, you kill off a part of you.

I must have done a pretty good job of convincing everyone that I was ok, because the next day a couple of women came from the rape crisis center and I impressed them so much with my reasonable responses, maturity, and resolve not to let it affect me, that they actually asked me if I'd like to volunteer at the center to help others. I know these women were not trained psychologists or anything, but I still find it hard to believe that they weren't trained to see through my act.

It did, of course, affect me. Though I had done a lot of partying and had previously had countless boyfriends and "made out" with who knows how many guys, I was actually the most prudish and sexually moral of all my friends, until the rape.

I was so determined not to let it affect me and screw me up sexually, I swung to the other side of the spectrum and became somewhat promiscuous, not by today's standards to be sure, but certainly more than I had been before the rape. I believed at the time that I was just making sure that I didn't become sexually dysfunctional and turn frigid like the rape victims on those "made for T.V. movies" always seemed to do.

I realize now that the rapist had taken the last thing I thought I had that had any value to me, or probably more importantly to me at the time, to a guy. Up until that incident sex had, at best, been the ultimate expression of love between two people; at the least, it was my best bargaining chip when it came to trying to find that healing love.

That rape showed me that sex could be taken from me against my will. My body could be violated in the most humiliating and hurtful way and I was helpless to prevent it. That which I had thought special and precious had now become worthless, much like the rest of me.

Sadly, I began to feel that I was almost obligated to sleep with a man if he made me feel wanted, as if their wanting me was such a great gift, one that I was so undeserving of that I had to somehow repay them for it. It felt to me as if it were some kind of favor that they found me attractive, so I owed them sex as some warped type of gratitude. Thank God I did not actually sleep with every man that wanted me, not even close, but I somehow felt guilty for dating all those men that I did not sleep with. The stupidest part of that was that I was actually very pretty, but that had nothing to do with how I felt about myself.

Well, after remaining home a few days to recover from the rape, I attempted to return to school and to work. On the way to school my first day back I rear-ended the car in front of me and trashed my car. I was off to a great start.

My step-dad, Bill, gave me a ride to work the next day since my car was, of course, out of commission. That afternoon at work Debbie received a letter from one of our former co-workers who had been told about our misfortune. Debbie read it aloud, sharing all the offers of sympathy and condolences that had been written to her with not a single mention of my name. Not one word was written to pass on those sentiments to me also.

That was so depressing for me that without an explanation I asked if I could please go home. I was unable to reach Bill so I simply began wandering around the mall where I worked, killing time until he might get home. As luck would have it, I ran into Danni and her new husband. She had been married the previous spring. I asked them if they would mind giving me a ride home. Danni was clearly annoyed as they had just gotten there and she said no. Her husband, who was a little older and had outgrown some of the self-centeredness that she, like all nineteen year olds, still possessed. He disregarded her wish and said immediately "Of course we'll give you a ride."

In the car I finally began to feel some of the pain of the whole ordeal and began to cry. I told them that I wished I had a boyfriend (big surprise) whom I could talk to. I didn't feel as though I had anyone to talk to about the incident. I didn't dare let on at home that I was upset. I feared that would just kill Mom. It never occurred to me that a boyfriend might care about me to the degree that it would also be painful for him to hear of my distress. Danni told me I was being ridiculous and made some other rather cold remarks about my being stupid until her husband told her to shut up.

I did not cry again for at least two years after that. I had shut down, turned off all the emotion I could, and died a little more.

chapter four

LATE TEENS/ EARLY ADULTHOOD

The rapist turned out to be a serial rapist who was eventually caught and sentenced to serve thirty-three years in prison. It seemed I had also been sentenced. I would remain in my own painful prison for many more years. I tell you all this sob story stuff to show you a pattern that was certain to destroy my self-esteem, my sense of self-worth. The pattern was set and I had begun making choices, at least on a sub-conscious level, that were certain to ensure that the pattern continued. After all, we build the life we believe we deserve, and by this time in my life I had become convinced that I had no real value and was fortunate to get even the crumbs the world had to offer. I believed I deserved little so I demanded little, little of the blessings life could bring and little of myself.

I gave up on high school completely. I took my mentally gifted I.Q. of 145 (though that number was unbeknownst to me at the time) and went home. I had gotten fired from the job I held when I was working with Debbie so I drifted for awhile, partying with the friends I should have graduated with. I had turned eighteen and house rules had pretty much gone out the window. Of course my mom requested that I call her if I was not coming home at night so she wouldn't worry, but other than that there were no holds barred. It was sure a much better set-up than I had when I was a couple of years younger. Then Anne and I would claim to be spending the night at a friend's house in order to make a particularly wild party, only to end up sleeping on the floor of the place where the party was being held.

I had not only given up on high school, but on any dreams I may have once held for any real success as well. I just kept looking for that one guy who would make me feel loved and lovable, whole and healed.

I took a variety of retail jobs and even tried my hand at selling cars for awhile. That didn't last too long. I got fired rather quickly for refusing to sleep with the boss and later had my heart broken by another car salesman who worked there (with whom I did sleep.) Eventually I tried junior college and got a part time job selling fine jewelry in a small, local jewelry store.

One evening a friend of mine fixed me up with a friend of her boyfriend. His name was (and still is for that matter) Steve. He was strong, handsome and arrogant (the single most attractive quality for me at the time). He had a decent job, a new car and owned his own home. *Bingo!* I had hit the jackpot!

Though I had become kind of promiscuous after the rape, I had enough sense to know when not to have sex, like when I really wanted to keep a guy. Even I knew if you allowed a guy to use you he would, and then he would discard you. I may not have had any respect for myself, but I knew sleeping with a guy too soon would ensure that he would not have any respect for me either. So I made him wait. It was only a month or so, but to him it probably seemed like an eternity. I had actually become quite practiced at the art of seduction but, let's face it, how much art does it take to seduce a twenty-year old guy? Waiting twenty minutes to get laid can seem like an eternity to a guy that age.

Perhaps making him wait was a bit manipulative on my part, but it worked. He fell in love, hard. Ok, it was mutual. I too was in love. I knew for the first time in my life what it was like to feel safe. I remember telling him that I felt like he could stop a Mack truck from hitting me.

Some years later while on a break at the mall where I worked I observed a little girl of about four or five with her father. She had fallen and had gotten the slightest bit hurt and was crying. He scooped her up in what must have seemed to her to be the biggest, strongest arms in the world and was able to instantly comfort her. She immediately stopped crying because Daddy had made everything alright. I was shocked at my reaction to that little scene. I felt an immediate and intense stab of envy. I realized then that that was what I had been searching for, longing for, my whole life. That father had worked absolute magic with his little girl. As long as she was with him she knew he could, and would, protect her from everything bad in the big world. She felt safe. It was that same feeling that I had felt early on in my relationship with Steve, that same feeling that I had never felt with my own father.

I had moved in with Steve two short months after having met him. Steve was quite a party guy so before long we had developed our own pattern. He had been temporarily layed off not too long after we met so we would stay up late and drink or get high and then sleep in late in the morning. I generally got up long after my first, and sometimes even my second, class had begun so it wasn't long before I dropped out of junior college. Oh, yeah. I was on the fast track; the fast track to nowhere.

Steve was pretty much a dinosaur when it came to women's lib. He preferred to have me at home where I could not be hit-on by any other guys and could cook and clean for him and be available to pamper him. (My still closest friend, Julie, referred to him as Fred Flintstone.)

I possessed no sense of self-discipline, having never developed one in high school. Heck, I could have been out really late drinking on a school night and I only had to tell my mom I didn't feel well the next morning and I was off the hook for school that day. That doesn't exactly teach you a work ethic, so I had none. That was one of the ways her leniency with me had done me no favors. I was by now nineteen and was still completely irresponsible. Soon I had quit my job which certainly didn't break Steve's heart.

Oh, eventually I found another job selling fine jewelry and just like that, my career choice (such as it was) had been made.

After having been with Steve for about six months, he proposed. It was not very romantic. We were in bed and I was tired and he wanted to fool around and it was the one way he figured he could get me to go along I guess. I have to admit it worked. Soon we set a wedding date, but a few months before it arrived Steve backed out. I was so hurt and angry that I left him because of it and moved back home with my parents, but it didn't take him too long to convince me to come back.

Eventually we set another wedding date, but again as it drew near, he backed out and again I left him. We fought an awful lot in our relationship so God knows I should have stayed gone, but I never could. Neither one of us were exactly emotionally healthy and he could never let me go and I could never remain gone. When life got scary without him or the next relationship failed, I'd give in to the pressure he exerted and would go back.

One time I managed to stay away for about a year. I had gotten my own apartment and had been actively dating a variety of handsome and successful guys, but had also gotten more involved with partying and was using a frightening amount of cocaine. One evening after work I was on my way to meet my latest boyfriend when someone cut me off as I was driving about fifty miles an hour. I hit my breaks and they locked up on me causing me to lose control of my car. It spun out and sent me hurtling into oncoming traffic, finally colliding with another car.

This was back in the days when seatbelts were more or less optional and I had opted not, so upon impact I flew up out of my seat and landed on the emergency break in between the two front seats. My back is still trashed, but other than that I was extremely fortunate and suffered little injury. A mutual friend told Steve what had happened and he showed up at my apartment at about three a.m. that morning.

Now, I still had the attention span of a gnat when it came to romance. Steve was the only exception, so soon I was bored with my newest boyfriend and had started entertaining the thought of dating Steve again. My intentions were only to date him, mind you, but it was enough to make my current boyfriend become another casualty of that attention span, and once again I was back at Steve's door.

We began dating and within a few weeks it was becoming clear that I would never be free of him. I would like to tell you it was because I was so madly in love with him, but though I truly loved him, it had far more to do with that safety net he provided than it did anything romantic and passionate. In fact, the only passion that really existed between us was evident only in our fights. We were actually getting along pretty well at this stage however, probably because we were only dating. I had laid down the ground rules and the major one was that I did not want to make a commitment until I was sure that we belonged together.

One evening I arrived at his house after work when he surprised me by informing me that he could no longer just date me. He told me that he was going to take a shower and that I had until he was done to decide whether I wanted to marry him or get out of his life for good. How romantic.

Of course I agreed to marry him. It was the safe thing to do. I had become extremely comfortable with the art of settling by then so it was a natural decision to choose the familiar over the unknown, the easy over the difficult, the safe over the scary.

A few short months later we were married. Julie was, of course, my matron of honor just as I had been in her wedding.

If you knew
when we were wed
how small
and balled up
my heart
had become,
I wonder
if you'd stay.
If you knew
how weary
and thread bare
my soul was,
I wonder
if you'd feel loved.
Or would you

> *look at me*
> *and see a bride*
> *that came with a sign*
> *hung around my neck*
> *that read*
> *"sold"?*

Steve and I should have realized after all the break-ups that we were not exactly made for each other, at least not in any healthy sense. He was incredibly controlling, chauvinistic and ill-tempered, while I was very rebellious, strong-willed and equally ill-tempered. Not exactly a match made in heaven.

Ironically enough I remember as a young girl idolizing all the soft, demure women like those in the fairytales I grew up with. I always wished I could be ultra-feminine and helpless like those women, for even though they were always pathetic victims, they always got the prince. Though I was certainly feminine enough and petite in stature, I was also very strong-willed and independent-minded. Even though I had certainly been victimized, I had never been the quiet, sweet natured little fluff that those women of the fairytales like Snow White and Cinderella had been. I always believed that this meant that there was something wrong with me because I had this rotten temper and I simply could not back down like a good little girl should, and Steve was certainly quick enough to tell me that there was plenty wrong with me. I was passionate and intense and so was he, so we fought bitterly and often.

Six months after our wedding, I was pregnant. Five months after giving birth to a beautiful baby girl we named Katie (after my grandmother who was by then dying of cancer), I was pregnant again. We named her Laura and she was the most delightful surprise (notice I did not say accident) I could have ever dreamed of. The timing was not exactly ideal. We had no medical insurance by then and Steve's paychecks were bouncing.

Needless to say what was not an ideal marriage in the best of times became a horrid marriage under the strain of these circumstances. After Laura was born the fighting continued to escalate and the marriage continued to deteriorate. Steve drank more and more and with two babies, I was trapped.

He had become a binge drinker and had proceeded to get more and more verbally, mentally and emotionally abusive. Sadly enough, I thought this was normal, that all women endured these kinds of marriages. I saw no options as more and more of me was dying inside.

I spend my hours
wasting my life
in a feeble attempt
to rectify some ancient situation
not of my making,
continuously haunted
by the need
to fix Daddy for Mommy
to reinvent my childhood,
transform my parents
by my fervent wishing
into what I dare to dream
I deserve.
I trudge through my days
paying penance
for the sins of the father,
diligently denying myself
joy and freedom,
stoically, meticulously
keeping the shackles of yesterday
firmly in place
around my heart.
I remain deeply committed
to the recreation
of my past,

> *the repetition of every error,*
> *unable to forgive myself*
> *for not having been raised*
> *by Ozzie and Harriet.*
> *I remarry my father,*
> *am reincarnated as my mother*
> *and gift my children*
> *with the familiar chaos*
> *of dysfunction,*
> *hide booze and bruises and God*
> *from my daughters*
> *and do not notice*
> *the cycle repeating.*

I had gone back to work part time to help augment the family income when the girls were two and three, respectively. Steve had only allowed it (yes, allowed it), because we desperately needed the money and the benefits since he had become self-employed as a painter. The jewelry store I had been working in had closed down and because I was the top salesperson there even though I worked only half the hours of everyone else, they had given me a job in another location rather than let me go.

The night before I was to start that new job, with a new boss and all new co-workers (just like starting over in a new school again), I sensed that Steve was about to go out and binge drink again. After a while you begin to recognize the signs of an impending binge even though the drinker often doesn't. I begged him to please come straight home after work. He came home at about three-thirty in the morning dead drunk instead.

Of course I had been unable to sleep alternating between worry and anger. My youngest daughter, Laura, who was three by then, had woken up about an hour before he came home and had gotten in my bed with me because she was not feeling well. When Steve finally came staggering in I completely lost it and started screaming at him.

Anyone who knows anything about drunk men with bad tempers knows that is not the smartest thing to do. He also completely lost it. He grabbed me by the hair and dragged me out of bed, throwing me to the floor while screaming every obscenity you could imagine and possibly some you couldn't. He was calling me every filthy name you pray your child never hears and he was doing it just a few feet from Laura. She also completely lost it and began crying hysterically. I recovered as quickly as I could and picked myself up off the floor and took her from the bed and carried her to her own. I climbed in next to her and frantically racked my brain for a way to keep this event from scarring her for life. I tried to comfort her by telling her it was ok, Mommy wasn't hurt and Daddy wasn't a bad man, that he'd just had too much to drink. I explained to her that Daddy didn't mean to do that to Mommy and that he would never do it again. Finally she calmed down and fell asleep. Eventually I cried myself to sleep as well.

The next morning, after only an hour or two of sleep, I got up and tried to hide the fact that my eyes were red and swollen from crying with Visine and make-up, and put on that all too familiar face of bravery and went to my new job. Once again I had to rely on my ability to bury pain and shame and go out into the world as though nothing had happened, but hey, it was no big deal. After all, practice makes perfect and God knows I'd had plenty of practice at pretending that I was ok when I wasn't.

I didn't tell anyone about that night, not even Julie. I was so ashamed of the fact that I could have been so stupid as to have married someone who could do that to me that I could not bear to confess the details of that night. I buried it along with the rape and the death of my father and every other unbearable event that had taken place in my life. I buried it as though it were dead and I knew somewhere deep inside me that my marriage had hit the floor with me that night and it too was dead, just as sure as I was dying.

chapter five

NOT QUITE MID-LIFE CRISIS

I tried to fix our marriage. I even convinced Steve to go with me to a marriage counselor. She told us that she held out little hope for our marriage because marriage counseling was for people who were willing to compromise, and clearly Steve was not willing to compromise. I had given him a list of things that he would have to change in order for me to stay. He not only did not change all of them, he did not change a single one of them. Oh, I know that there was a large part of the responsibility for the horrific state of our marriage on my shoulders too, but I sincerely believed that I could meet him half-way if he were willing to budge at all. He wasn't.

I spent the next six months walking around thinking *I'm thirty years old, my life is over, and I ruined it.* I could not support the girls on my own so I could not think of a way out. I had approached my mom a couple of years earlier and asked if I could take the girls and move into a condo she and Bill owned and had been renting out well below the market rate, a rate I could have afforded, and she turned me down. To be fair to her, she had no idea how bad my marriage was and that she was in effect sentencing me to more years of the kind of abuse I had been enduring. Furthermore, she was afraid I would only end up going back to Steve anyway and who could blame her for thinking that.

So, we stayed together and we kept fighting and the only way out I could see was suicide. I entertained the option many times because I was so desperate and hopeless, but I was also more of a survivor than a victim by nature and the very thought of leaving my girls was even more unbearable than the thought of staying with Steve.

He was never physically abusive to me after that night, perhaps because I had learned my lesson about yelling at him when he was drunk. It was certainly not because he had stopped getting drunk. The other forms of abuse though just continued to get worse. I remember more than a few times having been backed against a wall, cowering while Steve screamed at me, calling me stupid and worthless (two of his favorites), as well as a barrage of all the filthy names that he was also fond of using on me. He would scream those venomous insults, splattering me with his spittle as I cried, scared to death that he would get violent again.

I would try to make myself as small as I could, as small as I felt, wishing fervently that I could become small enough to slip through a crack in the floor. Whatever may have remained of my fragile ego when I entered that marriage had long since disappeared. He had completely destroyed any last remnants of self-esteem I might have still possessed. Nearly thirteen years of being told I was stupid and worthless, along with all the other lovely insults he hurled at me regularly had certainly made me believe them.

How can you continue
tearing me up,
wearing me down
as though I were something
you would rather
spit out?
You see only
what I can't do,
never all that I can.
You know only

> *what I am not,*
> *not what I am.*
> *What really scares me*
> *is that you have done this*
> *so well,*
> *for so long,*
> *you're making a believer*
> *out of me.*

For Katie's fifth birthday we went to Disneyland. It was the first real vacation I'd had in nine years. My whole family had decided to join us in the celebration. Steve and I had spoken no more than was absolutely necessary during the trip. I had been sharing a bed with Laura and he had been sharing his with Katie.

On the last night after the girls had gone to sleep he began pressuring me for sex. Now he was not above forcing himself upon me from time to time leaving me feeling completely enraged and helpless. There were also plenty of times when the pressure would become so intense, I would give in just to get him to leave me alone. Having the girls right there in the room though only made giving in even less of an option.

When I refused to submit, he blew up and told me that he wanted a divorce and he was leaving me there, five hundred miles from home with the rest of my family having already gone back the previous day. He stomped out of the hotel room door only to return a short while later and climb in bed with Katie where he went to sleep without a word.

On the way home the next day, although he didn't apologize (he never did), he told me he didn't really want a divorce. My heart sank. A few months later during another argument he again said he wanted a divorce. This time I prayed he would not take it back. I didn't have the self-esteem to leave him, but I hoped like hell that he would leave me.

I kept thinking of my daughters. I knew if I stayed they would grow up to think our marriage was normal. I was continuing along the road of dysfunction traveled by my parents before me and their parents before them. Steve was no stranger to a dysfunctional family either. His mother had been killed in a car crash when he was only two years old and he had been raised by his alcoholic father and a couple of different step-mothers who were as screwed up as his father. He had suffered more than his share of neglect and abuse. I could see this vicious cycle that would only be repeated by my daughters if I did not break it now. The thought of my precious little girls being treated by their husbands the way Steve treated me, because that would become what they considered normal and what would be familiar, was simply unacceptable to me.

I knew that I could not let Steve change his mind again and sentence them to repeat my history. Once I realized that the cycle of dysfunction was sure to be repeated if I didn't do something, I made a decision. Though I did not have the self-worth to leave for my sake, I had the sense of responsibility as a mother to leave for their sakes. They gave me the strength and the courage to get out of a situation I had become certain was a life sentence. My maternal instincts and the innate sense of responsibility that was part of those instincts, rather than any false sense of nobility, were what would end up saving me. I have to admit, once the decision was made, I was thrilled beyond anything I had felt in years. I recognize that what I was feeling was hope and it was way past due.

> *It's my soul*
> *sending forth*
> *a barely audible*
> *whisper in the dark.*
> *It's an attempt*
> *to stem my meltdown,*
> *to keep from falling*
> *into the abyss.*
> *It's to be a revelation*

> *that will sustain me,*
> *that will span my despair*
> *and revitalize me.*
> *It's a tiny voice*
> *within me*
> *swelling and rising up*
> *to infuse me with hope.*
> *It's the remnant*
> *of a distant dream,*
> *work left undone,*
> *and life yet unlived.*

So, my determination to give them a chance at a happy, healthy future gave me the nerve to come home from work that day and tell Steve that he was getting that divorce. By then, of course, he had changed his mind again, but I would not, could not, change mine. Within a few weeks I had gotten full time hours at work and since I was again the top salesperson I had been made assistant manager of the store as well. I found an apartment and a babysitter for the girls.

The night before I was to move the girls and me into our apartment, I gave Steve one last chance to try to work this out and to see another marriage counselor. I did this out of a feeling of obligation, not so much out of desire, as by that time, I honestly couldn't wait to get out of there. Much to my relief he was not willing to try any longer either.

I had left him the house, but it was a small price to pay for freedom and a new chance at happiness, at life. I inhaled the hope that permeated my new apartment. I could almost smell the impending joy. It was available and I wanted to breathe it in until I was intoxicated. Perhaps now, I thought, *I'll find real happiness, true and lasting love, Mr. Wonderful.* Is the word "pathetic" crossing your mind yet? It should be.

chapter six

NEW (IF NOT DIFFERENT) START

And now that the war is finally over
where do we turn in our search for peace?
God knows it never comes
right after the surrender.
And even though I lost,
the feelings of relief are much stronger
than any feelings defeat could bring.
And in our search we turn away
from the battle ground
unable to face the devastation.
We turn away from the mirrors
unable to face our consciences,
'cause we both know
we never fought fair.
Neither one of us holds our head up high,
for now we know
there can be no winner
in all out warfare
and these were no minor skirmishes.
And now two losers wander shell-shocked
still searching for peace

> *long after the explosions*
> *are just echoes within.*
> *And now that I'm free*
> *my resources are drained*
> *and I stand at the border of love and hate*
> *and wonder,*
> *Where do I turn in my search for peace?*

Life was still rough. I was trying to support myself and my two daughters on ten dollars an hour and four hundred dollars a month in child support. In the San Francisco Bay Area that was barely above the poverty level. Steve and I had initially been quite amicable about the details of the divorce. I just wanted my life and my girls and he was entertaining visions of his new bachelorhood and nearly foaming at the mouth over his prospects. We used one attorney and when the judge got the details of the financial arrangement we had made, he nearly dragged us into court. We had to have the attorney go in and convince the judge that I knew what I was doing because the child support was so low for the area. We had to sign all these special documents to prove that I was aware of my rights and truly was comfortable with the figure.

I was to receive a certain amount of cash over the next few years from the equity we had in our house. Traditionally, the wife would remain in the home, but I knew that I would never have owned a home at all had it not been for the small amount of money Steve had received just prior to meeting me from a life insurance policy on his mother. He had used it as a down payment for his first house, so it would never have been right to take that from him. A house was small consolation for having had no mother.

By the same token though, I was sure to be a few hundred dollars short each month for all my bills and knew my savings would only last so long by using it to make up the difference. That too, was a small price to pay for a chance at living, really living, rather than merely existing. It was a small price to pay to go from victim to survivor.

Financial difficulties were actually the least of my challenges. The girls were only four and five then and were completely dependent upon me for everything. They were not even big enough to pour themselves a glass of juice at the time, so my work load was heavy indeed. It wasn't that Steve had done much while we were together when it came to the demands of the children and the house, but at least I had only been working part time then and so I had many more hours in the day in which to get everything done. In the interest of being fair, I might add that Steve was madly in love with his little girls and did do things for them when he was around, at least once they passed the diaper stage. He certainly was not one to do anything as "womanly" as changing diapers. He used to joke that if one needed to be changed and I was not around for some reason, he would just take the baby out on the lawn and hose her off.

Anyone who has ever had children knows how demanding and challenging they can be, especially when they're little. If they were being particularly trying when I was married I could at least get Steve to take over for ten minutes or so in the evening so I could just leave the room to calm myself down. I always told people that I had ten times more patience than I ever thought I'd have, but only about ten percent of the patience that I needed. Sometimes that ten minute break could make the difference between my doing or saying something I might deeply regret and my being able to get a handle on my nasty little temper.

I can remember more than once sitting in my apartment late at night in tears and utterly exhausted from a long day. My alarm would go off at six a.m. which really sucked for me because my natural body clock is a truly nocturnal one wanting to be up late at night and get up late in the morning. Of course my grueling schedule would not allow me the luxury of my hours of preference so when the alarm went off I would rise, get myself ready (no small chore), and then get the girls up and dress them, a task that always presented a battle of wills. I would then get their breakfast ready, again a battle of wills was certain to ensue, forcing me to police their eating and the subsequent teeth brushing. Then it was off to the babysitter and on to a full day at work.

After the work day came the frustratingly long commute back

to the sitter's to pick them up, followed by cooking their dinner, doing the dishes, reading to them (which would soon enough turn into helping them with their homework), bathing them, and getting them ready for bed, which of course brought yet another battle of wills. I would hope and pray it would be a night that would see them fall asleep quickly and quietly and without fighting with each other. More often then not however, I made seemingly endless trips into their room to referee disagreements, remind them, scold them, bribe them or threaten them into closed eyes and closed mouths. Once they finally did fall into the dreamy world of la-la land it was time for housework and laundry and all too soon, making lunches for the next school day was added to the already too long list.

At last I was free to fall into my own bed. More times than I care to remember, it was past midnight by then. I was exhausted and yet so plagued by stress induced insomnia that I would often lie there haunted by nameless anxiety and dread over all the things I had to do the next day. I was completely unable to shut my mind down or even slow it to a bearable pace. I would lay there for hours before finally finding the elusive shadow of sleep at last falling over me, only to wake a couple of hours later, completely stunned by the ruthless noise of my alarm clock sounding reveille again.

On those nights when I was so wiped out and the weight of weariness was great enough to allow me to fall asleep quickly, I would wake a few hours later and toss and turn until the alarm sounded and cruelly rubbed my mind in the harsh reality that the cycle was immediately going to start all over again. I always seemed to awaken feeling as though I lacked the energy to even draw breath.

Nice pattern, huh! It was not the only pattern haunting me. I immediately began dating again; the eternal optimist in stubborn pursuit of the love that would heal me and make everything ok. This was quickly complicated by Steve, who had realized that bachelorhood was not all that he had dreamed of and had decided that I should never be allowed to date anyone else and should, in fact, come back to him. He had so many abandonment issues because of his background that he did not handle the divorce very well. Ok, that's kind of like saying the Titanic did not handle the iceberg very well. He pretty much lost it.

While I was busy exposing my raw heart to the bottoms of boots adorning the feet of each new man I placed my desperate hope for healing in, Steve was busy threatening to kill me if I didn't come back. Since he collected guns and had over a dozen of them, I always had hope that he might have trouble choosing among them, allowing me time to escape the trajectory of his bullet, if not his fury.

I definitely did not feel safe, nor was I having any success in my never ending search for true love. Once again suicide began rearing its' ugly head shouting "Try me, try me," insisting it was still my only viable option.

One Sunday, on my day off, the girls were playing in their bedroom while I sat crying in a chair in the living room, my own handgun lying in ominous silence on my closet shelf. I sat there trying to figure out what would happen to my little girls if I did it. I couldn't bear the thought of Steve raising them and God knows my mother had not exactly been "mother of the year." Though my mother had done some very good parenting along with her very lacking parenting, at this stage of her life she was certainly not at the top of the list of qualified candidates. Sadly enough however, she was at the top of the list of possible candidates. She had, after all, stepped up to the plate and had been caring for the girls for me one day a week in order to help offset some of the cost of my daycare. I certainly still needed the help in the areas of finance as I kept indulging in irresponsible luxuries like food and rent.

So I sat there with rivulets of tears striping my face in mascara (you would think by then I would have only bought waterproof mascara), and hopelessness shrouding my life when, as if right on cue, my mother called me. I don't remember why she called, she didn't call me often, but it may have been a lifesaver that day. Though I tried to clothe my words in the armor of that false courage I had worn so often, she saw through the thin veneer of my false bravado. I had learned early on that people were not for depending on and though I rarely admitted to anyone, let alone her, when I needed help, I broke down.

She convinced me to come over so I packed up the kids and went. Bill kept the girls occupied while my mother and I talked. She suggested I seek the help of a counselor and since I had Kaiser health coverage at the time, it would be affordable for a certain number of visits. It made sense and I agreed to go.

Now here's the insidious thing about low self-esteem; it is not dependent upon reality, only perception. I was not stupid, nor was I blind. I knew, logically speaking, that I was pretty, nearly beautiful. I also knew that I was quite intelligent. My sister Katrina's husband John, who had been around me since I was seven had gone to a great deal of trouble to get that across to me. In addition, I had spent my whole career working with the public and you cannot do that and not realize when there are huge gaps between your intelligence and that of the average consumer. I knew I had talents, my gift for writing poetry and my sales skills at least.

I could sit there and mentally acknowledge all these facts and yet not feel any pride in myself. I knew I had positive attributes and yet they had nothing to do with the way I felt about myself. I still felt completely undeserving of the very love that I had spent my whole life searching for. After all, if I was so lovable, wouldn't Prince Charming have come along by now? Wouldn't my father have come home every night to see me? Wouldn't he have told me of his love for me at least on his death bed?

I still felt like that spoiled, selfish brat my family had described me as so many times. I did not feel love for myself. I felt shame instead. What I *knew* had nothing to do with how I felt, nothing to do with reality, only with how I had always been conditioned to perceive myself.

One night Steve had called, as he often did, and I had broken down on the phone with him. (I sure was doing a lot of that "breaking down" garbage then.) I told him that I felt like a really pretty package, a beautiful present perfectly wrapped and wonderfully decorated, but if you were to strip away the bow and all the ribbon and remove all the pretty paper and open the box, you would find only dog doo inside. I'm not sure why I told him that. He was the least likely person for me to confide in at the time, but I was so vulnerable and he was being so kind at the moment.

So, I went to counseling for the ten or so sessions my insurance covered, made a little progress, garnered a little sympathy, gained a little wisdom, received a bit of understanding as to why I was so screwed up, and became certain I was "cured." Even the insomnia gradually began to ease and though I was definitely not even close to being healed, I felt better than I probably ever had and that was good enough for me. After all, I was quite used to settling for good enough.

Things were starting to look up. Steve had begun dating and seemed a little better adjusted to our split. He had even stopped crying in front of the girls on his nights with them. Though we had both agreed not to blame one another or tear the other one down in front of the children, knowing how harmful that would be to them, he had not strictly kept his end of that bargain.

It broke my heart, but I was willing to accept the blame, hoping that when they were older they would understand that for their sakes, as well as mine, I had to leave. I did not want to take away their natural hero-worship for their father. God knows mine had been stripped when I was all too young and every little girl deserves to have a hero for a father. So I tried not to tell them any of the real reasons I had to leave him. I tried to assure them that it was not their fault, that we both loved them more than anything, but that we fought too much and it wasn't good for any of us. I had to settle for promising them that they would understand it all better when they were older.

I allowed his whole family to blame me as well. I didn't mind losing contact with most of them, except his grandmother on his mother's side. She had been the greatest influence in his life and had probably been ultimately responsible for all the good there was in him. If she had known the truth of how he had treated me, it would have broken her heart and though I had been extremely close to her and missed her desperately, it was a sacrifice I had to make for her sake. I did not do these things because I was so noble or selfless. I am not trying to convince you that I was. It simply seemed to be the right thing to do and the only sensible option I had at the time.

The greatest surprise to come out of the divorce however came to my attention with startling clarity as I awoke one morning. I suddenly realized that I was not angry. I had become so used to being constantly angry, twenty-four hours a day, seven days a week, for more years than one would think bearable, that it was as though the sun had risen for the first time. It's lovely light illuminated a world filled with possibilities. It was a huge and heavy anchor that had at last become unchained and was no longer about my neck, or about my heart. I felt free. It was a true woo-hoo moment!

Some miracles whisper.
I'm sure I believed
that when I found happiness
it would sound like trumpets blaring
and symbols crashing.
But it crept in quietly,
like a gentle shadow.
It was my hope and freedom
that brought peace and joy,
and now I know
it was the anger
that made all the noise.

chapter seven

FROM BAD TO WORSE

Then came Rob. Now I had been unbelievably blessed in my life when it came to romance and passion, in spite of my not so romantic marriage with all its passions misplaced, and in spite of all of those dates that did not quite lead to relationships. I had managed to live a romantic life many women could only dream of, but then, that is where I had directed all of my energies since before I had even experienced my first French kiss at ten years old (sick, huh?). Seriously though, I had even been the bride in a lunch time wedding behind the portable classrooms when I was in the third grade. I ran off, leaving him standing at the altar in true drama-queen fashion.

I had built my entire existence out of fairytale romantic notions and had found it to be the number one source of validation for my value as I searched for the love of my father in every man I met. I was an addict and romance was my drug of choice.

I had culled the ability to portray a confident, independent and magnetic woman and had honed my skills at flirting into a razor sharp instrument that could cut away the resistance of most men. I was, after all, a saleswoman and had acquired excellent social skills. Because of all the work I had put into my romantic mission, I had led an exciting dating life, attracting and dating many handsome, successful and even wealthy men.

I understood the narcissistic nature of human beings and that made me a great date. I was practiced at keeping the conversation focused on my date without him realizing it. By the end of an evening I usually knew volumes about him while he knew very little about me, beyond the fact that I was a good conversationalist, mostly because I had become an attentive listener. You see, I understood that love, especially romantic love, has less to do with who the object of desire is (me) and more to do with how that object of desire makes the other person feel. This is especially true if said object is adept at making the other person feel particularly good about themselves. To be honest, I used the information I gained to qualify men for relationship potential, weeding out most immediately.

Possessing these skills led to numerous declarations of love and even multiple marriage proposals during my somewhat long, if not so distinguished, dating career. Let us not forget that my dating career spanned many years before meeting Steve, as I had begun dating and having boyfriends at about twelve, and also included many stretches of time during those turbulent years I spent with Steve when we were broken up. I see now that most of those "I love yous" and proposals likely came from emotionally unhealthy men who also desperately needed someone to make them feel good about themselves just as I did.

One would have thought with such a vast and interesting dating history that I could not have been so easily taken in by the blazingly romantic charms of an only moderately handsome, semi-successful man like Rob, but let us remember the pathetic desperation with which I had been seeking the cure for my devastatingly lonely, isolated past. Yes, I had made some progress in those counseling sessions, but was still oceans away from being emotionally healthy.

So when Rob waltzed into my life with a mouthful of magic beneath a pair of passions own bedroom eyes, more skilled at verbal seduction than I could have believed possible, than should have been legal, I was way beyond vulnerable to him. I was desperate for him. I had waited my whole life for him. You see, it wasn't just that I was looking for my fathers love in Rob, but he also possessed many of the very charming traits that my father had possessed.

If sales skills are hereditary, I have no doubts where I got mine.

My father could have charmed a snake right out of its skin. I think I probably only tried selling cars because my father had done it off and on for years in between his piano playing gigs. From what I'd heard he could persuade nearly any woman to sleep with him and the fact that he continued this behavior long after he had married my mother was not lost on her. I'm certain that it contributed a great deal to her drinking back then. She probably figured she had a much better chance at keeping him out of strange beds (not to mention jail) if she could keep him home at night, and keeping him home meant keeping the drinks coming.

Oh my father had plenty of other talents in addition to his charm, his powers of persuasion, and his musical talent. He had been published as a writer and was quite an artist as well. He excelled in photography too. His photographs had even been published by the local newspaper. His life was a tragic waste of all those gifts and abilities. Rob, however, only shared common traits with my father like that charm and power of persuasion, and those were the very ones that would come into play as I somehow recreated my parents' courtship.

I was not entirely blind to his brilliant charms. My instincts screamed out inside my gut in an effort to open my eyes. They were loud enough to get me to ask to see his driver's license a few weeks into our relationship. That old saying "If something seems too good to be true, it probably is," pretty much summed it up for me. Yet I continued headlong into the path of this romantic steam roller, convincing myself that I was only trying to sabotage this wonderful new chance at love.

My intuition was not alone in it's displeasure over Rob. Steve did not react to this new little endeavor of mine well either. In fact it probably brought him closer to following through on one of his many death threats than anything else had. He called me at work one night in an absolute rage after discovering that I'd had the nerve to have a friend watch the girls one evening so that I could go to dinner with Rob. This was the only time I had dated on one of the six out of seven nights that I had the girls and for that matter, Steve himself had tried to convince me to get someone else to watch them so that we could go out and talk, but you would have sworn I had just committed some great atrocity of abuse on them by doing this to see Rob.

When Steve called me at work that evening he told me that he had driven all the way out to the store where I worked to kill me, (with the girls in the car, mind you) but thank God, (and I do) he'd missed the exit in his irate state of mind and had driven home to call in his death threat instead. Later that night after I got off work, I had to go to his house to pick up the girls. When I arrived I found him sitting in the dark with a handgun on his lap, loaded of course, (oh, him too) and what little was left of a bottle of Jack Daniels at his feet. He barked at me to sit down. "I'm just here to get the girls and go" I said. "Sit down b——!" he yelled. He was so loud I was surprised that he hadn't awakened the girls who were sleeping in the next room since it was after ten p.m.

When a drunk man with a loaded gun yells at me, I figure it might be prudent to obey, so I did as I was told, hoping to find a way to diffuse the situation before it got really ugly. He slurred out "The way I see it, you've got three choices. I can kill you, you can kill me, or you can come back." I have to admit that the middle one was looking rather attractive to me, at least until he threw that handgun to me. (Or was it *at* me? I've never been quite sure.) "And I don't care which choice you make," he added.

Just as I had done during the rape and the subsequent trial and nearly every other traumatic event in my life, that phony act of courage came back to me and took over. It just happened to be February eleventh so as I set the gun down and rose, I calmly said, "Gee Steve, does this mean you're not sending me roses for valentines day this year?" To this day I don't know where I got the guts to say those words. This was way beyond the false bravado I normally experienced and I was probably as surprised as Steve when I said it. I pushed past him into the bedroom where the girls were sleeping. I picked them up, one at a time, placed one on each hip, and calmly walked out of the house.

I put them in my car and got in myself. I was more than a little relieved to see that he hadn't followed me and I swear I didn't breathe until I was safely down the street.

Though that was certainly not the last confrontation I had with Steve, it was probably the most dangerous. He was such a control freak, certainly because of the completely out of control way he was raised, he just simply could not cope with his inability to control me after all the years he had successfully managed to do just that.

Anyway, Rob had really put on the "full court press" in his efforts to win my heart. He lavished me with fine wines, four star restaurants, limousines, fancy hotels, whirlwind weekend getaways, and expensive gifts. As if that was not enough, he used music, poetry, roses and unparalleled passion, all topped off with explosive sex. I was helpless. If romance was my addiction, with Rob, I was main-lining it.

I fell in love hard and I fell in love fast. This love was unequaled in sheer passion alone by any love I had ever felt before.

Before our first year together was over however, there were countless signs of his infidelity that I chose both consciously and sub-consciously to ignore. I was an ostrich in love who would rather eat sand than face the looming truth. That first year saw numerous red flags go up in front of my closed eyes, destined to remain unseen by any vision but hindsight. Slowly, but surely however, his deft skill at selective truth did begin to become undeniably evident.

We become our own architects
drawing up plans
and crudely drafted dreams of love.
We become our own attorneys
as we construct contracts with our kisses
that will hopefully bind the hearts
more than the lips.
We become our own conductors
as though we are virtuosos
who could set our love to music
and orchestrate some eternal melody.
We end up as addicts,
mainlining one another,
unable to break free of the stranglehold
that romantic fix has on us.
There lies the difference

> *between love and need,*
> *for lovers do not make for qualified engineers*
> *and the needy*
> *do not make good lovers.*

Without even realizing it I had begun that survival trip without a compass through the forest of his words, trying to find my way through the maze of his mind as I attempted to separate the fact from the fiction in his stories.

As I wrestled with my ever growing suspicions, I had career problems to deal with as well. I had lost a couple more jobs due to store closures since the night that Steve came home drunk and attacked me. No matter how much I personally sold, it was never enough to carry a whole store during the slow down of luxury item sales that had been plaguing the fine jewelry business since the recession of the nineties had begun. I had been transferred after the last store I had worked in had closed and had even been promoted to store manager. The company I was working for was in serious financial trouble and had filed for bankruptcy, leaving all of us feeling more than a little insecure about our futures with them.

I worked hard to succeed as manager, all the while the forest of Robs lies became thicker, the red flags larger. (You could have probably wallpapered my apartment with them in fact.) One night he called me well after midnight to tell me that he had gone out of town on business for a couple of days and would be hard to reach. (This was long before cell phones were as common as the cold.)

It just so happened that the next day I had to leave work about six hours early. We were having a special event designed to bring in extra business and I needed to prepare all the food for it. I mentally wrestled with whether I should do the grocery shopping first or pick up the girls from their daycare. (One day soon I would come to realize that it was not me I was wrestling with in my head that day. The decision had already been made. I was just being convinced.) Anyway, the order in which I did both had created absolutely perfect timing to have me driving down a small side street just as Rob was coming up it in the opposite direction with his arm around a young lady in his passenger seat. Now it was my turn to go "Titanic" as they became the iceberg. I went ballistic, postal, Columbine even, to use a few of the latest, tasteless terms that have come to define "losing it."

I whipped a U-turn and chased them down, finally passing them on the right and cutting them off, effectively forcing them to stop. This little configuration was blocking the afternoon traffic, but I could have cared less. All I know is it's a good thing I wasn't armed. It was not a pretty scene as it was. With all the cars behind us honking their horns in frustration, he agreed to pull over into a nearby parking lot where we could talk.

I'm sure that talk was quite a scene for all those nearby, including his date. I probably sounded like a crazy, schizoid, raving maniac. God knows that's how I felt. His date must have thought I was completely certifiable since, as I learned later, he had told her I was his ex-girlfriend, rather than his current fiancé. (That's right, I was pathetic enough to have believed he was going to marry me.)

When I at last regained some small modicum of control, I returned to my car and went home in a complete daze. I got in my apartment and began vacuuming in my high heels and suit. I was in a complete state of shock. Finally I just sat down. I don't know how long I had remained there in that chair, unable to move, unable to function, unable to think, when it finally occurred to me that I still had all that food to prepare. Still, I just sat there, seemingly paralyzed and completely numb mentally. It was as if that last small part of me had finally died.

At last I rose and went to the phone to call Julie. She was unable to help me with the food as her son had a baseball game to play in and she was about to take him to the ball field. So I did what I had done before during a crisis. I called Katrina. I calmly explained the situation to her regarding the store event, the food I needed to prepare and, oh yeah, catching Rob with another woman, leaving me seemingly unable to function. She and John were at my door in less than thirty minutes.

chapter eight

CRASH AND ABOUT TO BURN

John took the girls out for pizza while Katrina helped me to prepare the food for the store event the following day. I can't recall a single sentence spoken between us as we worked in my small kitchen. I was likely emotionally paralyzed and unable to even acknowledge intellectually what had happened just a couple of long hours earlier. I realize that I probably spent a good deal of my childhood like that, for I had mastered the art of burying the unbearable long before that pivotal afternoon. Children simply do not have the emotional resources to handle traumatic pain, so if their parents are not available or capable of helping them through traumatic events, or worse, the cause of such events, children have little choice but to cope by denial while the effects of that event manifest themselves in other ways.

At some point John brought the girls back and I must have put them to bed, though I can't honestly recall that either. The next thing I do remember is Katrina, John, and me sitting at my kitchen table while they urged me to get counseling. I had been whining about having picked yet another loser. I can be a consummate and prolific whiner. I was, after all, the baby of the house, remember? They had suggested that I see the woman who had worked extensively with them. (Katrina and Danni both had seen counselors at one time or another to help them to resolve the issues in their lives that had resulted from our oh-so-cheery childhoods.)

I was droning on and on about my inability to make good choices and how my life never seems to get better, etcetera, etcetera, etcetera. You get the picture. In fact, I'm willing to bet you've said these same types of things yourself once or twice or a few hundred times.

I knew I had to do something because there was simply no way to keep this one buried. I suppose my internal dump was finally full and this little trauma was way too big. It hurt more than anything had ever hurt before and that is saying a lot. I simply could not avoid or escape feeling the overwhelming depth of the pain of this all-consuming betrayal. There was simply "no room at the inn" for a defeat of this magnitude. I had invested every ounce of my being into this romantic, dream-healing, and I was absolutely devastated at its tragic and brutal demise.

At least I already understood that I was responsible for my own life and that if I was going to start making better choices in my pursuit of happiness I needed to learn how. I also knew I needed to understand why I continually made the choices I did before I could learn how to make better ones.

I had, for my whole life, pursued wisdom with a passion and had always been the one to whom others turned for advice and emotional support. I was good at applying wisdom to the lives of others, but seemingly lacked the objectivity, not to mention the training, to address my own issues and apply that wisdom to my life, though I'm sure I believed I was doing just that. Now I needed wisdom, help and advice, well beyond anything I had ever given, but in my current situation I could not afford it. I still barely made ends meet even with the promotion at work. Katrina and John were not going to let that stand in the way. They insisted on paying for half and getting Mom to pay for the other half since they figured that she had contributed to my need for therapy. (To give her credit, my mom agreed to help pay without hesitation.)

I remember looking at John through my tear soaked eyes and saying, "I don't think I have the strength to dig up all the garbage I have buried and work through a whole lifetime of pain." He answered with what would turn out to be one of the truest statements I have ever heard. He said, "It takes a lot more strength and emotional energy to keep all that garbage buried while you try to ignore the pain and anger, than it will to finally deal with it." John had been one of the only people in the world who had never broken a promise to me. Right then he was promising me that fixing the problems would be easier than trying to keep them buried. He had a history of trying to do what was best for me so I believed him.

He went on to tell me that once I had worked through this, not only would my life get better, but so would I. (He was right. It's kind of annoying how often he is.) Katrina said she would make an appointment and amid hugs and tears and my gratitude, they said goodbye and left.

The weight of the pain I was buried under had made me feel more exhausted than I could ever remember being. I went to bed and fell asleep, for a while. Within a few hours I had awakened to that pain. It was just as fresh. The wound was just as raw as it had been the moment I first saw Rob with that girl in his car. I knew I had no hope of getting back to sleep so I called Rob and let him lie to me some more. It would be some time before my willingness to humiliate myself would know some boundaries.

I could recount many more such humiliating scenes between Rob and I that took place over the next week or two as I wrestled with the break up, but it wouldn't serve much use. I'm sure you get the picture, besides, I really haven't got the stomach for it. I doubt it matters much to you. I'm sure if we ever met you and I could swap horror stories such as these for longer than either one of us would care to.

As if the devastation caused by Rob were not enough, life (or God) had a bit more to throw at me. I got fired. That's right. Not layed off. Not let go. Fired! Though I'm sure it had more to do with the company's financial state than anything personal, they only cited reasons such as the stores electricity bill was too high. Knowing that my performance had been more than adequate did not help much to ease my despair.

I see now what a blessing it actually was losing that job. Even though it had been nearly two decades since I had briefly tried that "God thing," I still had enough respect for Him to recognize when He was trying hard to get my attention. It was clear to me He was in effect saying, "I've tried to reach you for almost twenty years. I've tried to get you to make different choices all along the way, but you have continued to ignore Me and constantly insisted upon doing things your own way. Well, look where it's gotten you. I'm done being subtle. If I have to crash your world and burn it to the ground to get you to listen, then I will."

He, in fact, had. I didn't need to hear an audible voice to get this message loud and clear. Again I remind you, I am not stupid. I knew instinctively in a way that defies logic that this was the will, if not the work, of God, as surely as I knew my own name. If I'd had any doubts back then I sure don't now. Years later I would also come to recognize the rest of the message He had tried to send me back then. I believe it was "This is the life you made, but it is not the life I have planned for you. You will rebuild your life, but you will do it out of different pieces, better pieces, pieces that I will provide for you."

Now I could have had another job in the jewelry industry the very next day with a single phone call. I likely could have had a few to pick from with a few phone calls. That's one good thing about a career in sales; there are almost always jobs for an experienced sales person in any given industry. I had been fortunate enough to have built a reputation locally within the jewelry business that would have practically guaranteed me employment even in those tough times. My lengthy experience was somewhat rare in the field and became more valuable when times were tough.

For that matter I probably could have had another man the next day as well, but I thank God (literally) that I had enough sense to at least recognize that it would have only made matters worse. Another job in jewelry and another man were the same pieces I had previously built my life out of and I needed a new life, so I realized that I needed new pieces. New pieces would only be found when I gained the tools to unearth them.

So, believe it or not, I actually took some advice from Steve who told me to take some much needed time off. It turned out to be an entire summer that I ended up taking off. Between my unemployment checks, my child support, no daycare costs since I was home, and my good pal Visa, we got by. It actually turned out to be the best investment I could have made in my relationship with my two beautiful daughters who were barely six and seven at the time. It was not such a bad investment in my relationship with myself either.

For months and months I'd endured long working hours, a stress and anger level that was way off the charts, and guilt over always being the last one to pick up my kids from the new daycare center they were in. (I had fired the babysitter, my new ex-friend, when she started sleeping with Steve, conflict of interest and all, you know.) The girls and I desperately needed some time to decompress, relax, and just hang out together.

That long and lazy summer unfolded without alarm clocks. What a gift! I had time to bond with Katie and Laura in a way I had been unable to do since leaving Steve. With the help of one of their friends I taught them how to swim. I taught them to hit a baseball (with no help), and to ride their bikes without the training wheels (Okay, I had a little help with that one too, but just a little).

We shared a cabin with Danni and her family, went camping with friends and even went to Disneyland with good old Visa and a neighbor. It was a priceless time that probably reversed a course that likely would have resulted in the continuity of that vicious cycle of dysfunction begun so many generations back in my family. The girls needed me and even though I tried to meet their every need and tried to always put those needs first, I had to work too much to make the bills and when I was with them I was stressed out, ticked off and basically emotionally unhealthy, if not unavailable. Add to that the huge distraction that Rob presented and no matter how much I loved them and how hard I tried to be a great mother, I could not have continued on in that way and have hoped to have succeeded.

No less importantly, I was finally making a real investment in myself, and my family had absolutely come through for me regardless of any past mistakes they may have made. While Katrina and my mom paid for my counseling, Danni stepped up and watched the girls for me during my sessions.

Well, so much for the sob story. Up until now you've been reading about the long road I took straight to rock bottom. Though I can't promise to completely omit any further sob stories, I can promise that this is where I truly began my journey to joy. I invite you to take me up on this invitation and come along with me now. I pray, again literally, that you will. You just might find a roadmap that will help you to navigate your own journey to joy.

Again I reiterate, I am not a psychotherapist. I am just a woman who, probably like you have, got tired of pain, of failure, of poor choices, of shame, of anger, and of being only reactive in my life instead of being proactive.

I finally got it! No one, not even a prince, could heal me. Only I could do that. It would take some time, it would take some work, and it would take some courage, but oh, what a payoff!

PART TWO

Therapy

We chase the demons
and monsters
from the dark and whispery
attics and cellars
in our minds.
We hunt for them
through the cobwebs
that hover in the
more neglected corners
and passageways,
armed with wooden stakes
and silver bullets.
We search with mere
flickers of light
from the torches
or candelabras that we carry
like a scene from some old
horror movie,
replete with every
wretched villain
that we can conjure up.
Some of us are content
just to keep the creatures
locked away,
behind faux walls
and beneath trap doors,
but there are those of us,
more daring,
more adventurous,

who openly pursue them,
drag them out
into the daylight
to expose them
for what they are.
We rip off masks
and disguises
until we have proved
to ourselves,
that we had created
our own monsters
from essentially
human seeds.
We twisted and warped
and buried them
ourselves.
And when we have exorcised
all the demons
from our minds
and cleaned out all
the poltergeists,
then,
and only then,
the spirits that remain
will be our own,
and they shall be as free
as wild angels,
for when you release the monsters,
you unlock your soul.

chapter nine

ACCOUNTABILITY / RECLAIMING YOUR POWER

I'm special! So are you. Each one of us is because God made each of us completely unique among all the billions of people He has created throughout time. One difference between you and I may be that I now understand that I am special. I believe it now because several years ago I made a choice to do whatever it would take to learn how to become happy. I accepted responsibility for my life and the quality of it. I decided to become proactive in seeking the joy I longed for.

One of the most important things I learned in beginning the process is that I am accountable for the choices I make and the results of those choices. No one else has the power to change my life, nor do they have the responsibility to do so. If I wanted to be happy it was up to me. Well, I wanted to be happy so I sought the tools I needed and then I used them to make the necessary changes within myself that led to better choices, better results, and a better life.

Your story is surely different than mine in the details and probably in the dynamics as well. Your history may have been harder, it may have been easier, but if you're still with me on the page, I'll bet the resulting feelings have been very similar. So many of us grow up knowing more guilt than good, more shame than assuredness, more self-loathing than self-love.

We don't have to make those feelings a life sentence. That punishment in no way fits the crime of simply having lived through emotionally traumatic events, or having been raised by emotionally unhealthy, or just unenlightened parents. Low self-esteem can be the product of many things and no matter what you attribute yours to, it gives you only a reason for having it, not an excuse for continuing to live with it. If you don't know what it's like to feel good about who you are then you don't know real peace and you can't know true joy and you deserve to know both.

Perhaps there were painful situations that occurred in your life that came to define you in a way that has the weight of shame and feelings of worthlessness strapped to your back, years, even decades later, until that weight has you feeling more like the hunchback of Notre Dame than a prince or princess.

Even if your parents did most of the right things in raising you, they may not have had any idea of how to foster good self-esteem in children. They may not have even known the term "self-esteem," let alone the importance of having it.

Suffering from feelings of inadequacy does not necessarily indicate that we had bad parents. Even very functional parents may have failed to instill good self-esteem in you, not out of cruelty or some lack of love, but simply because of the way they were raised. People often tend to parent by following the role models they had—their parents. They likely emulated their own parents who were never enlightened by Oprah or Dr. Phil. Your parents just may not have had an understanding of how to help you recognize your worth or how to help you to overcome the damage the outside world may have been causing to your sense of self-worth.

Most parents of past generations had enough on their plates just trying to survive. They may have been struggling through the depression or any one of the wars Americans have been involved in. Your parents and grandparents probably worked long, hard hours just to put food on the table and clothes on their children and a roof over the family. Who had time to work on emotional health when they had so many challenges to overcome just to maintain the physical health of their families, with a lot more disease around and a lot less medical knowledge and medicine? Life was different in past generations and in many ways it was harder.

My mother was certainly not a bad person, nor was her mother. They both however had been victimized in their lives and emotionally damaged because of it. They were simply ill-equipped to deal with emotional issues and were therefore incapable of enabling their children to cope with them. It is just the way the cycle of dysfunction works and perpetuates itself. This does not mean it is not our duty to ourselves and to future generations to break this cycle. On the contrary, it is our responsibility to break it, rather than to pass it on.

Most of us simply race through our days,
unaware that at any moment
we might hit the wall.
We should be instead taking time
to peel back the layers
and reveal who we are.
We should climb up into our consciousness
and strive to live there.
Instead we merely feel our way
through a sightless world
with our hands out in front,
trying desperately to distinguish
separate shapes and textures
in the blackness of the ignorance
that comes with blind acceptance.
We do not break free
from the slavery of fate.
We remain commanded by the puppetry
of circumstances,
uninspired, unenlightened, numeric.
Some days I want to go around asking people,
"How much would you charge for your soul,

or have you already gotten your price?"
For most of us just trudge along,
afraid of becoming social misfits and outcasts,
so we stay trapped beneath a roof
that is really no more than cellophane,
just an illusionary prison.
We waste whole lives
afraid of rising up
and being set free.

Charles Swindol wrote that, "Life is ten percent what happens to me and ninety percent how I react to it." It doesn't matter whose behavior led to your low self-esteem, it is still up to you to repair it. That may not be fair, but it's the truth.

The reason you are the only one who can heal yourself is because you are the only one whose behavior you can control. You cannot control anyone else's. Though you may not be able to choose how you will feel about another person's behavior, you can and must learn to control how you will react to it, how you will let it affect you, and how much power you will give it in your life.

If your self-esteem was damaged due to the behavior of others you must choose now to stop responding in the same way that you have been. You do have a viable alternative. There are skills you can learn and steps you can take to repair the emotional damage rather than continuing the same non-productive behaviors and the same rationalizations (excuses) for them. Doing nothing is the same as choosing to allow your past to continue to rule your life and inflict pain while preventing joy. Since every action you take in your life is a choice, so is every action you don't take.

Those choices bring consequences and those consequences directly affect the quality of your life. If those choices involve drinking or drugging yourself to avoid your pain they can also affect the length of your life. Your choices can reflect who you are, but may not reflect who you could be, who you are meant to be.

Many people use their past pain and abuses as excuses for fail-ure. My counselor once told me that it was no minor miracle that I was sitting in her office seeking help rather than turning tricks or doing drugs. Fortunately, those were choices I did not make. I had enough excuses to rationalize that type of failure at life if I had been so inclined. Thank God I wasn't, but I have met plenty of less fortu-nate women who were.

It would have been all too easy to wallow in self-pity and blame others for my mess of a life. I know just how easy because there were plenty of times when I did just that. As you read earlier, I kept wait-ing for some knight in shining armor to come and rescue me from my pain, from my past. That was not very joyful. It was not very helpful either. There was not a single knight out there who held the respon-sibility for making my life better. That responsibility fell squarely on the shoulders of this damaged damsel in distress.

A happy life must be built from the inside out. It requires you to strip away the excuses that by their very familiarity have offered a warped sense of comfort. Even though pain hurts, if it is all you're used to, you become comfortable with it as it becomes familiar, a known quantity as opposed to an unknown quantity. Pain can also give you excuses for your failures. No one expects much out of a vic-tim and victims tend not to expect much out of themselves. Often people get caught in a vicious cycle of feeling pain, which brings excuses for failure, such as not even trying or sabotaging their efforts. That brings even more pain. The familiar status of being a victim is then perpetuated. Giving up the comfort and convenience of the excuses that victim status affords you can be scary, even though they can be exchanged for peace and joy. It is human nature to find change frightening, even when it's for the better.

You may worry, "What if I do all this emotional archaeology and still fail?" Here's the indisputable truth. You can't fail because you can't lose any ground by trying if you are not happy to begin with. If you were happy, you probably would not be reading this book. So you have absolutely nothing to lose. If you are not happier after taking this journey, then you are certainly no worse off than you are right now, although I find it impossible to believe anyone truly seeking help will not get some from this book.

I am certain, however, that if you are diligent in learning and applying these skills, honest with yourself in assessing your feelings and your behavior choices, and courageous in facing your past, you will change the way you feel about yourself and that will change the quality of your life. Self-esteem equals confidence and confidence equals courage; the courage necessary for going after the life you truly desire, the life you truly deserve. But nothing in your life will ever improve if you do not take the initiative now to do what it takes to improve it at the very core level. That means you have to take some action and apply skills that will allow you to feel your self-worth, not just on the surface, not just when you're having a good day, but deep down in your soul every day.

Caught in the eye of the wave
during yet another life storm,
there are thoughts being born,
mere tiny mental grains
moving slowly through your brain
gathering momentum, growing into words,
the words connecting with other words,
forming themselves into sentences,
until the thought is whole and complete,
no longer moving like light through water,
but like clarity after a fog lifts,
until the breath stops in your chest
and your eyes become wide with the revelation
and you are suddenly aware
that your moment of truth is a lie
and that you are not now
and never have been
the one in control.
All at once you realize
that you've been but a row boat
being tossed about upon the sea of life.

> *You've lived without a rudder or sails.*
> *You've had no motor, not even any oars.*
> *You have remained at the mercy*
> *of the waves and the weather,*
> *all the people who have moved*
> *in and out of your life.*
> *Grasping this truth*
> *is the beginning of your birth,*
> *the first step you will take*
> *to reclaim your power,*
> *the power that will set you back on solid ground*
> *where you will choose the road you take*
> *and map out your own destination at last.*

If you have been carrying the baggage of old pain and low self-esteem around, you have given away the power in your life. Ironically enough, you have given it away to the very people who have proven themselves the least worthy of having it. You have given it to those who have already shown themselves to behave in ways that are not in your best interest. This allows you to continue to make choices that perpetuate pain and are self-destructive. These choices have you settling, out of fear and feelings of being undeserving, for things and relationships that are not fulfilling. Settling is to give in again and again to a powerless, reactive existence.

You can and must reclaim that power. You need to take it back from the people and situations that have hurt you in the past and those that may be hurting you in the present. You must not remain at the mercy of circumstances and the mercy of other people.

If you are dependent upon others to make you feel good about yourself because you are unable to recognize your own self-worth, you have given away your power. If you are allowing people to mistreat you and take advantage of you, you have given away your power. If you wallow in self-pity because you have had it so rough, you have given away your power. If you abuse drugs or alcohol, you have given away your power. If you do anything to a severely excessive degree (work, spend, date, have sex, primp, eat, diet, exercise, remain busy, carry other peoples burdens, etc…), in an attempt to avoid your feelings of pain and inadequacy, you have given away your power.

If you have given away your power you are not in control of your own life. That can lead to anxiety because of that decreased control. You likely feel greater pain because you probably personalize everything bad that happens to you. Furthermore, you may feel greater hopelessness due to believing that you have no ability to affect any positive changes in your life.

You do have that ability. The power to direct your life is inherent in all people. You just need to learn how to do so. You must learn how to make choices that are in your best interest, choices that will put your life back on the track on which it was meant to be. That means you must also come to understand the reasons you make the choices you have been making. It is likely because of your unrecognized, but desperate need to feel good about who you are. You have probably made countless attempts to find that quick fix for the emotional pain that accompanies poor self-esteem. I have named many such examples two paragraphs back. They are all just temporary measures and amount to no more than a band-aid for a bullet hole. There is no quick fix.

But there is hope. You're reading it. It will require some work, but the paycheck will be immeasurable. You will need to examine your own life, your history, your feelings, and your patterns. You must be ready to face all of these and truly assess them. You need to be willing to process any unresolved feelings, to recognize and replace all those berating tapes in your head with encouraging ones, and to nurture yourself and become your own biggest supporter, your own friend and advocate. You must learn to set boundaries to protect yourself from future avoidable injustices and to let go of the past ones rather than allowing them to continue to inflict pain, self-doubt, and the poison of anger.

How do you do this? Open your mind and your heart and read on. When should you begin? Yesterday!

chapter ten

URGENCY

What's the rush? Why yesterday? I'll answer those questions with a question. What is the single resource you have that is absolutely finite? Give up? Time. You cannot retrieve lost time. You can always make more money if you go broke, but you can never make any more time. Every minute that passes, passes away. You cannot stop the process or even slow it down. You cannot alter it in any way. It is an indisputable fact that time moves even when you stay still.

I say this because it is vital that you not only decide to begin this healing process immediately, but that you actually begin it immediately. If you're like most people you have great intentions, but poor follow through. You probably always mean to fix that leaky faucet, or organize your closet, but it never quite makes it to the top of your priority list. Those things just don't have the same sense of urgency as the immediate demands of the day like getting to work, feeding the kids, paying the bills, etc...

So you figure when you get some free time, you'll get around to it. We all know there really is no such thing as free time. It costs time to spend it doing anything and no matter how much free time we think we will have, there is always far more that needs to be done than we have hours in which to do it. As for those long stretches we plan to use so constructively, like vacation time and weekends and such, they still have a way of ending up packed with more urgent, or at least more entertaining activities. We always manage to fill our time up while the list of "should do's" just gets longer and pushed even further down the road of tomorrow's.

If only we were half as prudent with our time as most of us tend to be with our money. How many hours do we spend watching inane sitcoms on television? Too many. Don't get me wrong. I am not one of those anti-television, intellectual snobs. I love my T.V. It's a great tool for relaxing and decompressing and everyone deserves to indulge in a little insipid programming sometimes. I like to dumb down with some occasional low grade brain candy as much as the next guy or gal. And hey, in the great age of cable, you can even learn something from T.V. I just don't recommend a steady diet of network programming that excludes the more productive endeavors you might engage in. Spending all of your free time watching T.V. is more foolish than emptying your bank account and giving it to some guy in a trench coat who is promising to sell you the Brooklyn Bridge. You can make money to fill your bank account again, but there is no piggy bank for time. What you use stays gone forever.

I do not advocate being busy all the time either. We all need some down time. It's as vital to our well being as work and food. You may be one of those people who never sits around. Perhaps you are on the move constantly, filling your time with endless tasks that keep you working on a perpetual list of "urgent" things to do, your hands always busy, your mind always distracted. That is not much more valuable than being a T.V. drone. Either extreme consumes vast quantities of your most precious and limited resource and neither does anything to enhance the quality of your life.

My point is simply that you need to use your time wisely and strive to maintain a balance in how you spend it. I cannot personally think of a wiser way to use your time than investing in you, your life, your happiness. So choose to spend time right now doing the most important work of your life, the inner work, the examining and processing of your feelings, patterns and history. It is not all that time consuming of a process and yet is the most constructive thing you can do for yourself, as well as your family. Everyone benefits from being around a happy, productive person and positive role model.

The sense of urgency in actually beginning your journey to joy comes not only from my wanting you to use your time wisely. It also comes from knowing life offers no guarantees on its length. So don't wait until tomorrow. You never know how many tomorrows you may have.

Let me tell you about a couple of friends of mine. They were both clients I met on my job. The first one saw my name on his invoice not long after I took over the territory and called me to set up a meeting. The meeting really wasn't necessary, but he said later that he felt compelled to meet me. I guess the name Victoria sounded far more alluring to him than the name Vince, his former sales reps name. We connected quickly (not that way) and developed a wonderful friendship. I was thirty-five at the time and he was close to sixty.

One day over lunch he confessed to me that he and his grown daughter had not been on speaking terms for many months. He described the incident that had led to their falling out and I believed that he was justified in his anger, but he was quite distraught over the split. I suggested that he would do better to apologize, even if he was right, in order to bridge the existing chasm. I was able to convince him that being happy was more important than being right.

He put his ego aside and took my advice and apologized, which not only re-opened the dialogue between them, but also enabled him to resume a loving relationship with his daughter. It is not rare to find good advice, but it is quite rare to find someone who is willing to follow that good advice. For some reason, unbeknownst to me, but not to God, Darryl was one of those rare people who listened to and actually acted upon the advice I gave him. He even followed my advice on his love life, or should I say the lack there of?

I asked him one day, again over lunch, if he was content to grow old alone. He had been divorced for well over a decade and had done little, if anything, to find any love and companionship since. I'm certain that is why he had bonded to me as he did, for it was not only romance that he had not invested himself in, but people in general. He was very independent and self-sufficient and had not gone to any more effort to make friends than he had gone to in pursuit of romance. Sure he had plenty of acquaintances, but not what you would call real, true friends. That had to be lonely at times. Much to my surprise he would eventually come to refer to me as his best friend. I am extremely honored that he chose to let me in and that he got so close to me, but it is sad that he waited so long to begin creating true friendships again.

Anyway, I told him that if he didn't want to grow old and die alone he would have to go out and actively try to meet women he might like to date. "Ms. Right is not going to come knock on your door one night and announce herself as eligible and interested and enter your living room and your life." I said.

Darryl loved the horse races and one day not long after that conversation he approached a woman there named Emily. They connected on a much deeper level (yes, that way), and were married within a year or two. Had Darryl ignored my advice he would never have made the effort to meet Emily and he would have continued to exist in the same unfulfilling way that he had for years, and that's how he would have died. You see, Darryl contracted a form of cancer of the blood and died a few short years later.

The good news is, Emily is a Christian woman of great faith and God was able to use her to help re-establish a long broken connection between Darryl and Him. Darryl died a man of faith, sure of his future and the eternal life promised in Christ.

I know in my heart that God brought Darryl and me together because He knew Darryl's time was short and He wanted him to live that time in joy and to leave that time in peace.

I was fortunate enough to have had Darryl tell me how I had changed his life by urging him to heal the relationship with his estranged daughter and to seek out love in his life. The truth is, I didn't change Darryl's life. Darryl changed his own life. Imagine if he had not even ignored my advice, but only procrastinated. He could have easily wasted his last precious years intending to get around to it, only to find it too late.

He could have died never having met the love of his life, having missed out on the grand joy, exhilarating passion, and blessed comfort that Emily gifted him with. He could have died never having reconciled with his daughter, never having given her away at her wedding, never having enjoyed those last years of love between a father and his daughter. What a tragedy that would have been.

> *Pondering this opportunity*
> *has me reflecting on all those*
> *aborted attempts,*
> *all those moments when I stood*
> *sometimes determined, sometimes uncertain,*
> *but unable to move,*
> *not forward, not backward,*
> *just frozen in time,*
> *paralyzed in place and trapped*
> *in the fire of burning indecision.*
> *Even making a mistake,*
> *if done with initiative,*
> *is far preferable to remaining*
> *safely ensconced in the thick mud*
> *of cowardice.*
> *Life must be led with courage,*
> *lest we die buried*
> *beneath a mountain of regrets.*
> *Hell is*
> *"I should have."*

If that story did not encourage you to act immediately, perhaps this one will. Rick, like Daryl, was also a client who had become a friend. He was married when I first met him, not happily, but married nonetheless. He and his wife had a young son of about four whom Rick positively adored. Rick came home from work one day to be blindsided by his wife's demand that he leave and give her a divorce. Rick had worked very hard to provide for his family and had just bought a big, new house that his wife had insisted upon having. Rick ended up renting a room from a stranger, while his wife kept their son and enjoyed the luxury of that beautiful home.

Before long she was dragging him through nasty battles over custody and property and money. Greedily and deceptively she used every trick in the book, including their little boy, to gain the financial advantage.

After months and months of this legal and emotional wrangling, Rick fell in love with a sweet and wonderful woman with whom he had worked and with whom he had been friends for quite some time. They were making plans for a future together. Rick had rented an apartment large enough for the two of them and his cherished son and they had begun putting money away for a wedding and a home of their own.

Rick was happier than he had been in many years. On his son's fifth birthday, Rick had spent the day playing with him as hard as any kid would have played, much to the delight of his adoring little boy. Later on that evening Rick complained to his fiancé of severe back pain. She insisted upon taking him to the hospital where he died of a massive heart attack an hour or so later. He had been in excellent shape and had lived a very healthy lifestyle and yet he died. He was forty-five.

I ask you; do you know how many tomorrows you have left? When do you think you should begin building a happier you, a happier life? If you are blessed with far greater longevity than either of these two men, how do you want to spend that time? If you have fifty years, would you rather spend them stuck in the quagmire of blindly surviving pain, dissatisfaction and the feelings of worthlessness, or would you rather spend them fulfilled and joyful?

Okay. So now you get the sense of urgency, but how do you find the time to do that inner work? You make it! You make yourself a priority for maybe the first time in your life.

For years my mantra was "I want time to write." Time for a few poems on a Saturday morning was simply not enough. I dreamed of the time when my daughters would go off to college (even though I shall miss them like crazy), so that I could have more free time to enjoy my passion for writing. I planned out the way I would fill an extra bedroom with my desk and computer and my vast collection of poetry books and my books on the craft of writing. My husband and I have always intended to sell our house when the kids left home and buy something in the country where we could enjoy the lush surroundings of nature rather than the stressful surroundings the San

Francisco Bay Area offers. Of course I would not consider moving before they graduate. I promised them, as well as myself, that they would remain in the school district they started out in and never have to deal with losing their friends and starting over, well at least not until college.

Anyway, we figure we will eventually be able to give up our high stress careers for part time jobs or a small business if we don't have to endure the high price of housing that exists here and keeps us tied to the higher salaries the area offers. Then I will finally have time to write. We've talked about maybe having a little cottage on the property where I could while away the hours indulging in my great passion. I felt certain I could get so much more writing done in a room in the country, my creativity inspired by all my books and all that greenery.

That is still my dream, but it is no longer my excuse for not writing more. I understand now that I was overwhelmed and intimidated by the prospect of writing anything more than my poems, small pieces quick to have an ending. I was equally unsure of my ability to write anything but poetry. I had been lucky enough to have somehow talked my way into being paid to write a half-page weekly column for a local sports magazine devoted to the Raiders football team (another one of my passions), when the girls were little, but beyond that I had never really written anything besides business letters and my poems.

Anyway, with a full time career, two teenage daughters whose lives I am extremely involved in, a commitment to help out those in need within our community, and an active church and social life, when was I going to find the time to write more?

Well, I am writing this in the family room (instead of my dream office), while we all watch T.V. I am writing this in the car when my husband drives us anywhere that will take more than thirty minutes. I am writing this on Saturdays and Sundays in my bedroom or kitchen, or backyard. I am writing this on weeknights after work. I am writing this any time and any place I can get a few free minutes.

I tell you this because you need to recognize that anytime you put off doing something that is decidedly constructive, such as taking the first steps on your own journey to joy, you are likely making excuses to avoid beginning something that is unfamiliar and thereby intimidating. Furthermore, I learned that you can always find time for something you are really motivated to do. It is simply a matter of prioritizing the way to spend the time that you do have.

I can't make you find the time, nor can I do any better job at motivating you, but I can at least remove some of the element of risk that may seem to exist in this unfamiliar process. It does not involve huge amounts of time. You can examine your particulars for a little while at night before you go to bed and on weekends you could schedule a small block of time in between the "absolutely have to get done things" You must simply make this, too, an "absolutely have to get done thing."

Heck, it doesn't even cost money. Even if you decide you need the professional help of a qualified therapist to deal with something that seems too painful or complicated to deal with on your own, many counselors will work on a sliding scale if you need them to. The only real investment you have to make is to commit to learning and applying the skills and tools that I describe for you.

So what are you waiting for? Turn the page!

chapter eleven

EGO VS. SELF-ESTEEM

Many people confuse the words ego and arrogant with self-esteem and confidence. Some fear that building up their self-esteem will make them unbearable egotists. They may believe that being modest and humble is far more important than being confident. Wrong on both points. There are enormous differences between ego and self-esteem and being confident is the very core of our ability to not only truly be humble, but to enjoy and succeed in life, no matter what the endeavors are that we pursue. Being humble is important, such as being humble before God and knowing our practical limitations so that we can accurately assess when we need help. For example, I am humbled when I need legal advice and seek out a lawyer. This of course does not mean I am stupid. It only indicates that I am not educated in legal matters. Being arrogant and egotistical sometimes makes people too afraid to admit, even to themselves, that they may not be equipped to handle something. That can create a lot of trouble, especially with God.

People often confuse a good show of ego with healthy self-esteem. They are truly quite the opposite and you may not even know for certain which you possess. Ego commonly manifests itself in the form of arrogance. That can sometimes be mistaken for self-esteem to the casual observer, but is often more a sign of insecurity than anything else.

Rob was a classic example of an arrogant man and was one of the most insecure men I've ever known. I didn't realize this at first of course, but it is crystal clear to me now. He was quick to brag of all his grand accomplishments. Rob often spoke of all the great businesses he had built, all the beautiful women he had been involved with, his great athletic prowess and his superior intelligence. He made a great show of buying expensive wine and champagne in restaurants, especially if we were with people he wanted to impress.

Early on in our relationship he showered me with expensive and lavish gifts. He even bought a brand new color television for me as a token gift on our fourth or fifth date to replace the small black and white I had in my bedroom. As I mentioned in a previous chapter, he pulled out all the stops when it came to those early dates, spoiling me with the most impressive hotels and restaurants and all the costly trimmings you could add to a date, up to and including planes, trains and fancy automobiles.

This lavish treatment is even more impressive (or really less) when you consider that he only rented a room from a woman (with whom he also slept) in an affluent town not far from the town in which I could at least afford to rent an entire apartment. I remember him even being ashamed to admit to people at a party in the very exclusive community of Blackhawk, that I lived in the city I did because it was definitely not impressive.

I learned further into the relationship that he had maxed out all his credit cards to wine me and dine me as he did. Apparently Rob never believed that I might have fallen in love with him if he had been a man just squeaking out a living like me. He felt he had to create this grand illusion that he was some huge financial and social success in order to impress me and win my heart.

Furthermore, I learned that every business he had ever built had gone on to fail. In fact, he had managed to sabotage every business and every relationship he had ever been in, including of course, ours.

He was all about image and convincing people that he was what he believed he needed to be in order to win their respect and affection. (I guess he believed that everyone was as shallow as he was.) You see for all his bragging and showmanship, he clearly did not believe that he deserved respect or love based on who he truly was, so he spent immeasurable amounts of energy and who knows how much money he could ill afford to spend, to create the illusion that he was someone he believed would be worthy.

I'm certain his infidelity was yet another manifestation of his insecurity. I believe he needed to prove his desirability over and over again to none other than himself. I later learned that when he would travel on business to conventions and such he would often bring this blonde bimbo with her store bought, big bust to impress his associates. I was clearly not only not quite impressive enough, but I had a job and two kids and was certainly not available to travel with him. How convenient for him.

To casually know Rob you would likely be sure he was brimming with confidence. If you looked a little deeper however, you would see a man desperate to prove himself worthy and unable to convince the most important person of all of his worthiness: himself. If you spent a little time with him you would also see that he fed his ego off of the shortcomings of others. Rob was quick to put others down as a way to make himself look superior to them. Because he did not actually feel superior, the only way he could look superior was to make others look inferior.

He had also perfected the game of one-up-manship so that no matter who had what story to tell, he could top it and steal the glory. Whatever another had accomplished he was certain to have done it better.

Another way ego can manifest itself is in the inability to admit being wrong. This was one of the ways Steve's ego showed itself. He could never afford to acknowledge any weaknesses or failures. His ego demanded that he always be right.

Self-esteem on the other hand is comfortable with apologies and admissions of error when they are applicable. Not that anyone enjoys being wrong, but a person with healthy self-esteem realizes that being wrong does not devalue them. At worst it humanizes them. Making mistakes is as much a part of the human experience as triumph is. I added the "when applicable" phrase because the opposite can be true in people of low self-esteem. Some people irrationally take the blame for everything and are so certain they can never be right that they apologize for everything, no matter how illogical that may actually be.

An egotistical person will probably not be very generous in handing out compliments either for fear that building another up may make the other person look superior to them. On the other hand, a person with healthy self-esteem will be pretty comfortable complimenting others and not see another person's strength as a threat to them. For an egotistical person, any act that makes someone else look good becomes internalized and warped into a way that they perceive as making them look bad.

Healthy self-esteem means having an honest, rational, and good self-image. It means you do not view life as a contest that constantly pits you against others and causes you to be afraid to risk being found inferior in a comparison. When you like who you are, you have no desire to see others be made to look bad, nor do you attempt to steal their limelight by working at making yourself look better than them. If you are truly comfortable with yourself you are able to enjoy the freedom of not worrying about whether others recognize your worth or not. You waste no time trying to prove your value to other people. The opinions others have of you do not affect your opinion of yourself. They are unrelated and you understand that. Of course it's always nice to be appreciated and thought well of, but you are not dependent upon others recognizing your worth for you to feel your worth.

If you are worried about others knowing how great you are then you probably do not believe you are great yourself. If you desperately need the admiration and validation of others it is surely because you are unable to provide that validation for yourself and you are probably directing enormous energy in the wrong areas as you try to get that validation.

If you recognize any of the common traits that egotistical people have, as being traits you exhibit, this may be a little bit of a rude awakening for you. If this book is sounding that alarm clock for you, it is to wake you up to a new day, a day filled with the rewards that healing your self-esteem will bring.

One of the many rewards of healthy self-esteem is the very removal of the ego that causes you far more social damage than you may know. As you begin to change the way you feel about yourself and become happy and confident with who you are, you will find that you will enjoy your own company more and so will others. People are naturally drawn to happy, confident people, but are loathe to be around egotistical, insecure people. As you heal your self-esteem you will likely find a more rewarding social life begins to emerge as well.

Now after all you've read about Rob, you might think it would have been easy to walk away from him and never look back. It was anything but. Although I was beginning to discover that the man I had fallen in love with did not actually exist, the dream of having that illusion turn real was mighty powerful stuff, and besides, the actual man who did exist did not want to let me go. I don't know if it's because he really did love me and regretted sabotaging yet another relationship, or if he simply did not like to lose. The most pathetic part of all, especially where I am concerned, is that he continued to pursue me and I continued to give in. He also continued to see the girl I had caught him with as well. Since she was only twenty-one, I use the term "girl" quite intentionally.

Though our relationship had drastically changed and was more than severely damaged, Rob relentlessly chased me, turning the romance and the charm on full blast in an effort to keep me in his life. He cast us as the tragic, star crossed lovers who could not work things out, yet could not remain apart. How trite. It's rather difficult to work things out when there are three of you in a relationship.

I had already attended a few counseling sessions, as I sought help in unraveling my past and its power over my choices. I knew that it was definitely not in my best interest to continue any form of communication with Rob, but I simply had not progressed to the point where I could resist his constant pressure. As devastated as I had been by his infidelity, I was still desperate to be loved by him. I believe I was terrified of discovering that perhaps he had not loved me after all, or that it was somehow my fault that he could not remain faithful to me, that I was not pretty enough, sexy enough, or good enough in bed. Factor in that he owed me over two thousand dollars and I still had incentive to talk with him. (I know, how much more pathetic could I have been?) Oh, occasionally my resolve would hold and I'd not give in to seeing him, but early on after the split, I'd relent, if for no other reason than I was hooked on the physical part of the relationship.

Seeing Rob was not the only thing I was doing that was not in my best interest. I had begun smoking again after eight years as a non-smoker. It started innocently enough. I'd been having a drink with my sister, Danni, one afternoon at her house when she surprised me by lighting up. Apparently she was one of those smokers who could indulge in a cigarette occasionally with a drink and not pick them up again for weeks. I figured after all the time I had not smoked, I could do the same. Wrong! Within a few weeks I was buying them by the carton again.

Now, I drink in moderation with no problem. I may have a drink every couple of months or so, but that's about it. Now with smoking, that's another story. I can't smoke in moderation anymore than an alcoholic can drink in moderation. Nope, not me. I'm a hard core, pack-a-day smoker.

Well, this might seem insignificant to you, but it was not to me. You see, like my mother did (believe it or not), I possess an innate sense of responsibility. With my life having been so effectively destroyed by the loss of Rob and my job (hey, that rhymes), practically in the same week, what I really wanted was some magic pill that would allow me a complete escape from all the pain and humiliation I was feeling. I wanted to just float away on some happy cloud while someone else did all the painful work with my counselor.

Of course, that was not an option. Being so responsible and having two small daughters to take care of, I could ill afford to check out of reality on drugs or alcohol no matter how much I may have wished I could. Though I have always believed my mother was an alcoholic, at least until her health forced her to give up drinking, she was what many would refer to as a functioning alcoholic. No matter how much she had drank the night before, she always got up and went to work the next day. Perhaps if I had liked drinking more, I might have turned into a functioning alcoholic myself under the circumstances, but I did not really like to get drunk, a little tipsy from time to time, but not drunk. So turning to alcohol was truly not an option for me. Besides, I had a deep fear of becoming addicted.

This did not surprise my counselor. She explained to me that many children of alcoholics grow up to be what she called hyper-vigilant and terrified of losing control to a substance. I had long ago given up any other form of recreational drugs besides alcohol and had even become cautious about my drinking. I hated it when I occasionally overindulged and lost any control for even a single night. The thought of losing control of my life on a full time basis to an addictive, narcotic substance the way addicts do deeply frightened me.

So the most rebellious, independent, comforting thing I could do, was to smoke. The only drug I could allow myself was one that took the edge off without altering my consciousness and for me that was nicotine. Much like I had when I was twelve and first smoking, I snuck around to smoke. The only difference was that when I was a kid, I was afraid of being caught by my mother. Now that I was a mother, I was afraid of being caught by my kids. (I did not think smoking would set a very good example.)

We forced our independence
down into our lungs
out behind the farthest building on campus,
gingerly drawing on cigarettes
I had sneaked away from my mother
when my rebellion was burning at its hottest,
leaving me a mess of contradictions
with defiance screaming inside of me,
convincing me that I was mature
well beyond my barely pubescent age
and should do as I pleased,
alongside that river of fear
snaking its way through my veins,
haunting me with the threat
of being caught,
and worse yet,
discovering that my mother
might really know best after all.

> *So we hurriedly and furtively*
> *worked on those cigarettes,*
> *gently sucking the dirty smoke in*
> *and quickly blowing it back out,*
> *both proud and excited*
> *that we were wild enough to smoke*
> *and yet not really liking*
> *the thick, hot, heavy feel*
> *of that ashy tasting smoke*
> *squeezing tight our small, pink lungs*
> *while we were not yet as addicted*
> *to the smoking*
> *as the sneaking.*

Besides occasionally still seeing Rob, the smoking was the worst I could allow myself to do as I devoted myself to the process of healing all those old wounds that had, for decades, been bleeding all over my life.

chapter twelve

THOUGHT CONTROL

This is how the process works;
Change your thoughts,
you change your feelings.
Change your feelings,
you change your behavior.
Change your behavior,
you change your life.

This is not complicated, but it can be challenging. It requires diligence and a commitment on your part. It means that you need to become aware of the way you think of yourself, the way you speak to yourself, the way you feel about yourself, and the way you treat yourself.

In my case, as I stated earlier, I knew on an intellectual level at least, that I possessed certain attributes and yet that knowledge existed entirely independent of my feelings. Even though I knew on one level that I had several valuable traits, I still felt horrible inside and was completely unable to love myself. This is a common example of how irrational the connection between reality and our warped perceptions of ourselves can be.

What you choose to look at determines also what you do not see. This statement will be repeated throughout other chapters because it is so true, and in regard to your self-image and your life, it is so applicable. For instance, if you are busy looking back over your shoulder you will not see a bus coming straight at you. You may have the future flying up the road, but if you're too focused on the past, it might just smash into you. That future is a bus that could carry you over the rainbow, but if you don't see it, it can run you over instead.

We rarely look in more than one direction at a time, so if you are completely focused on your bad qualities (whether they are real or only what you perceive) you will not see all your good qualities. As I stated earlier, I was aware that I had some gifts and abilities, yet I spent no mental energy thinking about them or focusing on those positive qualities. Instead, I continually reminded myself of my faults. That is where I kept my focus and hence those faults are what I saw and what I responded to emotionally.

I did not recognize my own inherent value, but believed that my value was dependent upon being perfect. Again, this illustrates how irrational my perceptions were. I always felt that I had to be perfect. If I was not perfect, that meant I was garbage. There was no gray area in between those black and white extremes. I was either one or the other. Obviously I was not, and never could be, perfect. Of course that is an impossible standard for anyone to set for themselves. Yet that is what I expected and demanded of myself. Talk about an unrealistic goal. As would everyone, I fell short again and again and this contin-ued to feed my long list of failures. I could not accept that there was tons of gray area in between perfection and garbage, and that though I was certainly not perfect, I was also certainly not garbage. It seri-ously did not occur to me that I could be so flawed, so imperfect, and still be a wonderful person who had been perfectly planned by God to be exactly who I was.

I still saw myself and defined myself as the spoiled, rotten, selfish brat that I had been labeled as when I was a child. To be fair, there was a lot of truth in that label when I was a kid, but it had more to do with my age, my mother's indulgence, and my desperate need for attention than because that was who I was truly meant to be.

There in my early thirties, as a hard-working divorced mother, I was certainly not spoiled. I always put my daughter's needs ahead of my own, so I was certainly not selfish. I tried incredibly hard never to hurt anyone, so I was certainly not rotten. I do admit to occasionally throwing temper tantrums, but still, I was truly not a brat.

I can look back and see the logic of these true statements, but at the time I did not see it. I never let the facts get in the way of my emotions. I felt unworthy of love when I was a child and I felt unworthy of love as an adult. I'm sure if I had felt more loved as a kid, I would not have been such a brat. It's hard, though, to feel loved by a father who doesn't tell you that he loves you, who doesn't come home to you every night, who commands you to remain in another room when he is home so that he can drink undisturbed, who doesn't visit you after a divorce, who abandons you permanently without professing his love for you, even when given that last chance on his deathbed.

If I was lovable, wouldn't I have been given that message rather than all those messages that I was not lovable? If I was lovable wouldn't my mother have paid attention when I was failing in high school the way she did when I was sick or harassing my poor sisters? If I was lovable would I have been such a brat?

Do you see the connection, the cycle? This became the way I learned to feel about myself and the way I had come to define myself; as a brat. Somehow, on some level, I had decided the only way to make up for having been that brat, was to be perfect. Anything less was still a brat. So I set myself up for failure by setting up this ridiculously impossible standard. The more I failed to meet that standard of perfection, the more despicable I felt.

I simply did not feel as though I were a good person no matter how good I was. I could never have been good enough to have changed the warped way I saw myself. I could never have received enough love to have made up for the feeling that I did not deserve it. Consequently, though I looked for that love everywhere with desperation, I only saw the men who rejected me, the jobs I lost, the friends who criticized me. I did not focus on the love I did receive, I focused only on the love I didn't. I did not focus on my successes, I focused only on my failures.

Let me show you another example of this type of illogical self-perception, as I am certainly not alone in having had an irrational view of myself. I have a friend named Jackie. She is beautiful, intelligent, successful and talented. She travels all over the country as the vice-president of a successful company. She makes a six-figure income doing that job, I might add. Jackie has an amazing singing voice that could melt the heart of an angel and directs the worship at her church. She has a wonderful marriage and family and loads of friends who adore her. Jackie is not only hard working and successful, but incredibly kind and generous. She has a quick wit and makes a great conversationalist.

The first workshop I ever held on building self-esteem was at a women's retreat for the women of her church. At the end of the session I asked all the women to list several of their good qualities on their papers. I wanted to help them to recognize and acknowledge their attributes.

Jackie's paper was blank. She could not think of a single good quality that she possessed. The other women spoke up incredulously and asked her, "What about your vocal talent? What about your career, your beauty, your generosity, etc...?" She just shook her head. She could not be convinced that she had any gifts or talents. How she felt about herself had absolutely no basis in reality and yet was deeply etched in the stone of her mind.

I had worked with her prior to that retreat in an effort to help her to find joy in her life, in who she is. Sadly, she is one of those people who have not taken a single step on that journey to joy regardless of my best efforts and encouragement.

Happily, I have a story that represents quite the opposite of Jackie's. I have worked with many women who have begun the battle against addiction. I hold group sessions at a drug and alcohol rehabilitation house twice a month. Some of the women I know from this house have been positively inspiring to me. One such woman is a very large African-American woman struggling to recover from addiction to crack cocaine. She has shared some of the things she did in her addiction in order to finance that drug use. They include things as deplorable as stealing form her own mother while her mother was dying in the hospital and a sordid variety of other crimes.

There is another woman I met there on the day of her arrival. She had lost her career, not to mention every ounce of her self-respect because of her addiction. I remember when I was introduced to her, she could not even look me in the eye. Nor was she able to look herself in the eye. She later confessed that she could not bear to see herself in the mirror. This sweet, bright woman was so filled with shame and self-loathing, she could not stand to see her own reflection. She had resorted to having sex with men that were repulsive to her, men that in sobriety she could not have even stood to be in the same room with. This woman was so thin from years of choosing drugs over food and had cut her hair so short because she had been unable to take care of it; I remember not even being quite sure of her gender at first. My only clue was that this house only took in women.

Both of these women, as have many others from this house, have gone on to truly change their lives. They are now both drug free and hold their heads up high. The first one I described is taking classes at a local college to enable her to become a substance abuse counselor and the second one I described left the program after ninety days and is doing great. She is self-sufficient and continues her treatment programs on an out-patient basis and is rebuilding her life with purpose and confidence.

These women had far more to feel ashamed of than does Jackie and yet they were able to begin moving down the road on their journeys to joy while Jackie was not. These contrasting stories illustrate how illogical the affliction of low self-esteem can be. Here are two women, far from society's ideal standard of beauty and success, who had led lives filled with shameful behavior, and yet they have been able to change that behavior and their lives as they changed the way they felt about themselves. Compare that to Jackie, who did fit into societies ideal standard of beauty and success, who has lived a life filled with kindness and accomplishment and yet cannot find any redeeming qualities in herself.

These recovering drug addicts who have very little financially, families that are no longer intact, and awaken every day to a battle with their desire to use, are happier by far than this beautiful, successful, talented woman that Jackie is. The difference is that these women from the rehabilitation house became proactive in their own lives and made decisions to become happy and then did the work necessary to make that happen. Jackie did not. Talk about a shame! What a waste to take the life God gives you and choose to spend it with far less joy than you could have. That is not His desire for you.

While these women in recovery have stopped beating themselves up for their shortcomings and their past behaviors, Jackie continues to berate herself for her imperfections and remains unable to identify her many gifts. Why? Because as I said before, *what you choose to look at determines also what you do not see.* Jackie focuses on her flaws while the other two women focus on their strengths. Jackie focuses on what she cannot and has not done, while the other two women focus on what they can and have done. It's all a matter of perspective. Jackie's irrational, the others rational.

The women who graduate from that rehabilitation house are those who have forgiven themselves and have let go of the anchor of guilt that they could have continued to drag around with them everywhere they went, everywhere except into their new lives as healthy, happy, healed women. Those who have succeeded have learned to love and appreciate themselves for who they are rather than hate themselves. They do not expect or demand perfection from themselves, but instead they accept themselves as being wonderful, but fallible human beings created by God to be a unique blend of gifts and frailties, deserving of love, of God's love, and their own. They have come very far indeed on their journey's to joy. Jackie, on the other hand, has never been able to see herself as she truly is, only as she irrationally and inaccurately has convinced herself she is. She is convinced that she is unlovable, because she does not feel love for herself.

This will probably sound strange to you, perhaps even rubber room, straight jacket, shock treatment kind of certifiably crazy to you, but here goes: *Love is not strictly a feeling. Infatuation is strictly a feeling. Love is really a choice.* We make this choice by choosing to focus on a person's good qualities as opposed to their weaknesses. If we are talking about your spouse for instance, you must make this choice every day to sustain a loving relationship. Of course both their strengths and weaknesses are present every day no matter which are being exhibited in any given situation, but you maintain your loving feelings for them by overlooking the weaknesses and reminding yourself of all the good qualities they possess. This does not mean that you are not aware that they have flaws, it only means that you choose to focus on their strengths.

If you change that focus and direct it toward your spouse's faults your love eventually begins to erode as your feelings become changed by your thinking of the bad instead of the good. Soon you are able to justify treating your spouse poorly because they are no longer held in high esteem by you, but are now considered to be disdainful and unworthy of good treatment. It is not because they have changed, but because you have changed how you see them. Poor treatment by you brings poor treatment by your spouse in return and before long the relationship erodes like the love.

Even the more instinctive, unconditional love we feel for our family members can be deeply damaged and occasionally even destroyed if we continually focus only on their negatives and never on their positives.

This process applies to your relationship with yourself the same exact way. Regardless of what or who caused you to warp your focus and see only your weaknesses (real or perceived), as opposed to your strengths, you need to change that focus and that means you need to begin with your thoughts. Your thoughts are the main way you communicate with yourself. They are the way you send yourself messages, either negative or positive.

I'm betting the things you say to yourself most often are decidedly negative and insulting. You probably have no real idea how often you entertain these types of thoughts. You may have never stopped to think about how often you insult yourself, beat yourself up, call yourself names, and put yourself down. You probably have countless ways of doing this to yourself.

The first step you must take on your journey to joy is to learn to recognize all the thoughts that you indulge in that contribute to your warped perception that you are unlovable. These negative, self-defeating, berating, insulting, and even abusive thoughts can become so insidious, and may have been the norm for you for so long you may not even notice them anymore. I have had numerous women in that group I teach at the rehab house insist in their first few sessions that they do not beat themselves up, only to later begin to confess many of those negative thoughts as they learn to become aware of them.

It is these thoughts that have a great deal to do with why you remain convinced, often long after a damaging event or relationship may have passed, that you are unlovable and are whatever negative image or label from the past that has stuck with you. Just as I had not seen that I had not been that spoiled brat for over two decades, you may not see that you are not that loser that some old message tells you that you are. We continue to perpetuate the vicious cycle of mental abuse often without needing any help from others. Damaged people produce damaged thoughts. They have had their perspectives damaged by people or events that caused lasting changes in the way they see, think of, and feel about themselves.

Only as we begin to recognize and dismantle the insulting messages that we send ourselves in our thoughts, are we then able to replace them with loving, encouraging messages. But first we must start paying attention to how we speak to ourselves mentally. If you are not aware of it, you cannot change it.

How did the women recovering from addiction learn to see themselves accurately and change their focus from their faults to their gifts? It begins with changing their thoughts. We assume that we cannot control what we think. While it's true that we cannot control every thought that pops into our heads, we can control how we deal with them as they do. We can train ourselves to recognize them and to stop them and to prevent ourselves from finishing them and embellishing upon them. We can learn to dismiss them immediately and to replace them with uplifting, inspiring thoughts.

Just as years of negative and abusive thinking have changed the way you feel about yourself, eroding your sense of self-worth and your ability to have a healthy relationship with yourself, a concerted effort to change those negative thoughts to positive thoughts can also change your feelings of disdain into feelings of love for yourself. The good news is, it won't take years or decades to undo the damage your typical thought pattern has inflicted. The bad news is, it will take time, effort and diligence.

You need to make the choice to do this every day. It is the choice of love. You will have to make positive, loving, encouraging thoughts a habit just as the negative thoughts have become.

Perhaps your self-esteem or self-image was damaged in a long, slow, continuous process, as in my case. Maybe it was a single, pivotal event. It may have been one person, or many people, one cruel comment, or a steady barrage of name calling, teasing, and insults.

Everyone has experienced the pain of being humiliated at one time or another, but some of us may have been more vulnerable than others to suffering lasting consequences due to that pain. Some of us have allowed those situations inordinate amounts of power in our lives. For those of us who came from families where our self-esteem was not fostered or perhaps even damaged, we are extremely vulnerable to the cruel remarks of others, especially when we are young and trying to fit in and to discover who we are. That was certainly my case and as a result, every mean comment stuck, each defeat became a permanent scar on my psyche, every failure was further proof of my worthlessness.

If you look at the insults you hurl at yourself. I bet you will recognize some of them as those that were hurled at you by others. If you call yourself stupid often, I bet there was someone in your background who called you that. It may have been someone whose opinion mattered to you or someone who sent you that message repeatedly. Just as your first grade teacher told you over and over that two and two make four, with no previous knowledge, no other frame of reference with which to question this truth, you simply accepted it as fact. Regardless of the specific situation in which you were called stupid, you probably accepted it as fact and began to define yourself as such.

You need to examine the things you call yourself as well as the typical circumstances under which you call yourself these derogatory things. Some people call themselves the same few names again and again. Others are not even picky and seemingly never run out of nasty insults for themselves.

For some, however, the habit of speaking badly to themselves becomes so automatic and frequent, the thoughts no longer even come in the form of specific words that form sentences. Sometimes the message becomes almost subliminal and needs no language. It can be so ingrained and habitual that it simply triggers the feeling that would follow such a negative message. I suspect this is often true in the case of the women who have not been at the rehab house for long and deny that they beat themselves up.

This more subtle way we attack ourselves can be the result of such constant self-abuse that the feelings of worthlessness and shame just come like flashes to leave an instantaneous message that we're losers. It works like other things that have become such a force of habit that we no longer require language to talk us through the process.

Take brushing your teeth for example. You do not need to specifically tell yourself to take out your toothbrush and toothpaste, to unscrew the cap on the tube, to squeeze a small amount of toothpaste onto the bristles of your toothbrush, to put the toothbrush in your mouth, to move it briskly across your teeth, etc. You get the picture. You don't require words to repeat this process twice a day, you just do it without really thinking about it. Try to notice if this same word-less process happens in regards to your self-abuse, leaving you feeling that little burst of shame without having consciously thought out an insult.

Negative comments often pervade everything we do, diminishing our joy and increasing our shame. Just to help get you thinking and paying attention to your mental talk, let me give you some typical examples of some of the ways you might beat yourself up. If you are cooking dinner and become distracted by a phone call and burn what's on the stove, think about how you would likely talk to yourself. You would probably say something like "You stupid idiot! Now look what you did. You can't do anything right!" (At least that's probably what I would have said to myself a while back.)

If a man you were dating stopped calling you, you would probably assume it was your fault and due to all that you lacked. You may say things to yourself like, "It was bound to happen. What made me think this one would be any different? It never takes long for men to get bored with me. I'm never smart enough, or interesting enough, or pretty enough to keep any man around. It's because I'm so fat. Who would want to look at these thighs all the time? He probably found someone prettier, thinner, younger, etc…"

Sound familiar? When looking for a job, do you gravitate toward those menial, dead-end jobs because when you see a listing for one that seems exciting, you assume you're not qualified? Do you tell yourself not to bother and say things like, "I could never get a job like that. I'm not smart enough. I was too lazy or dumb to go to college. I'll always be stuck with these crumby, entry level positions. I guess I get just what I deserve."

When you look in the mirror do you focus on every flaw and berate yourself for them? Do you say things like "I hate my body. I'm so fat (or so skinny)! I hate my gut!" Perhaps you tell yourself how ugly you are or how old and wrinkled you look. Maybe you criticize your smile or your hair or the way you are dressed. Maybe you just avoid the mirror altogether, much like you would avoid a case of head lice.

When things go wrong do you automatically take the blame even when it's unreasonable to believe you could have had anything to do with the situation? Do you just assume the responsibility was yours and you must have therefore been at fault? When I caught Rob cheating on me I was not as angry at him as I was at myself for having been so stupid as to have trusted him despite all the red flags. I hated myself for not having pressed him for better explanations when I voiced suspicions. I hated myself for being so naïve and for being too eager to believe his lies rather than face the devastating truth. I hated myself for loving him.

How unreasonable was that? He was (and probably still is) a lying, cheating, arrogant, phony son-of-a-butt, and yet I hated me. I internalized the anger and directed it at myself, automatically blaming myself for being stupid rather than him for being a scumbag.

I used to find myself agonizing over every situation that went wrong, searching for my culpability, certain that I had caused, or at least contributed to the failure. If I lost a sale at work I was usually sure that I had said the wrong thing or showed the wrong item. Most of the time I simply could not convince myself that perhaps we just didn't have what the customer wanted or that the customer just wasn't actually ready to buy.

These are some examples of how we beat ourselves up in our self-talk. We have conversations with ourselves nearly constantly and whether we realize it or not, these things we say to ourselves have far more impact than things others say to us, because once our self-image is warped to the point where we feel unlovable, we believe everything negative that is said, by ourselves or others, and nearly nothing positive that others might say. We often crave hearing compliments more than anything, yet we dismiss them as baloney.

We challenge every compliment paid to us when we should be instead challenging all our disdainful self-talk. Just as I, in hindsight, was able to look back at the belief I had held firmly for so long that I was a spoiled brat, only to find no credible evidence to back that belief up, you will also discover that all the nasty things you believe about yourself and tell yourself do not hold up to the light of reason.

You must not only begin to pay attention to the mean things you say to yourself so that you can recognize them, but you must also examine them in an objective and reasonable manner so that you see that they are not accurate perceptions of yourself.

If you're still denying that you beat yourself up, you're either reading the wrong book, or perhaps you're one of those people so practiced at the art of distraction through constant busyness that you keep most of your thoughts limited to the task at hand and allow as little time for random thinking as possible in order to avoid these unpleasant thoughts.

Drugs and alcohol are not the only ways in this society we can dull down our internal pain. In this day and age it is quite easy to be so busy that we remain distracted from our thoughts and can be nearly completely out of touch with our feelings. There are so many demands that we can become immersed in and shielded by such as our careers, our families, our social lives, our homes, and every other kind of commitment you can bury yourself beneath. We can easily get caught up in such a whirlwind of activity that our thoughts are held at a superficial level enabling us to avoid everything that occurs on a deeper, more real level within us.

If this describes your lifestyle, you need to set aside some alone time to sit still and unclutter your mind of all the shallow thoughts that generally surround this flurry of activity so that you can get in touch with what's really going on inside you. You need to know and address the thoughts that occur on a more substantial level. Are they negative? Are they painful? Do you find that you are uncomfortable with the thoughts that creep in when you are still and undistracted?

Perhaps you find being alone with your thoughts so painful you avoid solitude as much as possible. You may constantly seek out companionship even when that companionship is of poor quality or the resulting relationship is decidedly unhealthy for you. This can be yet another type of distraction you indulge in to keep from facing your inner-self. Sometimes no matter how much we may dislike a person we invite into our lives to fill our time, it is not as much as we dislike ourselves and therefore it becomes our choice as the lesser of the two evils.

Maybe you are more like the women in the rehab house and have turned to an overindulgence in alcohol or the use of drugs, prescription or otherwise, to soften and blur the brittle edges of the pain that permeates the lives of those with poor self-esteem. Intoxication can dull down the sharp pain until it becomes a more harmless surface that can be skimmed over and rendered unable to cut into your heart.

It will, of course, only work temporarily. Sadly the drugs or alcohol used to quiet the mind and buffer the heart ultimately only serve to further ravage them. Using and abusing any narcotic inevitably causes further destruction in your life, leading you to make more poor choices that end up piling more guilt and shame upon you. You then use this guilt and shame to further beat yourself up as it becomes yet another source of pain and brings more feelings of failure. This creates another vicious cycle.

You may use anything you can to keep yourself from wandering through your mind and risking bumping into those jagged thoughts, but you cannot feel joy if you do not allow yourself to feel anything at all in an effort to avoid feeling pain. You cannot identify negative thoughts, process unresolved issues and feelings, and change what is not working to create joy in you and your life, if you do not really face what is truly going on inside you.

You have to recognize and erase those hurtful thoughts, changing them from active messages being sent to you on different levels to just old tapes that used to plague you, but are no longer played on the radio station in your mind.

Introspection

With little more
than our dogged determination
we begin the process that moves us
from fear to hope.
With hands of love
we begin to heal
all of life's wounds,
even those that have been
self-inflicted.
We embark on that
spiritual adventure,
forging feelings of tranquility
out of the molten anger
that had been hardening
in our hearts.
We begin unfolding
the life force within us.
We start to hear
the music of our beating hearts
and begin to discover
the art of living
as we start to color
our seasons with love
and begin crafting a friendship
with our thoughts.
It's an exaltation
of our soul.
It's like giving birth
to ourselves.

chapter thirteen

TREAT YOURSELF LIKE A FRIEND

You need to learn to speak to yourself differently, to speak to yourself as you would speak to a friend. As with any other relationship you wish to begin, you must treat the other person with kindness and courtesy. You would never make any friends if you spoke to them the way you are probably currently speaking to yourself.

Let me illustrate what I mean. Think back to the first example I used in pointing out common ways we beat ourselves up. Instead of you cooking dinner and burning it while being distracted by a phone call, let's put a friend of yours in that same situation. We'll have you imagine that you are the person that calls her while she's cooking. When she gasps and exclaims that she has just burned dinner, you would certainly not say to her, "You stupid idiot! You screwed up again. You can't do anything right!" You would far more likely say something like, "Don't worry about it. It's no big deal, it happens to all of us. That's what take-out is for."

Do you see the difference? You would immediately forgive your friend for making a mistake and would never dream of adding insult to injury by belittling and berating her for being human. Why do we think it is ok to do this to ourselves? If a friend lost her job you would not tell her that she didn't deserve the job or was not smart enough, or was a loser.

You would try to comfort her and encourage her. This is the way you must learn to speak to yourself. A friend would try to help, not hurt. If your friend came to you upset because she had been dumped by some guy, you would want to tell her that she is an amazing, wonderful woman, whether he recognized it or not, and that just because a relationship doesn't work out doesn't mean she is not lovable or that the next one won't work out. A friend would offer a rational way of seeing the situation, not an irrational, nasty little blame game.

You wouldn't even talk to a total stranger the way you likely talk to yourself. You may often treat yourself more like a bitter enemy than a friend.

The irony here is that you need to be your own friend more than you need any other friendship, because you can never escape yourself. You are always with you. Imagine how helpful it would be to always have your staunchest supporter with you, someone to cheer you on and congratulate your successes while forgiving your mishaps. How wonderful would it be to have someone who offered you comfort every time you needed it?

I spoke in the last chapter of becoming aware of the derogatory statements you make to yourself. As you recognize them forming, stop them immediately! Stop mid-sentence and replace the insulting statement you were in the process of making with a positive statement instead. You are probably so out of the habit of saying anything nice to yourself you need to have a statement prepared and memorized and ready to go at all times. If you have to think one up impulsively you may not do it quickly enough to be effective.

This positive affirmation should be said far more often than only the times when you are attempting to correct and reverse a habitual negative comment. It needs to be said a hundred times a day at least. It should be said over and over before you go to sleep at night and again and again as you awaken in the morning. You need to say it as you groom in front of the mirror, while waiting at red lights or in lines, and during commercials as you watch T.V. and as many other times as you can. You cannot hear this new, positive tape too many times. There are undoubtedly years and years of negative messages to make up for.

It needs to become the new habit you will use to replace the old habit of beating yourself up. It should be something simple, no more than a couple of lines that will be easy to memorize and recite. You should recite it aloud when you are alone as well as silently when you're not. It must speak specifically to your priceless value and absolute lovability. It should not be too specific, for example focusing only on a single attribute. Don't make it something like, "I have a good sense of humor." Even Jeffrey Dahmer might have had a good sense of humor. That alone would not have made him a good person. A positive affirmation should convey that you have more than just one attribute. One attribute alone doesn't make you lovable. Thankfully, no one has only one attribute. Even Jeffrey Dahmer probably had a couple, and I can assure you that you are way ahead of him. Your positive affirmation needs to be broad ranged and very basic. It needs to speak of your inherent value and lovability.

I developed the habit of telling myself "I'm a good person. I deserve good things." Feel free to use that one if you wish, rather than trying to make up your own right now. (I promise not to sue you for copyright infringement.) Do this exercise diligently and faithfully and repetitively.

I know it sounds simplistic, but I am living proof that it works. You see, I had believed for my whole life that I was not a good person and that I did not deserve good things. This new perspective was a foreign concept to me initially. I had never even considered the possibility that I was actually good or deserving of things that were.

The sad thing is, we make choices in life that are certain to give us what we believe we deserve. This is usually done on a sub-conscious level, but it is done time and time again. It's heartbreaking, but unbelievably consistent, that people who don't believe they are capable of achieving or deserving of having all the good things life can offer, sub-consciously create for themselves lives which will prove them right and offer pain and hardship instead of the many blessings we could be reaping.

Some people with low self-esteem do respond by becoming over-achievers, but they often only end up obsessed with achieving things in their effort to try to prove their feelings of worthlessness wrong, and to gain the approval of others that they are not able to provide for themselves. Sadly this does not work to change their feelings because no accomplishment will make you feel lovable if you have never learned to love yourself. Not only will it not change the way you feel about yourself, it will not change your thinking either. That must be done on a conscious level and that requires intentional effort.

Another example of a positive affirmation you can use to change your thinking is, "I am worthy and deserving of love and have been perfectly planned by God." Don't be timid about choosing a statement that speaks boldly and unapologetically about how wonderful and deserving you are.

There will be times when you feel low and seem unable to tell yourself what may feel at the time to be such an outrageous lie. Those are the very times when you need to say your positive affirmation the most.

As I said, I am living proof that changing the way you speak to yourself can begin to change your life. After several weeks of working at developing this new habit and taking other steps to heal myself, I found the courage to begin looking for a new job, not in jewelry, as I had done for years, but in a completely different field. I decided to go into outside sales instead of retail sales.

This took far more confidence than I had only a couple of months before. Changing careers for anyone in their thirties is scary, especially as the sole supporter of two daughters. I was beginning to believe though that I deserved a better life and that included a better job. I possessed excellent sales skills, but without a college degree it was likely to be challenging finding someone to take a chance on me. It is not always easy for salespeople to make the transition from retail to outside sales, but I believed I could do it. I wanted the chance to increase and control my income. I loved the thought of no more nights and weekends as well as the autonomy I would enjoy out in the field as opposed to being confined to the same space for eight hours a day.

Working to consciously change my thoughts had taught me to focus on my ability to sell, my intelligence, and the things that would enable me to adapt to the changes that this new career would require. Before beginning the inner work on my journey to joy I would have focused only on my lack of experience in outside sales and my lack of a college degree. I would never have considered the idea being focused only on my limitations as opposed to my talents. I would never have found the courage it took to foray into something so risky, so challenging, so unknown.

I had even begun to be able to resist Rob, not every time he put on the pressure, but most of the time. I had once again begun dating (big surprise), and was ever hopeful of finding a good relationship. At least I had grown enough by then to begin to understand that there was no relationship on earth that would heal me. Only my honest, hard work could do that.

You stand before me with your smile,
a smile you believe to be
a prize you are gifting me with.
You are teasing and tugging,
trying to gently force your way
back into my head,
trying to script more of your story
across the parchment of my heart,
gazing at me as if there were still poems
in my eyes.
But I am no longer filled
with all that childlike love
that once had my eyes begging,
even while yours were closed.
For you are just a dream peddler
with a heart no more than a tomb,
a heart filled only with old relics
and the crumbled ruins
of some ancient love.
You can no longer enter
the temple of my dreams.
You will never again dwell
in the palace of my heart.
There will not even be any thoughts of mine

> *in which you could warm your hands.*
> *For I once lived in the dark of the unknowing,*
> *believing you to be someone else.*
> *I believed you were the man*
> *that I had fallen in love with,*
> *one that I bought with my raspberry kisses.*
> *Now I know one true thing;*
> *the man I loved*
> *I have never met.*
> *So away from you I move,*
> *back into my life,*
> *for you are just one more*
> *of yesterday's mistakes.*

It has been said "The definition of insanity is doing the same thing over and over and expecting different results." I think we can safely assume that up to now your life has not been working for you in a way that makes you happy. Therefore you must change the way you're doing things in order to become happy.

Remember that happiness comes from the inside out. If you are happy with who you are, you will be happy where you are, but if you are not happy with who you are, you will not be happy anywhere. Circumstances are fluid and ever changing, while your sense of self and your ability to love yourself will be with you everywhere and are virtually inescapable.

I have addressed the need to change your thoughts and the way you speak to yourself, as well as the method for doing so. I have also told you of the need to treat yourself like a friend. Learning to treat yourself like a friend goes beyond the way you speak to yourself. That is only one aspect of friendship. How many of your friends would you keep if you spoke to them nicely, but did other destructive things to them? You must not only speak kindly, but also behave kindly toward your friends.

The way I described the process at the beginning of the previous chapter is true;

Change your thoughts and you change your feelings.
Change your feelings and you change your behavior.
Change your behavior and you change your life.

This is absolutely, fundamentally, unequivocally true. It is also true, however, that the very action of changing your behavior can also help to change your feelings and your thoughts and your life. You see, the process works in both directions because thoughts, feelings and behavior are all interconnected and interdependent and are all the specific components that determine the quality of your life.

Behaviors can become habits over time and can change the way we think and feel. The women I work with in the addiction recovery house are doing just that. They have entered into a program where they are severely restricted in all aspects of their behavior and are therefore exhibiting the behavior of the clean and sober even though inside they are craving their drug of choice twenty-four/seven. Their thoughts are still on drugs and alcohol, their feelings are still those of an addict, and yet their behavior is forced to change if they are to remain in the program. Though their behavior is the first thing that begins to change, the changes do not stop there. After working the program and behaving like a non-user for a while, their thoughts and feelings begin to change also.

Staying drug free and establishing, or re-establishing, a connection between themselves and God, even after only a few days, makes them begin to feel better about themselves. They feel far more proud of praying, reading the bible and doing the early inner work than they did about using drugs or alcohol. Being honest with themselves and about themselves, as well as encouraging the other women in the house, all work to make them feel better about themselves.

As they are being taught about recovery they begin thinking about the lessons they are learning and hoping that mastering those lessons will set them free from the chains of addiction. With each small milestone they reach and every success they enjoy they begin to feel better about themselves. So even before attending one of my self-esteem groups they have already begun to increase their self-esteem. These women are some of the most extreme examples of how this process works.

It can work for you too. You do not have to wait for your positive affirmations to change your thoughts and feelings to begin to change your behavior. You should be working on changing your behavior simultaneously. The entire process should be a multi-pronged approach.

Start by recognizing and acknowledging some of your most destructive behaviors. For me, one was dating, especially dating Rob. I needed to stop doing that and start replacing that behavior with a more constructive one.

Let's say as an example, one of the things that you do and are ashamed of is sleeping with your own "Rob," someone who you know is not good for you. Perhaps he or she is using you, but you continue to see him or her because it is better than feeling lonely, better than being left alone with your thoughts and the pain that generally accompanies them.

When he or she calls, take a deep breath and muster up all your courage, and tell them "no." If you can still breathe after getting that word out, tell them the truth; *that you deserve better.* Even if you do not truly believe it at the time, resisting that person, that drink, or whatever your crutch is, and toughing it out will be a source of pride and can act as a step in your healing process. It will make you feel better about yourself. Every positive thought and every constructive action are building blocks that add up and change your feelings about yourself and ultimately change your life.

Like all journeys, a journey to joy is made one step at a time, one building block upon another. So instead of drinking alcohol, or overeating, or sleeping with a louse, or whatever your destructive habit may be, do something positive instead. Attacking your poor self-esteem from both sides, thoughts and behavior, will be infinitely more effective than just working from one angle.

So do something nice for yourself. Perhaps you can take a relaxing, scented bubble bath with a good book and your favorite music playing in the background. Maybe you should treat yourself to going to a movie or getting for yourself a slightly indulgent, yet affordable gift like a CD or a DVD you could enjoy. Two of my favorite indulgences are lingerie and fragrance. They are great pick-me-ups. (No, not that kind, well I guess they couldn't hurt, but that's not the reason I indulge in them.) Those things make me feel prettier, sexier, more alluring, and when I'm feeling low, that definitely helps. I never purchased those items for myself prior to my divorce because they seemed like luxuries that should be received as gifts. I finally realized that gifts *for* me could also come *from* me. You could even splurge on a massage or a facial or a makeover, or have dinner with a supportive, encouraging friend.

Maybe you could do something kind for someone you know who is also in need of some type of help. That always makes us feel good about ourselves and it benefits the other person or people as well. Or you could do something really constructive like going online and signing up for a night class that will further your career or take a class on a subject you have always been interested in. Go for a walk or get some other type of exercise. For most of us this is a grossly neglected area of our lives and our self-image is so often dependent upon our body image that engaging in physical activity can be hugely rewarding to both our psyches as well as our bodies.

You may feel uncomfortable with indulging in activities that pamper you, especially if they take your time away from others who may have become used to being the recipients of all your pampering and time. You may even worry that it is selfish. I can assure you that it is not only not selfish, it is an absolutely necessary part of caring for our emotional health. We have to get used to a balance in our priorities that will address our needs and not just the needs of others. Often people of low self-esteem focus way too little time and energy on themselves. I'm not advocating selfishness, just balance.

You may meet some resistance from your family if creating a healthy balance in your life means taking more time for being good to you and consequently having a little less time for others. This may be especially true if you have *always* put the needs of others before your own. Often, we busy ourselves with the demands of others to distract us from our own thoughts, needs, and lives.

Now I am not telling you to disregard the true needs of your family. I do not mean if you have small children, for example, to take that bubble bath and tell them to cook their own dinner while you soak. Remember, I said balance. It means that you may have to wait until after the kids go to bed to indulge in that bath. It may mean that you have someone you trust care for the kids for an evening while you and your husband go on a date, or you visit with a friend, or do whatever it is that you would find to be a treat, as long as it is not destructive to you or your journey in any way. It means honestly and objectively addressing your own needs and wishes and taking real action to meet them in a healthy, positive way.

It may mean a redistribution of the work load so that you are able to secure a little more free time for yourself by requiring each family member to contribute a little more. You may have to actually schedule this time for you to make it happen. While it's wonderful to be spontaneous, if you're like me and you wait for the conditions to be right for you to indulge in a couple of hours of special time for yourself, you will not likely find many opportunities.

If you are one of those type-A, busyness addicts, you will need to review your time commitments to make sure that you are not over-extending yourself. You may even have to get a little more practice in saying "no" to ensure yourself some precious free time. Spending inordinate amounts of time doing favors for others, does no favors for you. Ironically enough, it ends up in the long run actually doing no favors for others either. You can burn out, become overstressed and angry and resentful, and even allow your health to suffer, causing you to be unhappy and ineffective at best, and out of commission due to physical strain and resulting health problems at worst. You end up not much good to anyone when you are not much good to yourself.

Some of us actually depend on gaining our validation from being so busy and so needed. We can become almost addicted to being needed by others and to ministering to their needs. This is not uncommon to those of us with poor self-esteem who are unable to validate ourselves from within. It is the root of co-dependency. Many of us surround ourselves with others who are in even greater need than ourselves so that we feel of value as we care for them (sometimes so that we can even feel superior to them). The more dependent others may be upon us, the more value we feel we have.

As I said a few pages back, it's completely normal to feel good when we are helping others, but if this is the only source of your self-worth, you may very well be doing this to an extreme in order to get that pat on the back that you cannot give yourself. If you are not over-doing it in this area, but are nonetheless dependent upon it for your validation, than you are probably unhappy a good deal of the time. Either way, I need to remind you, it's all about balance. Helping others is fine. It's great, in fact, as long as it doesn't keep you from taking care of yourself or turn you into a martyr. Martyr syndrome (oh, poor, put-upon me) is another common by-product of low self-esteem and being a martyr is definitely not joyful.

As for me, I was an advice-giving junkie. As I grew more emotionally healthy I learned to draw boundaries and limited myself to being available in that regard only to those who were not only truly in need, but were serious about seeking advice. I dropped many people who only took advantage of my time by wanting someone to whine to, but never did anything I, or anyone else, suggested to improve their situation. I will always try to help any of my friends now who occasionally need a shoulder, with or without advice, because I no longer have any friends who only want to complain, and yet refuse to help themselves. Everyone goes through a rough time now and then, but I tend to choose friends now that are basically emotionally healthy or are at least serious about becoming so, like you.

So go ahead and do good deeds. Volunteer for your favorite charity if you like and enjoy the good feeling it brings. Just don't do it to the extent that it takes up all the time you need for taking care of yourself and don't allow that to be the only time you feel good about yourself. Your value is constant and exists no matter what you may or may not be doing in any given moment. It is not dependent upon any one activity. You do not only have value on the day you volunteer at your kids school, but none when you are absent the next day shopping or working. You need to come to know this deep down in your core.

The important thing is that as you begin treating yourself better you will be in the process of learning to recognize your value and learning to feel your worth. As you progress in this process you will begin to understand that your value is innate and constant. It does not ebb and flow like the tide.

So schedule a babysitter if it is the only way to get some free time. You need that time and soon you will come to realize that you deserve it. When my girls were little, I switched off with friends from my Lamaze class just to make certain we each had an afternoon to ourselves every week or two. Perhaps you can arrange for your husband to take over on Saturday afternoons. As selfish as Steve was, I was eventually able to convince him to watch the girls one evening a week so I could attend Weight Watchers and later a creative writing class. See, I was not a complete doormat and Steve was not a complete jerk. There was lots of gray area in both of us.

My point is: You need to be diligent in making yourself a priority, even if this means occasionally requiring others in your life make some adjustments in order for you to do so. You need to begin caring for yourself if you are ever to expect others to care for you. If you do not treat yourself with love and respect, no one else will. We set the standards for the way people treat us by the way we treat ourselves. Just as if we do not protect ourselves from being taken advantage of, we will be taken advantage of; if we are not good and loving to ourselves, others will not be good and loving to us either. We must invest in ourselves and give to ourselves if we are to have anything worthwhile to give to others. Happy, healthy, well-adjusted people even set good examples that encourage and inspire others.

Remember also, if you have children, you are their role model. Just as I was aware that Katie and Laura would likely grow up to emulate my and Steve's behavior in marriage, you must be aware that your children also will grow up and emulate your behavior in your marriage, as well as in other relationships, including the relationship you have with yourself. You teach your children how to treat themselves and how to allow other people to treat them by the way you behave. So your investment in your own emotional health, even if you do not have children now, is an investment in the emotional health of those around you now and in the future.

It may take some time getting used to behaving in a manner that is good for and to you, but behavioral changes are a necessary part of becoming emotionally healthy.

So be diligent in resisting your urges to repeat destructive behavior. If you used to find comfort in things that were harmful to you, you will find a reason to feel proud in resisting them. Remember, those destructive behaviors were temporary measures that may have temporarily eased the symptoms of your pain, but did nothing to treat the disease, so try to avoid repeating those things that are not in your best interest and will only bring on more unnecessary guilt and shame.

If you fall, and you will, forgive yourself just as you would forgive a friend. Pick yourself up and move on, but do not underestimate the value of doing nice things for yourself and treating yourself kindly. It is part of the process of convincing yourself that you deserve to be treated kindly, part of getting used to it. Remember, we get the treatment we expect and believe we deserve. We can command good treatment or we can settle for lousy treatment. It is vital that you begin to make outward expressions of your value, even before you may actually recognize your value.

While I was learning how to treat myself better, the world had not made quite enough progress in that area. After having successfully made the transition from retail sales to outside sales, I was quickly slammed back down to the mat by a corporate merger that resulted in the closing of the branch in which I was working. With only months of experience in my new field and the responsibility of those two little girls to consider, I was devastated to have lost yet another job, especially after having gone to such great lengths to avoid having that happen again. All those store closures that cost me jobs that I was powerless to have saved had contributed greatly to my decision to change careers, and yet, here I was again.

It felt like a huge blow and truly depressed me. I'd been depressed before on occasion, especially when I was married to Steve, (Shocking, huh?) but it was generally not in my nature for my feelings to sink that low. Oh, I'd felt deep pain and despair, even devastation at certain times (at least until I was able to bury it), but very rarely had I felt the long, lingering hopelessness that comes with depression and slowly sucks the very air from your lungs. This time I truly did not know if I had the strength to pick myself up again. I didn't even answer my phone for a couple of weeks. If it was Julie or my mom I would call them back, but I did not have the energy to pretend everything was alright to the rest of the world and I was not one to admit it to most people when things were not alright. I needed every ounce of energy I would have had to expend making jovial small talk for talking with possible future employers.

Eventually I had lined up three pretty certain job offers. I don't recall why I dismissed the first one, but I had narrowed it down to two. I wanted one job more than the other, but the final details of the offer had to be worked out by a man whose wife was about to give birth to their first child and was consequently out of the office much of the time. I grew more and more impatient as my impending unemployment grew closer and closer.

The company I had relegated to a distant second choice called again and upped their offer and promised to make the medical benefits retroactive so that my daughters would not be uninsured. The owner's sensitivity to the needs of my family won me over at last and I gave up on waiting out that baby's slow birthing timetable.

I started the job the first of April and landed my first account by the first of May. What I sold that facility is of absolutely no consequence, but the person to whom I sold the product was one who would help to change my life. His name is Matthew. He is a Christian. He was soon to become my good friend.

chapter fourteen

PROCESSING EMOTIONS

One of the largest and most important steps in this process involves learning from our pasts. We cannot break those destructive patterns if we don't understand why we began them and have continued to hang onto them. We need to carefully examine our deepest needs if we are to get a grasp of the true motivations behind our behaviors. This means stripping away all the justifications we have relied upon all this time and addressing instead what we are really trying to accomplish with our actions.

For instance, it is not a drink, it is comfort. It is not sex, it is love and affection. Once you discover your true needs, you can begin to find constructive ways to fill them as opposed to the destructive ways you have been using to try to fill those needs.

We all make a lot of bad choices that are truly not in our best interest. Many are made on a subconscious level, a level that escapes the light of reason and instead just drives us blindly to get our needs met with little awareness of the cost that certain behaviors will incur. We make choices based on what is familiar to us regardless of what is actually good for us. Comfort accompanies the familiar, even the familiar that is harmful to us, while apprehension accompanies the unknown, even when the unknown is good for us. If we are used to chaos, pain and humiliation, we will choose people and circumstances sure to bring those things to our lives. The behavior that leads to the duplication of our pasts is often so natural and ingrained in us that it becomes a habit that we do not think about anymore than we think about the habit of brushing our teeth as I illustrated in chapter twelve.

We must begin consciously processing our choices and behaviors, examining them honestly and objectively and subjecting to reason. As we become consciously aware of the true needs that drive our choices, the needs that truly exist in our inner selves, we become able to change our actions, our courses, our attitudes, our self-esteem, our patterns, and our lives. This is probably the purest and most necessary form of our learning. This is learning *from* our own life *how* to live our own life well.

Understanding what you truly desire is a learned skill for most people. We often confuse what we think we want in life with what we desire to feel. For example, how often have you been convinced that once you got something, say a promotion or a new sports car or a nicer home, you would be happy, only to find that once you acquired the object or achieved that goal, the satisfaction was short lived? The happiness quickly faded and you were left with the same sense of dis-satisfaction and longing that you had before.

The truth is what you needed to be happy was not the car or pro-motion, but the feeling that you believed they would bring. Perhaps you believed the car would bring you respect and admiration, the feeling of pride that such an outward symbol of success should bring. Surprise! If you did not feel like a success and feel proud of your-self before the car, you will not feel like a success and feel proud of yourself after the car. If you do not respect yourself and your abilities before a promotion, you will not respect yourself and your abilities after a promotion.

Being dependent upon the admiration of others to validate your worth is a never ending roller coaster ride that has you completely out of control and totally at the mercy of the whims of those around you. There will be some highs, but there will be guaranteed lows as well. You must realize that you can never control the other people and the external forces that exist and occur in the world. No where is that truth said better than in the Serenity Prayer, the prayer used by the twelve step programs for overcoming addiction.

God grant me the serenity to accept the things I cannot change, the wisdom to change the things I can, and the courage to know the difference.

You can only control yourself and even then you will only be able to do this successfully (happily) when you have an understanding of yourself and your life. I will go more deeply into this later. For now I recommend that if you do not already know the Serenity Prayer, you learn it and memorize it. You may want to repeat it to yourself when you are butting your head against the brick wall of life by trying to control what you can't control.

One thing you can't control is getting others to feel, let alone express, admiration. Admiration from others feels good whether you have healthy self-esteem or not. That's a fact. But if all the world gathered to tell you that they are proud of you and respect you it would still not give you the feeling of joy and peace that comes from respecting yourself and feeling proud of who you are. That can only come from you. Recognizing that self-respect is your first and most basic emotional need is a huge step toward getting the joy and peace you have been seeking in all those indirect ways that are sometimes quite self-destructive. Understanding the need to change your behavior means that you cannot continue to expect to reap apples if all you have planted are orange trees.

If it is the feeling of pride in who you are that you actually seek, then you need to realize that you must learn to give that feeling to yourself and no amount of success, material accumulation, or admiration will do that for you, certainly not in any way that truly lasts or really matters.

So, how do you produce that sense of well being, that pride in who you are, that healthy self-esteem? You must begin at the beginning which means learning to recognize and identify the feelings that exist within you. You cannot meet needs until you know what they are. Without that knowledge you are only making ignorant, knee-jerk, reactionary choices; the ones that have been failing you so far.

When you objectively look back at the pattern of choices you've made you will likely notice a theme. There has probably been a lengthy list of attempts at finding that thing, person, or level of accomplishment that would meet your need and produce the feelings of self-worth and lasting joy you have been seeking. That lengthy list of attempts to produce that feeling of well-being is actually an equally lengthy list of failures, not because you are a failure. It is because you've been continually looking outside for those feelings instead of within. You were trying to produce your validation in others rather than in yourself. In other words; you were trying to pick apples from an orange tree.

If you have a history of unresolved pain and anger (they are usually inextricably linked) those unresolved feelings will dominate your life demanding to be handled while you in turn demand their silence in your effort to ignore them as you seek happiness. If there is garbage in your heart all the perfume in the world (external, quick fixes) will not drown out the stench for any length of time.

If your self-esteem was damaged as a child you could not have possessed the emotional and mental resources to truly handle and fully process the feelings that resulted from the event or events. Furthermore, if you did not have parents who were able and available to help you to deal with those emotions, you probably ended up compartmentalizing them. You put them away in a place in your heart where they could not touch you. It's called denial: pretending that everything is ok and that you were not hurt by the event or events when you were actually forever changed by them.

If the damage was caused by one or both of your parents, that pain has been compounded by the fact that they not only did not help you through it, but actually perpetrated it. To a child, a parent causing them deep emotional pain is rejection of the most damaging kind. The rejection of a parent is the most powerful message of a child's "unworthiness" and "unlovableness" that can be received by that child. (How's "unlovableness" for a word I think I just made up?)

Those children often go through life, as I did, trying desperately to find someone who can convince them that they are worthy of love, but not believing it no matter how often people show them love.

Some children who grow up feeling unlovable will even go through life with the same desperation directed toward proving that message of their unworthiness right. If you have sabotaged your best efforts in school, on the job, or in relationships with bad behaviors, you may well be one of those people who are trying on some sub-conscious level to prove your worthlessness. It can be a self-defense measure you employ to beat any possible rejecters to the punch. Sometimes it is also the way you ensure yourself never having much expected from you because you keep yourself constantly victimized by all the failures that "just seem to follow you."

Regardless of which way you may handle unresolved feelings of rejection and pain from your childhood, you likely have an inordinate amount of anger, as well as fear and anxiety. You may not even be aware of these feelings. You may instead feel more numb and detached or perhaps you often feel sad and depressed. You might even be one of the really lucky ones who feels D: all of the above.

These emotions are all quite interrelated and generally have one emotion in common at their core: pain. You see, anger is often born out of pain. It is a natural response when hurt to be angry and even to want vindication. Of course what you really want is more likely to have that pain removed or healed, rather than some kind of revenge. It is easier though to turn pain into anger, even vengeful anger. Anger feels safer, stronger, and more like a position of power than pain. Pain is a feeling more of loss and fear and helplessness, which is far less comfortable.

This seems even more common in men. For men in our society, there are really only two emotions that are truly acceptable. They are anger and happiness, so any emotion that is negative often gets all mixed up and lumped in with anger and that anger is how those feelings are generally manifested. Since pain and fear are looked upon largely (especially among other men) as weaknesses, the normal tendency, particularly for unenlightened men, is to turn those feelings into that seemingly more powerful emotion of anger. Sadly this tendency is often taught to little boys by the male role models in their lives which may be their father or other relatives and is often reinforced by both fictional heroes and non-fiction heroes like the sports stars of today.

Many people have unresolved emotions festering in their hearts like emotionally infected wounds, unaware of what they truly are and how they are affecting their behavior, and for men those feelings can be even more convoluted.

You need to examine the feelings that are manifested in your behavior. Those underlying emotions are what produce your actions. You must learn to recognize the connection between those feelings and your behavior, the choices you have been making in an effort to either appease or avoid those feelings.

They are there deep inside and are controlling your life and doing a rather poor job of it. Instead of controlling you in ways that help you to deal with the garbage of those crummy feelings, they just perpetuate a vicious cycle that brings on more pain, more anger, more fear. The emotions must be resolved and processed so they can no longer drive you to make blind choices, bad choices, because your perception is warped.

You cannot fix what you don't understand. For you to try to repair the damage caused by all those unresolved emotions that you have held within for so long is like me trying to fix my computer when it crashes. Just because I can operate it (sort of) does not mean I have an understanding of how it works that is great enough to be able to repair it when it fails. I am not too stupid to know how to fix it. It's just that I have not been taught how to fix it.

That same principle applies to your life as well. They do not teach us in school how to deal with our emotions or our histories, though I wish they would. How can you fix what is broken if you do not even know how it would work if it were running perfectly? We have no frame of reference with which to even understand that there are problems with the choices we make, unless we at least learn that our happiness is the greatest gauge of how a healthy, well maintained, smooth running life goes.

If you are to learn how to make good choices, then you must learn to understand the way you work. That is the only way to break the cycle you have been caught in. That means facing, truly and honestly facing, the emotions that you have carried around and tried to repress all this time and the situations that caused them. This is the way you take away the power you gave them. You must revisit the event or events that led to the damage of your emotional health and development, especially those that you were unable to really deal with at the time.

If you were forced to bury those feelings as a child, to deny or ignore them, you may have developed a habit of using this tactic as your standard way of handling pain. You may have developed other inappropriate and ineffective ways of dealing with hurt as well.

Unfortunately, the only way to get past pain is through it. You cannot keep trying to find ways to go around it. You have to face it, identify it, research it, come to understand it, and feel it. Only by doing each of those things can you ever let that garbage go and free yourself.

> *Life is meant for movement*
> *more through time*
> *than across it,*
> *and as we move we grow*
> *we change, we learn.*
> *We learn to love and to lose.*
> *We learn about succeeding*
> *and failing*
> *and what those things truly are,*
> *what really matters*
> *and what doesn't,*
> *what to hold onto*
> *and what to let go of.*
> *We learn to hold onto love*
> *and let go of hate,*
> *to hold onto friends*
> *and let go of grudges,*
> *to hold onto joyful moments*
> *and let go of painful memories,*
> *to hold onto peace*
> *and let go of anger,*
> *to hold onto wisdom*
> *and let go of youth,*
> *to hold onto our giving side*
> *and let go of our taking side.*

> *We learn to hold onto tolerance*
> *and let go of prejudice,*
> *to hold onto change*
> *and let go of ruts,*
> *to hold onto our children*
> *and let go of control over them,*
> *to hold onto our dreams*
> *and let go of our disappointments,*
> *to hold onto life*
> *and let go of our limitations,*
> *to hold onto God*
> *and let go of the world.*

In order to begin the process of facing your feelings, you must set aside some time, sooner rather than later, to be alone and still, so you can intentionally begin to explore what is swimming around in your head. If you need to schedule time to do this, do it, but make it non-negotiable. Do not let anyone, including yourself, come between you and this vitally necessary appointment. Find a quiet place where you will be comfortable and can be undisturbed for preferably as long as it takes. You may need only a couple of hours or so, but some of you may need to schedule a few sessions for this.

You need to have a pen and a notebook with you. Try not to become distracted with the busy demands of your life. Don't allow your mind to go off making a grocery list or thinking about a project at work. If you are one of those type-A people it may take you quite some time to relax and get your mind to empty itself of all the superfluous stuff that normally fills it, but keep at it. Close your eyes and float down the river that is your mind. Ask yourself questions about how you feel until you get to a thought that is significant and pertains to the quality of your life. It may be a thought like, *I wish I didn't have to go to work tomorrow. I hate my job.* If it has anything to do with the quality of your life, write it down.

Write down every one of those thoughts you have. Try to leave a couple of lines in between each thought for you to fill in later. After you have filled several pages with your thoughts, go back and begin asking yourself how each written thought makes you feel. Then ask yourself why you feel that way. To the best of your ability write about how and why you feel as you do in regard to those written thoughts. Write down these answers in the lines you left blank. Remember there are no right or wrong answers in these exercises. You are dealing with feelings and they are not black or white or even close to anything logical. This is about exploring them and excavating all those that you have buried in your heart turning the soil of your life infertile.

If a painful memory begins to surface, let it. Embrace it and try to focus on it. Go to a blank page and write about the event that you are remembering, trying to recall and write down as much detail as you can about it. When you have written down all you can remember about it, reread it. If more comes back to you, add it in. When you are able to recall no more, ask yourself how you felt when the event occurred. Really go back to that moment and relive it, wallow in it if you need to. It's important to get back the feelings that the event evoked in you. If you are sad, concentrate on that sadness. If it hurt and makes you feel like crying, cry your eyes out. Feel all the depth of the emotion that comes up as though it were fresh. In many ways it is.

When my counselor suggested I do this, I was terrified. I feared that if I allowed that pain to take center stage, even for a few moments, it would never leave, that the curtain would never come down on the tragic production of my past. I was certain that if I began crying over painful things in my history, I would never be able to stop. I was afraid that I would float away on my tears until I drowned in them. I feared that someone would eventually have to send the police looking for me when I failed to appear at some expected time and place. It seemed certain that the police would then call for the men in the little white coats to take me, a water-logged mess in a puddle of tears, to some institution.

I did it though and guess what? I did not drown or get carried away in a straight jacket. I cried a reasonable amount of time and stopped, all cried out, just like that. Pain will not kill you, but your attempts to avoid feeling it may. I actually experienced this enormous sense of relief as the weight of all that pain I had been dragging around my whole life began to lessen, to dissipate until the burden of it became no more than an impotent memory.

We must cry
for life should not be seen
as some tragic joke
that just echoes within
the deafening silence.
We must set free our tears,
for they are what connects us
to our humanity.
Tears are life giving
and life affirming,
for tears are born of love.
They are the product
of our own pure pain.
They are the blood of the soul.
We need to become at ease with them,
to see them as able
to wash away our walls.
For the walls we build to protect,
become the walls that divide
and eyes that do not cry
are surely sightless eyes.

As you begin to feel the pain of your past you must go with it. You must accept that whatever caused it, happened and it cannot be undone. You can, however, destroy the power it has had over you. Before you know it the pain will start to fade and begin to lose its intensity. When this happens it means you have dealt with it and can, and must, let it go and move on.

Does this mean it will never make you sad to recall the event that caused that pain? Of course not. For instance, it was sad that I lost my father. It is still sad that I lost my father. But that sadness is now only a fact, not a life sentence. It is still a truth, but it is now only a shadow of a feeling, a memory of that pain. It is no longer the overwhelming, all consuming monster of emotion that overwhelmed me the morning the hospital called, nor is it that sneaky, deceitful villain that once convinced me to make horrible choices that would only punish me for his death instead of relieving the pain buried within me.

Because my grieving period was forcibly so limited, I had not fully processed my grief. Though I was eleven when he died, I was in my thirties when I finally processed my grief. That pain would not have gone away no matter how long I waited and no matter how many men professed undying love for me. Old emotions do not dissipate. They linger and loiter like thieves in the dark, stealing your joy and pilfering your peace. Unprocessed feelings act like slow poison in your soul, unnamed and unacknowledged, but devastatingly destructive just the same.

Until I faced it and dealt with it honestly and completely, allowing the full intensity of those feelings to run their course and be felt, I could not let them go and move past them. I wrote my father a six page letter stained with all the tears I sobbed during its composition. I will describe the process of releasing past pains in this manner later. Writing that letter allowed me to truly process (understand and feel) the pain that had so long incited me to make bad choices as I subconsciously tried to find healing by replacing my father with a man who would love me and not abandon me, a man who would guide me and protect me. Only after finally fully processing it, was that pain no longer able to chase me into the arms of countless men who could never have healed a pain they did not cause.

It was through this process that I finally understood that it was his problems, not mine, that made him unable to love me in the way an emotionally healthy father should. It was about his inability to genuinely, honestly, and intimately give love, not about whether or not I was lovable. I had punished myself for his shortcomings and his issues my whole life.

Concentrate on your past as long as you need to. Think back to your childhood. I know how much this sounds like every therapists psycho-babble, but if you're self-esteem was damaged, you need to go back to the beginning of the event or events that caused the damage and it probably began when you were a kid or a teen and the most vulnerable.

When you're done with the "painful past" exercise, you can move on to the next exercise. You may want to do this at another time just to give yourself a chance to sort of ruminate about the exercise you have just completed.

When you are ready to move on ask yourself what you would change about you and about your life now if you had a magic wand with which to do so. Yes, write down those things also. Do this too, for as long as you can. Next, examine those things you've written in that section. This can form the blueprint, the plan, for how you would like to grow and how you would like your life to be. It is just to open your eyes to all the possibilities.

Ask yourself now, "Is it possible that I could be like this, that my life could be like this?" Hold it to the light of reason. There is no reason that you cannot, with careful planning and effort, make your dreams come true. You do, however, want to be practical. For example, you do not want to make a decision to become a pop star if you're fifty years old and can't sing, act, or dance. There is nothing wrong however with deciding to pursue acting in your church drama ministry or singing in the choir.

You also do not want to decide you want to be completely laid back if that is simply not in your nature. It is great though to decide that you want to be *more* laid back and to decide to work on handling things in a more realistic and calm manner. This exercise is designed just to get you thinking more about the future and who you can be and how you can live.

Again, you type-A's may have a hard time staying focused on your deeper thoughts, but you must stay on that level of thinking, for that is where you really live. It is on the level of thoughts that reflect your feelings that your choices are made, whether you're truly aware of them or not. It is only on that deeper level of thinking that any changes can be made in you or your life. This is commonly known as "getting in touch with your feelings." (There goes that psycho-babble again.)

In the next chapter we will go further into your past and the reasons for your difficulty. We will also, in later chapters, delve deeper into getting to know who you were truly born to be and how to truly live the life you were born to have. But it is important for you, as you deal with that painful and angry past, to have an idea of where you are headed when you come out the other side.

chapter fifteen

UNRAVELING THE PAST

Buried, unresolved anger, even justified anger, spills over into your life and infects and poisons your relationships, no matter how deep your denial of those bitter feelings may run. In facing that anger, identifying and acknowledging it, lies the power to dislodge and release it. Too many people hold onto their past pains and use them as a built-in excuse to avoid taking responsibility for the current condition of their lives.

In order to be free of that poisonous anger you've carried from your past you do not have to go back and find the playground bully who beat you up in the third grade to release it, nor do you have to confront every person who has ever hurt you. In fact, you do not actually have to confront anyone, but you must get in touch with that anger so that you can at least direct it towards the correct source and assign it to the right person if you are ever to be free of it. You have to determine what and who has really hurt you and made you angry. It is just like when you get into a huge argument with your spouse over some minor detail like whose turn it is to take out the garbage, you are probably not really fighting over the garbage at all, but likely some much bigger issue. You need to identify the real issue at the heart of that excessive anger toward your spouse in order to solve it and that anger is also often the manifestation of hurt.

Anger is not a quiet, easily buried emotion. It will find an outlet and manifest itself in any way it can, toward anyone who is handy. We have all been subject to engaging in a fit of road rage at one time or another and most of us would agree that we were likely in a bad mood, stressed out, and angry to begin with when some poor, unwitting driver accidentally cut us off and became the recipient of a few loud, choice words and maybe even a little sign language exclamation point. Chances are the action on the part of the other driver in no way deserved the amount of rage we felt and expressed at the time and if the same incident had occurred when we were in a good, laid back mood, we might have responded with no more than a little sigh of annoyance.

Buried anger works in much the same way. It tends to leave us with little or no patience and can have us lashing out at people who really do not deserve it, but may have just been in the wrong place at the wrong time, like in the same room at the same time that we were.

When I was first divorced from Steve and the girls were young, I had no patience with them and screamed at them way too often and way too loudly. Part of this was due to my stress level and part was due to my exhaustion, but the majority of my anger was unresolved anger I'd been dragging around; anger that I too often misdirected at my daughters. Remember back to the chapter that covered my life soon after my divorce, when I woke up surprised that I was not angry anymore? Having removed myself from Steve's presence at least put me in a place where my psyche was no longer having more and more anger and resentment added to its already over-stuffed compartment. That was the first step toward disarming some of my overloaded supply of anger.

The next and most important one took place some time into my therapy when I became aware of how angry I had always been toward my father. This anger had been very hard to recognize because it had become all tangled up with the natural tendency of a child to not want to be disloyal to their parent, especially when all they have left of that parent is a memory. On one hand, as an eleven year old kid I was furious for all the ways my father had failed me as a parent, the ultimate failure coming in the form of his death, but on the other hand, I also felt horribly guilty for being so angry with my dead father. It felt like such a cruel betrayal to harbor those feelings. So I did what I had always done, what I had done with the pain of my grief when he died, I buried the anger and the guilt right alongside it.

Now that I had identified those unresolved emotions, I needed to deal with them, to feel them, and to release them, but how? Usually when you find that you are angry with a person, you can discuss it with that person and hopefully, if that person is in the wrong, they will admit it and apologize, making a way for you to forgive them. This is not possible when the recipient of that anger has been deceased for over twenty years.

My counselor suggested that I write my father a letter. She explained that it would not only be helpful in my being able to clarify, and therefore understand, the complex, intertwined feelings that I had held deep within for so long, but that it would also be a way to fully feel them and to expel them in a tangible way onto the paper. Of course I would never send the letter. I would be writing it for my benefit only, but it would likely be a cathartic experience for me even if I only tore it up afterward.

It truly was. Fortunately I didn't tear it up afterward. It turned out to be one of the most important pieces of the puzzle of my life and did for me exactly what she had said it would. It dug up all those messy feelings, that as an eleven year old I had been unable to deal with and process, but as a thirty-three year old, I was not only capable of handling, but desperate to handle. I cried nearly all the way through it, but by the end, I had learned that as much as I had suffered because of his alcoholism and his inability to be close and loving to me, he had suffered much more, and as much as I had lost out on a father, he had lost out on much more: me.

Just as I instructed you to do in the previous chapter, schedule some time when you are sure to be uninterrupted in a quiet place and begin writing to the people that have hurt you, the people that you are angry with. If you need to, get your writings from the last chapter and begin rereading them to access the information you have already uncovered. This should help to get you back in touch with the core of feelings you need to process.

I know, it's easy for a writer to clarify feelings through writing, but what about all of you who hate to write or think you're no good at it? You don't have to be good at it. You're not getting graded on it. No one else is likely to ever even see it unless you decide to share it. Don't worry about spelling, grammar, punctuation or how it sounds. None of that matters in the least. Even if you hate to write and are not likely to win the Pulitzer Prize, it is still the most efficient way of taking a jumbled, confusing mess of unknown feelings, and processing them in a way that allows you to acknowledge and identify those feelings, and to express them in a lucid and understandable format. Writing requires language, and language enables you to clarify all the complex junk you've had buried within you.

It is a very educational and enlightening process that enables you to get to the stuff that has been haunting you from the deepest level of your mind. This lets you take the ghosts from the dark cellar of your memories and drag them into the light of the present, where you can examine them and finally exorcise them from your life.

I remind you, you do not ever need to send it to the person or people you are writing about, so don't worry about finding the address of that playground bully. It isn't a necessary part of this exercise that you send it. In fact, I don't really recommend mailing it. If you are concerned that someone will see it, it may change what you write. Only the certainty of having no audience frees you up to truly empty your heart onto the page.

You may decide to burn it in a little ceremony as part of your decision to release those feelings and to move on after you have identified and processed them. It can be very beneficial to perform a physical action in relation to the process of letting the garbage go so that you can move forward.

You may even find that you are able to forgive the person. That is the ultimate and ideal act of releasing those feelings and the power they have had over you for so long. I was able to forgive my father because I was able to at last see things from a perspective other than my eleven year old mind. You may find a gift like this too.

You may discover that you have grown to a level of emotional maturity that allows you to see things from another perspective as well, one that may even show you that the actual event no longer justifies the amount of hurt and anger you have held because of it.

Anger, like negative thoughts, can also become a habit that needs to be consciously changed. Furthermore, anger is poison only to you and does nothing to punish the person responsible for inciting it, so I highly recommend you strive for forgiveness. Anger is a feeling, but forgiveness is a choice. It is not warm and fuzzy. It is practical and deliberate and it is also tremendously liberating. We will look more deeply at forgiveness in an upcoming chapter.

What do you do if the person, or people, who have hurt you and have left you holding the bag of rage are still accessible and forgiveness does not feel like an option, at least not right now, and you would really like to confront them? Should you confront them in person? Probably not. I still believe the process of writing the letter is far more helpful than a face to face confrontation. Not only does it help you to clarify what you are feeling, but what your position is as well.

This exercise is designed to provide you with a calm, quiet atmosphere in which you intentionally explore situations that have hurt you so that you will process all the feelings that those situations bring up. If you are led to tears, you are free to cry them, where if you were in a confrontational situation, you may not want to break down and cry, even if you need to. Also, you will surely have your train of thought interrupted by the other person, who is likely to argue in an attempt to defend themselves. This would be distracting and possibly confusing to you when what you truly need is to get to the heart of your feelings right now, not theirs. Writing is a safe way to face whatever is within you regarding the people and events that have affected you in ways that you may be just now beginning to understand.

It is better to write the letter first, process (feel) and become familiar with those feelings, and get comfortable with the memories. If, after you have done this and have allowed some time to pass, you still wish to confront the person, that is up to you. Be prepared, however, that you may have fantasized about this confrontation many times, but it is not likely to go as you have envisioned. The person is likely to become very defensive and may even deny your version of the truth altogether. This can be very upsetting. There is a very good chance the result of any confrontation will be a heated argument that will not truly resolve anything. You are not likely to get the apology you are hoping for, and probably deserve, and you may be very disappointed.

This does not mean that there are never opportunities to discuss the contents of the letter with the person. Sometimes both people can have a calm, rational discussion and are able to come to understand each other's point of view regarding the situation. You may even receive an apology from the offender, but this is definitely a "best case scenario" and likely to be more the exception than the rule. So attempt a discussion of the matter only if you are fairly certain that it is necessary and may produce positive results.

I have provided the contents of the letter I wrote to my father below because I hope it will inspire you to do this exercise by seeing how my tangled feelings were clarified and because it provides you with a sample that may give you an idea of how to start:

Daddy,

I'm writing this in hope of making some contact with the feelings that lie so deep within me. They are feelings I recognize to be rage, humiliation, pain and fear, enormous amounts of fear. These emotions have driven me all of my life, and for the most part, they have driven me to make very painful mistakes.

You see, I have spent my whole life trying desperately to find someone to take care of me, to make me feel safe, secure, and protected. I've tried to find someone who could convince me I was worth loving, that I deserved love.

These are things you should have done! But you didn't bother. You were never there for me. You never hugged me, you never said you loved me, worst of all, you never did anything to show me you loved me.

You drank. It was more important to you than your wife or your home or your own children. I never knew if you were coming home, let alone when. Most of the time you were home you just locked us away from you so that you could drink more. What was it about that despicable bottle that could mean more to you than your own children?

You should never have procreated! You had no right to bring

children into this world that you weren't capable of nurturing, or loving, or even providing for. You couldn't even keep a job, so we were always moving and having to start over.

How could you have had me; this bright, beautiful, little girl who looked so much like you, and not have wanted to hold me, cuddle me, love me? I was just a baby, a victim of your drinking. I had dire health problems and still you weren't there for me.

I got none of your time, none of your affection, and none of your love. You selfish, spineless piece of garbage! You were weak and spineless and now I've had to have a hundred times more strength than you did, just to survive. I looked for your love every-where, even in the bed of an abusive man for thirteen years of my life!

When your drinking cost you your marriage, you didn't even bother to call me! You lived in the same city and yet you never even visited me for nearly a year. It was just an extended version of your disappearing act.

I will never understand a man who could live without his own children. As if it wasn't bad enough that you neglected me, you even took my mother away from me. She was always so consumed with taking care of you she never had any time for caring for me.

So the adults wallowed in their booze-filled world leaving their children to fend for themselves. I hate you for that! I deserved bet-ter than that. Yet you made me feel as though I deserved nothing, cause that's all you gave me.

It's an absolute shame you never really got to see what a beau-tiful person you brought into this world. I'm very sorry for you. You never got to experience the tremendous pride and joy you should have felt. You were never able to receive my love either. You denied yourself the greatest gift you could have gotten.

If you could see me now, you would be very, very proud, cause Daddy, I am very, very lovable.

Your Daughter,
Vikki

What I discovered as I finished writing this letter was surprising

and liberating. Once I acknowledged the pain of having a father who had been so unavailable to me, and was ultimately made permanently unavailable, I discovered the greater sadness was what he had denied himself. He passed away at forty years old, never having the opportunity to experience all the love and closeness that he could have gleaned from having a healthy relationship with me. I had inherited so many of his gifts and talents, not to mention his big brown eyes and small stature. I not only looked the most like him, but I am bright and creative, witty and magnetic like he was. I write and draw and even sell like he did. We would have had so much in common that he could have nurtured and enjoyed.

After realizing this, it enabled me to forgive him and to let go of the anger that had been punishing me for so long. God knows he had already punished himself with all that he had denied himself. I was able to see all that he had lost while he chased that ever enticing bottle. I began to see the whole picture, not just my portion of it, and that new perspective helped me to be free of the hell that had long existed in my damaged psyche.

My Father

How tragic
that such a huge mind was thrust
into such a small frame,
that you could be so grand
while your hands sailed across the sea
of ivory keys,
and while color danced
from the tip of your paintbrush
in great strokes of flourish,
or while your words waltzed
over a paper landscape,
merely hinting at the brilliance
that lit your life.

How heart wrenching
that such great love bloomed
in your floral heart,
that you could live so large
in the skyscape of your passion
as a lover,
all the while being so miserly
with your love as a spouse
and being so ruthlessly negligent
in sharing your love
as a father.
How soul saddening
that even as you embodied
this wild wit, this unending charm,
this untamed, yet calculated charisma,
you would trade talent again and again
for liquor,
that you would barter your body with God,
choosing over and over
to punish your body.
Perhaps because it was only five foot six
it had cheated your enormous gifts
out of a proper,
respect commanding form.
Is that why you lived so hard,
so fast,
so desperately?
Were you always in some silent contest,
some deeply driven way
to win at life?
How ironic
that while you lived life as a sprinter,
racing through it in such swift style,
you would keep your family
on the sidelines,
watching helplessly alone
in a crowd of strangers,

as you staggered and stumbled
your way toward a finish line
that no one else could see.
All the while you were running,
you were running right past what mattered,
denying yourself the blessings that lay
in the pink kisses of your daughters,
in the warm arms of your wife,
in the lasting love of the Lord.
How pathetic
that you never learned
that early on
you had dropped the baton
that you were to pass on to your children
and that all the talent in the world
amounts to nothing in the grave,
and that liquor
is not a fair trade
for love.
You sprinted unaware
that life is not a dash,
but a marathon
and you had written your story,
your destiny,
across a cocktail napkin
in such small letters
that you would drop out of the race
at forty.
How tragic.

My rage had turned to pity somewhere during the process of writing that letter. Now I can't promise you the same results. Each situation and every person involved in it is different, but I can promise you it is worth the effort.

As for my mom, that was a little more complicated for me. I

had developed a real love-hate relationship with her. On one hand, I loved her more than any other woman in the world, and recognized the ways in which she had really come through for me. On the other hand, I was furious with her for the ways that she hadn't. One huge thing that I had learned in my therapy was that I was very angry with her because after the rape, I desperately needed to be taken care of as any woman, let alone a teenager, would have. Instead of reaching for that comfort, I felt compelled to disregard my needs (bury, deny, and ignore) in order to spare my mother a pain I was afraid she could not bear.

I needed a mother whose loving arms I could fall into and find comfort, safety and security in. I needed to be tenderly nurtured through the aftermath of one of the most traumatic events possible, but I knew if she saw me that hurt and needy she would lose it, and I knew I could not have withstood that on top of everything else.

How did I know this? As a sickly, asthmatic girl, I had seen her in a crisis way too many times. In fact, by the time I was fourteen or so, I had stopped telling her when I was having an asthma attack because my fear of her hysteria had become more intense than my fear of dying of asthma. I taught myself how to relax during an attack until it passed (after using my inhaler, of course). I gladly risked the consequences, because it meant I could avoid her screaming for my stepfather to hurry up and get me to the hospital and the sheer panic the fear of anything happening to me brought her. I understand that she panicked because she loved me so much, but that kind of expression of love was just too hard to bear.

Then there were all the other mixed messages: the back-handed compliments like "That's a pretty dress. You look a little heavy in it though." There were mixed messages like the intensity of her attention when I was sick, but the lack of her attention when I was running around partying instead of getting an education, and not helping me out of that horrible marriage of mine the first time I came to her, but helping take care of the girls after I finally did leave.

Not long after I wrote that letter to my father, I also wrote one to my mother with no intention of ever sending it to her. It was filled with anger and expletives and it did not heal my relationship with my mother, but it did help me to understand the dynamics of it. It also helped me to recognize, face and even release some of the anger that I had inside for her. It would be a little while before I had matured emotionally to the point where I could truly see from her perspective, which would ultimately allow me the compassion and forgiveness to actually heal this relationship, but writing that letter was certainly the first step in the process.

Writing these types of letters can go a long way toward unraveling all your tangled feelings, and deciphering any mixed messages you may have received. They can become a map that you can at last navigate by, instead of just using the faulty compass and broken rudder that your warped perception of yourself and your unresolved emotions have left you steering your life with.

If doing any of these exercises brings up things that are too traumatic for you to sort through on your own, such as sexual or physical abuse, I cannot urge you strongly enough to seek out the help of a professional therapist, such as a psychologist or a psychiatrist, who can offer actual therapy and help you work through that past trauma. I also urge you to seek out a professional who has all the latest medical and psychological treatments to offer you if you suffer from depression. It can be a very dangerous and even life threatening disorder, but it can also be a disorder that can be very effectively treated by a professional, so that you do not have to continue to suffer from it.

Let me remind you again that I am not a psychologist. This book is not intended to, designed to, or capable of replacing real therapy. It is not a cure-all, nor will utilizing all the information in this book solve every challenge in your life. It is only a sharing of the things that damaged my self-esteem and the things that healed it. I believe whole-heartedly that these same skills and exercises can help repair your damaged self-esteem also, but if your problems are too enormous or traumatic, then please seek qualified help in the form of counseling by a professional as I did.

As I began to put the pieces of my past together I began finally to solve the riddle of my unhappiness and to break that vicious cycle of dysfunction. I was becoming a calmer, happier person and that meant I was also becoming a calmer, happier mother, the kind of mother my beautiful little girls had always deserved. Thank God!

chapter sixteen

RELATIONSHIPS

Being proactive, rather than reactive, is especially important in relationships. Until you can recognize and then calmly, but firmly, assert
your needs, you are giving away the power in your own life. So many
people are so desperate for validation due to their lack of self-esteem,
that they will give over the power in their lives by becoming simply
reactive in many, if not all, of their relationships. They are likely to put
up with a variety of abuses and mistreatments, because they are more
afraid of being alone than they are of being in a miserable relationship. This is yet another way people of low self-esteem sometimes fail
to take responsibility for their lives, and allow their emotional health
to continue to deteriorate.

Self-esteem pretty much amounts to power in your life. Assert-
ing power will also further bolster your self-esteem. This is a good
cycle. I spent my childhood, and a large part of my adult life as well,
afraid to stand up for myself. You know that feeling of horror and
panic you experience during a nightmare when you are facing some
kind of terror, but can't scream, no matter how badly you want to or
how hard you try? Well, that's how it felt for me to be tolerating some
kind of injustice while I stood silently by, nearly paralyzed with fear.

As a child this mute response led to further teasing and even an
occasional thrashing at the hands of some cruel girl who smelled the

fear in me. As an adult it meant being taken advantage of, allowing various forms of mistreatment ranging from verbal abuse to job loss. This is not to say that I never stood up for myself. My marriage to Steve was certainly proof that I was not adverse to a good argument. I had also learned to project confidence even when none existed, so often I was quite assertive, but only in limited circumstances, never when I was in a circumstance where I was not comfortable or there was anything of value at stake.

I can easily identify experiences from early in my life that probably caused this behavior, this inability to defend myself. I remember, for instance, being about five and having my mom take my prized pennies and pretending that she would not give them back to me because she thought it was amusing to watch me get so angry. This made me feel helpless because I could not get them back from her. Standing up for myself, at least as much as I could, by pleading and demanding seemed ineffective and a waste of time. I did not have any power in that situation. My mother had all the power, so I could not make her give back my pennies. Of course, she did return them to me later, probably not even much later, but it was a time of her choosing, not mine. This was just one situation in a long line of them that likely sent me a message that made me feel unable to affect the results in a conflict.

I tried to stand up for myself other times as a kid, even against a variety of teachers. I had one teacher in the second grade who I remember in particular. I got so angry with her one day I just left. That's right, I got up, walked out of the classroom, and went home. I don't recall what she had done, perhaps it was one of the many great ruler trips she took across my knuckles. We never really saw eye to eye. The principal, politically correctly, called it a personality conflict, but the truth of the matter was, we hated each other.

I'm not sure why she disliked me so much, considering the fact that I was out ill much of the year. Anyway, I got all the way home when it occurred to me that I had no idea what to do next. Surely I would get in trouble from my grandmother for just coming home in the middle of the school day, so I just sat down on the front porch to think. I'm not sure how much time had passed before my grandmother opened the door to inform me that the school had called.

I guess they didn't approve of "flex-time" in the second grade. Of course my grandmother sent me straight back to school. Imagine my humiliation as I had to slink back into the classroom in utter defeat, in such contrast to the great degree of pride with which I had made my grand and dramatic exit.

I could fascinate you (or bore you) with many such tales, but the point is that I started life with a fiery nature and a fierce sense of justice. If I felt I was being treated unfairly, my temper would ignite and I was quick to flare. But after many experiences in which life and people simply beat me down, the world had proven to me that people could mistreat me and get away with it. I could be taken advantage of and forced to go back for more. I could be angry, and totally justified in that anger, and yet be totally helpless to do anything to affect the situation or its outcome. Eventually I learned that even my body could be taken and used against my will. What was the point in standing up for myself? No wonder I rarely tried.

Not standing up for yourself should not be confused with simply being kind. There is a fine line we must learn to walk between being kind and being taken advantage of, between being loving and being victimized. That fine line is made of healthy boundaries that enable you to give, but do not allow you to get taken. When you give, it builds you up and you feel good about it. When you are taken advantage of, it generally means that you give something that you would rather not give, but because somehow you feel a warped sense of obligation to do so, you give even though you end up angry and resentful afterwards.

A good example of this type of "giving" would be how I had described my promiscuity after the rape back in the first part of the book. Do you recall that I explained how I often felt this distorted sense of obligation to have sex with a man I was dating, just because I was grateful that he found me that attractive? When I did "give in" to this warped way of seeing his pressure, I did not feel good afterward, but instead generally felt kind of humiliated and used. I had convinced myself that I was using them the same way a man uses a woman, but it really didn't do much to minimize the humiliation.

This type of feeling is certainly not exclusive to having been used sexually. It is the same way we often feel after we have been taken advantage of by acquiescing to a request or demand that we truly do not want to give in to. Another example of a situation that may leave you feeling this way would be if a friend, relative, or lover asked to borrow money from you. Let's say you know from their track record that they are not likely to pay it back, and that lending it amounts to a gift that you would never really desire to give them had they not put you in this awkward position by asking. Let's also assume that you are not really in a financial position to give away your money like that, but you don't want to seem unkind or selfish, so you give in and then feel resentful towards the person and angry at yourself for being pushed over yet again.

People of low self-esteem often seem to have other people in their lives who are continually requesting things from them that they would rather not give. Those things are certainly not limited to material things alone, but can be anything from sex to favors that cost you precious personal time. Giving out of a sense of obligation that is misplaced and undeserved is another way of giving away the power in your life. Anything that people ask or demand from you, that leaves you feeling taken advantage of, or that robs you of your dignity, is something that you need to learn not to give away. That means establishing emotionally healthy boundaries and learning to say "no."

This can be especially hard if you feel poorly about yourself. You probably worry way too much about what others think of you, and are likely always afraid of being rejected. Often you will sacrifice your dignity in hope of retaining a relationship. This is often because you are lonely when you are alone and lacking the distraction from your negative thoughts and unhappy feelings that companionship offers you.

This too often means settling for an unhealthy relationship with someone who may clearly not be good for you or to you. It may be a romantic relationship that does not bring you the joy that a healthy love should, but you resign yourself to it because you are convinced that you do not deserve any better and that you cannot do any better. You probably chose this person with the same desperation to find validation and love that you have based most of your life choices on.

Your choices in people that you become involved with are often perfect examples of the warped perception you have of yourself. You likely settle for poor treatment from a person who probably has his or her own emotional issues, and you probably end up feeling even worse about yourself as you get twirled around in the dizzying dance of yet another vicious cycle.

Initially romantic relationships are the ultimate pick-me-up. You get all this attention and, particularly in the early stages of courting, it usually comes with all these flowery phrases and compliments that can become a powerful narcotic to someone who never compliments themselves. You don't believe the compliments and yet you absolutely cannot get enough of them. It is as though you feel if you hear them enough they will come true, when the reality of it is, that they already are true, but you just can't see it. It is why I tried to teach you first and foremost that you need to retrain your brain so that you can rid yourself of the distorted and inaccurate vision you have of yourself and see the real you in all your glory.

Right after my divorce I dated a man who was in a relationship that he swore was not going anywhere and he was about to end. He even credited me with giving him a reason to finally just get it over with and succumb to the inevitability of the break up. That was ten years ago. They have been married for five years now. I ended it when I finally faced the fact that he was not getting out of his relationship anytime soon, and as needy as I was, I was not morally comfortable with dating someone who belonged to someone else. The sad thing is that he actually sought the help of a counselor not long after we stopped dating. Because he had a long standing pattern of being unfaithful in his relationships and had two divorces with a child from each marriage to show for it, he sought help. His counselor told him that he was very good at beginning relationships, but was very bad at sustaining them.

He had poor self-esteem and was addicted to those early stages of romance when everything was magical and the compliments and attention were like pure elixir to him. Sound familiar?

The biggest problem with this courtship addiction that so often plagues people of poor self-esteem is that early courtship is temporary and it can take no more than a single disagreement to wipe out every compliment and all the positive attention that came before. After all, you never really believed all that mushy stuff to begin with,

l you? That's another one of the problems with having low
...em, you never believe anything positive that anyone says
about you no matter how true it actually is, and yet you believe everything negative anyone says including all those nasty things you say to
yourself, no matter how untrue they actually are. That is why all those
compliments can dissipate like a puff of smoke on a windy day when
the first sign of trouble arrives. You never believed the compliments
or felt that you deserved that love to begin with, so you do not expect
it to survive a disagreement.

Chances are if you have become involved with a real quality person, you will sabotage the relationship yourself, but if the person is
also damaged in some way, and can be further damaging to you, you
will probably feel vaguely comfortable and settle right in. I hope the
very irony of this is not lost on you and I wish that either of these
scenarios were far less common than they are.

Too often we get caught up in mediocre or down right destructive relationships, and become so dependent on the other person for
our validation that we even end up dependent on them for our moods
as well. When things are going well and they are being loving to us,
it's like a ticket to heaven and we are up. When things are not going
well, either due to arguing or just the natural ebb and flow that exists
in every relationship, we are down. We can become almost manic-
depressive in the extremes our moods can reach when relationships
strap us back into that roller coaster. Too often we allow ourselves to
be completely at the mercy of that person to whom we have given
away our power.

This can be devastating when the relationship ends, as most do.
Let's face it, like the old saying predicts, we all have to kiss a lot of
toads before we find our prince. If you are emotionally unhealthy, you
are likely to pass over the prince and spend your life either serving
or chasing any number of toads. The relationship may end with a big
bang like an explosive argument fueled by those desperate emotional
needs and irrational fears that demolish the fragile structure of it.
Maybe it will end by the slow poison of time and neglect and the
often inevitable attrition of passion that destroys romance and deteriorates relationships.

Either way, you are likely to end up with more emotional scarring and residual pain that may further intensify your feelings of rejection and worthlessness. Even if you're the one that chose to end it, you are probably an expert at finding a way, rational or not, to internalize the failure of the relationship and take the blame for it. You may begin a whole new list of "if onlys," or just rehash the same old ones. You know the drill: "If only I was prettier, smarter, nicer, more interesting, more successful, etc…"

Even if the other person was a total loser and was addicted or abusive or unfaithful, or even D: all of the above, you will still likely berate yourself over the demise of the relationship. This may happen to you every time a relationship ends, compounding your problems with your self-image. You assume your ensuing misery is your fault, and it may well be, but not because you are not good enough. It is because *you don't believe* you are good enough.

You need to look at the situation logically and objectively. In the light of reason, I doubt you would be able to find any particular quality that you are lacking that would have fixed the relationship. Relationships begin and end for all kinds of reasons that mostly just add up to the fact that two particular people are not right for each other. This does not mean that you are not right, just not right together.

The most common relationship challenge we face when we feel badly about ourselves isn't even the end of a relationship, but hanging on to relationships that should end. We settle for a partner who is unsuited for us, and for that matter, who is unsuited for anyone. We ignore all kinds of red flags, like the ones practically draped around Rob that nearly shouted about his blatant infidelity. Just as I did, you probably ignore them and choose instead to deny those bad behaviors exist. Again; *what you choose to look at, determines also what you do not see.* So you focus only on the things that you want to see, or the things that you want to believe you see.

Remember back when I described love as a choice and you first read that line about *what you choose to look at*, I explained that if you focus only on the flaws in a person, you will not be able to love them because you will not see the good qualities. It works both ways. If you focus only on the good qualities, real or imagined, and convince yourself that the flaws are not there, or are not that bad, you are cheating yourself out of the whole, accurate picture of that person, and may be blindly hanging onto a deeply flawed person who is incapable of having a healthy relationship.

That is one of the reasons wise people do not rush into marriage. They understand that they need to see the whole picture before they can make an intelligent decision and that it takes time to get that whole picture. Everyone can be on their best behavior for awhile. Remember when you were a kid and Grandma came to visit? You were probably quiet and polite and everything your mother made you promise to be. What if Grandma had moved in with you as mine did? How long before she would have seen you talk with your mouth full and fight with your siblings?

Wise people wait for the "sibling rivalry" to start, or for the manners to begin to get sloppy before making the decision to trust their life to that person. If you have poor self-esteem you may be so desperate to secure that "love" that you rush in and give your heart away no matter what the risks are, even when the risks would be obvious to anyone else. You use that person's attention voraciously to medicate your feelings of worthlessness. It doesn't matter if that person has immense problems, all that matters is that you are not alone and someone is validating you.

You may spend the majority of your time involved with that person feeling used, humiliated and taken advantage of, but are still willing to settle for them because you so fear being alone and are so convinced that this is the best you can do.

You may be suffering emotional, mental, or verbal abuse, but are willing to remain and take it as though you deserve it, often even believing you deserve it. You might even be willing to endure physical abuse rather than get out. Perhaps you have yourself convinced that there is no way out, even though there are safe shelters in almost every city for abused women and their children to run to where they can be protected and helped to get back on their feet without that torment. Remember if you are in this situation and have children, you are teaching them how to be treated, and may even be allowing them to receive that same treatment now by remaining with that person. You absolutely need to understand that you do not deserve it, and that they sure as heck, do not deserve it. You do have a choice, no matter how difficult that choice is, and no matter how hopeless it may seem, but they do not have a choice. They are depending on you to make the right one for them.

> We lap up all the love
> that drips and falls around us.
> We live on our knees
> as the desperate often do.
> We clamor for the crumbs
> that even a worthless man
> might throw us.
> We trade our dignity
> for attention
> and give away our independence
> with our open hands
> as a peace offering
> like it could buy us love.
> We lose our hope
> and lose our way
> and find ourselves
> all black and blue.
> We wipe up their drunkenness
> with our dishrag hearts
> and sometimes
> with our flesh and bones.
> Yes, we would even trade
> our blood
> to have someone
> come home to us.
> We lose all shreds
> of our pride
> as well as our identities.
> We lose our days,
> we lose our dreams
> and sometimes
> we even lose our lives.

Maybe you're a saboteur, someone so certain you don't deserve love and happiness that you do things to undermine the chances of success for the relationship. These things are likely done on a sub-conscious level, where you're not even aware that you're doing them. You may withhold emotional intimacy, keeping your partner at a frustrating distance, or start arguments, goading them into saying negative things about you that will somehow prove you right in your feelings of unworthiness.

Perhaps you begin searching for a replacement when things get too close and begin to scare you. Maybe you are like Rob or the other man I described just a bit ago, and you are the one who cannot stay faithful. It may be that you just get bored very quickly and move on before any real chance of a deep and lasting bond can form. You may start looking for problems where none exist or you might begin focusing on your partner's flaws, convincing yourself that he or she is not right for you, completely blind to the fact that the only problem is that you are not right with you.

There are countless ways that we can sabotage a potentially good relationship and we can be quite creative about it. We are capable of producing numerous excuses for why we should get out of a rela-tionship, and you may have some that I have not mentioned or even thought of.

Maybe you're not into sabotage, but are a desperate clinger, even when your partner is not worth clinging to. Perhaps your partner is not abusive or unfaithful or anything horrible, but is just not some-one who brings you the happiness that being with your soul mate would, and should, bring. Maybe the relationship is not terrible, but is certainly not fulfilling either. You don't dare assume that you deserve to be happy and should wait for a person who really is all that you may have dreamed of finding. You are surely not willing to risk being alone until you find the right one, so you stay in a ho-hum relationship with a ho-hum partner. This of course ruins your chances of being available for a great partner, let alone your being proactive in seeking one.

Perhaps the person is okay, but just not right for you. You may even be caught up in trying to be right for him or her, though you are being completely untrue to yourself in your efforts to fit into the mold of the person that you believe he or she wants you to be. You might even be so out of touch with your feelings, and who you truly are on the deeper level of your psyche where the real you actually lives, that you are not even aware that this is what you are doing. You could have this image that you should be an outdoorsy type and continually choose athletic types, or perhaps you think you should be an outdoorsy type because you have chosen an athletic partner. Either way, you may actually be more fulfilled curled up on the couch with popcorn and a good book or a classic movie than you are jet skiing or rock climbing.

How can you really be happy with someone that you have little or nothing in common with? Harder still, how can you be truly happy trying to be someone who you really aren't? Eventually, playing a role will get very old, and the dissatisfaction will begin to erode the relationship. You both may get resentful and tired of the enormous amounts of compromise it takes to maintain a relationship where the two people involved are just not right for each other.

It may simply be that you have settled for a partner whom you just have no chemistry with. Perhaps there are no sparks, an essential piece of the romance puzzle. I am not talking about the effects of a long term relationship where the sparks were there, but have died down and need to be revived. (Passions fires need to be stoked in a conscious way, just as you need to keep love alive by choosing to focus on the good instead of the bad.) Too often we enter into relationships where there are no sparks, no passion even from the start, but we rush in anyway, because it offers us some precious security against the horrifying prospect of being alone. Then we cling to this mediocre relationship, trading real excitement and happiness for that same security.

> *I wash the truth from my hands,*
> *wring out the pity,*
> *dry off the anger*
> *and walk out alone*

through the closing door of me.
I replace my face
with that of a lover's,
carefully conceal the resentment
that haunts our togetherness
and defies the farce
that exists between us.
I enter, braced and steeled,
back into my dogged denial,
close my eyes
and take back your hand,
re-soiling my own.
I resettle into my settling,
resigned to this love masquerade,
nearly consciously choosing
the mediocrity of us
over the terror
of solitude.

It doesn't matter what your style is, beyond your need to recognize and address it. The end result is always the same; a failed relationship that you thought would save you, but that only succeeded in leaving you filled with even less self-esteem, more pain, and more guilt and shame, as you shoulder the blame for yet another failure, and a few new feelings of rejection that you use to prove to yourself once again, that you are not good enough.

Here's one more bit of irony about all this relationship stuff; we tend to attract people of fairly equal levels of emotional health. This should not surprise you. When you think about the way we attract members of the opposite sex you'll realize that we generally attract those who are on, or quite close to, our same level of attractiveness. You rarely see someone who is an eight or nine on a "one to ten" scale of good looks with say a five or a four. Sure, you sometimes will see it in a couple who has been together a very long time, but I'll bet you they both started out about the same, but one aged better than the other. Most of the time you see a person who's an eight with a romantic partner who is probably somewhere in the seven to nine range, and you'll see that person who's a four or five with another person who is about the same.

This is rarely done on a conscious level; it is just kind of automatic. The phenomenon of attracting romantic partners of equal emotional health works this same way, but often even more sub-consciously. My ex-husband serves as a perfect example of this. After we split up we both ended up in relationships with partners who had serious emotional issues. Of course both relationships failed, but the difference came about when Rob and I fell apart and I got help and dealt with my garbage, changing the things that had been leading me straight into the oncoming train of failure, while Steve did nothing. It was as if he had been riding this broken bicycle all his life and every time it crashes it gets a little more damaged, but he just gets up and hops back on that same old bike and rides on down that same old road.

I ended up eventually choosing a partner who had also tired of failed relationships. He had grown as a person and had made adjustments to his behavior that, combined with my own personal growth, have enabled us to have a wonderfully healthy and fulfilling relationship. Steve, who did nothing proactive to address his issues, moved on to a bleached blonde he met in a bar who had no job, no car, and no drivers license. She was, and still is, an alcoholic who came from a long line of addicts and dysfunction. She entered his life with a huge trunk full of emotional baggage and entered his home with only a duffle bag full of belongings.

One of Steve's issues was a need to rescue, which is what he thought he was doing, and may have been doing in some weird way, every time we got back together. This woman was in desperate need of being rescued. Their emotional issues fitted perfectly together like two pieces of an emotional jigsaw puzzle to form this unhealthy bond. They went on to spend five years off and on, bouncing about in the depth of battles and breaks in this sick drama they had produced, before Steve finally moved on from the woman.

Think back over your own romantic history. I'll bet you will find a similar pattern in your own past. You have probably been involved with people who have had plenty of their own issues, and have likely stubbornly pushed onward trying to make the sinking ships of those relationships float, even though they were probably not very good relationships. I will also bet that you have attracted more than your share of losers and have been unable to attract or retain, or have been uninterested in keeping, many partners who have really had it together and have really treated you well. Emotionally healthy people are far more likely to recognize red flags, those signals that the other person has problems and issues that will cause nightmares in a relationship. The emotionally healthy person will quickly retreat from a potential relationship with an emotionally needy person.

This does not mean that every time two emotionally healthy people begin a relationship that they will automatically enjoy a fulfilling and lasting relationship. They may simply not be well suited for one another. Perhaps they just have too many fundamental differences in their beliefs, goals and values. When relationships do end for emotionally healthy people they usually do not fall apart and wallow in blame, guilt, shame and self-pity. They rarely take the split too personally and do not tend to believe that they have been rejected because they deserve to be rejected.

Though they are surely disappointed, they are far more likely to see the situation in a clear and rational manner. That means understanding that successful relationships require a certain combination of features in the two people involved that will allow them to properly fit together. People with healthy self-esteem seem to know that if two pieces in a jigsaw puzzle do not fit together, it does not mean that either of the two pieces are defective, only that they will fit somewhere else. They may need to go back to the "box" and keep searching for a piece that will fit next to them correctly. A person with low self-esteem will likely assume when a relationship fails that it did so because they were unlovable, where a person with high self-esteem will understand that if that person did not love them, it just means that they were with the wrong person. No one can float everyone's boat.

Changing the way you feel about yourself will change the way you behave in relationships, as well as the way you feel about their role in your life. It can change the way you deal with all the people you are involved with, not just the ones you're involved with romantically.

Once you realize that you are worth fighting for and deserve to be treated well, you will fight for your rights when necessary and command being treated well. You will begin setting healthy boundaries and that leads to healthier relationships. And as you become able to see relationships and those involved in a rational way, and to see yourself as a valuable human being, you cease to be dependent upon others for your validation. When that happens you are no longer unreasonably afraid of rejection, and therefore you gain the courage to establish healthy boundaries in your relationships and involvements.

I am no longer afraid of confrontation when it means standing up for myself or standing up for any injustice for that matter. This does not mean I go around starting arguments. I have not become offensive or aggressive in my courage, only assertive. I am not overly defensive either, always looking for a hint that someone is mistreating me, but when a situation does arise that demands that I take a stand and voice my opinion to prevent being taken advantage of, I am not afraid or hesitant to do so.

I try to remain calm and rational and try not to escalate the situation with a raised voice or inflammatory remarks. I attempt to solve situations that require a conversation that involves a disagreement with as much tact and diplomacy as is possible, rather than just angrily attacking the other person. Don't get me wrong. I am not a saint. I do not always succeed at this by any stretch. When I am angry I am still subject to fits of temper and outburst. As I stated earlier, improving your self-esteem will not give you a problem free life. It will, however, leave you better equipped to handle the problems that do arise.

When a situation comes up that requires you to stand your ground, I urge you to do so with rational anger and clear communication. I use these terms with utter intent. Rational anger suggests an element of control. This means you do not go postal, grab weapons, fly into an uncontrollable rage that leaves you flailing, hitting, and/or screaming obscenities and derogatory names. That is not productive and can, in fact, be dangerous, not to mention illegal and embarrassing.

I say clear communication because that means calmly and reasonably stating your case, while open-mindedly listening to the other person's point of view. Do not use excess volume. That does nothing to change a person's mind, and will generally only result in escalating the situation, making it impossible for either one of you to get your point across. Try to remember there are always two sides to every argument. Often the infraction, or perceived infraction, has been caused unintentionally, not because the other person actually meant to harm you. You should also try to remain calm during a disagreement. If both people do so, there is a much better chance at arriving at a compromise.

Compromise is not always possible, but should always be attempted. If it is not possible, you need to learn that it is often more valuable to just agree to disagree than it is to continue to try to change the other person's mind. You may find that you need to simply apologize or to just forgive the other person.

Then again, occasionally there are circumstances where you may have been subjected to behavior that is so selfish, that it falls just short of being malicious, or perhaps on a rare occasion, you may find that it actually was malicious. If the person is not genuinely remorseful, and is unwilling to right the wrong, you may have to accept that this may be someone you need out of your life. At the very least, you may need to keep them from being in a position where they can cause any further harm to you. You need to protect yourself from people who present a high risk of being destructive to you.

When you improve your self-esteem you will find that you are able to respond to people and situations in a more appropriate manner. When you recognize a relationship to be unhealthy, one in which you are being taken advantage of or mistreated in, whether it is romantic or otherwise, you will be far better equipped and inspired to force a change or to end it if necessary.

If you find you need to end such a relationship, expect to feel some pain as you grieve its passing. If the relationship is a romantic one there is additional disappointment to deal with. When a romance dies, dreams die with it and dreams die hard. We all have hopes when we get involved romantically of it becoming the right relationship. Even people with the highest self-esteem still hope to find their soul mate. This is not any kind of a sign of weakness. It is the way God hardwired us so that our species would propagate and continue.

I had finally made enough progress in my therapy to begin establishing healthy boundaries that would not allow people to take advantage of me. I was no longer desperate to keep people in my life to distract or to validate me, so I was finally able to end the last fragments of my relationship with Rob. As my self-esteem grew there was a definite shift in power that accompanied the growth. I found I no longer had even the slightest bit of patience with those half-truths of his that required my ability to separate the fact from the fiction when we spoke. I recognized that the man I had fallen in love with truly did not exist, at least not in Rob, not even a little. Rob was the pathetic one, not me, and I deserved better and was not willing to settle for one more day with one more jerk.

I concentrated my time and energy on the girls and my new career. I was enjoying great success because of my greater confidence and that was leading to even more confidence. I was focusing on my accomplishments now, and that was a powerful pick-me-up. I was landing accounts that no one had ever been able to land, though many had tried over the company's sixty-five year history. I was the first female salesperson ever hired by the company because it was such a male dominated industry, and there I was breaking sales records. I had been able to break through the "good old boys" club mentality that had, for decades, permeated the industrial cleaning chemical business.

I was actually happy and I had built that happiness from the inside out. Courage had enabled me to build a life that further contributed to my happiness. My new confidence had brought me that courage, and I used it to take chances that would pay off in happiness. After decades of being hopelessly trapped in a dysfunctional cycle, I was at last whirling around in a healthy, happy cycle. Remember, it all starts with convincing yourself that you deserve a happy life.

chapter seventeen

YOU ARE NOT YOUR BAD BEHAVIOR

The real definition of love is truly desiring what is best for the recipient of that love, even when doing what's best for that person requires some level of sacrifice. For example, a good friend would discourage you from doing drugs. If you had become dependent, a true friend would do all that they could to help you to overcome your addiction. They might even bring in your family for intervention, knowing full well that you would be extremely angry at them for doing so.

A friend of convenience would not bother to try to prevent you from making this mistake. In fact, it is often this type of friend who is the one encouraging you to join them in this kind of destructive activity. This holds true in romantic relationships as well. A partner who truly cares about you will encourage your constructive behaviors and discourage those destructive behaviors.

This is also true in your relationship with yourself. I've brought this "relationship with yourself" term up before, and it probably sounded a bit vague and like some new age trend in psychotherapy. It is not a trend, old or new. It is an inevitability. I covered a good portion of what this relationship you have with yourself consists of when I spoke about your thoughts and how they are manifested in the way you speak to yourself and how that translates into the way you feel about yourself. You cannot avoid having a relationship with yourself, no matter how much you may have been distracted by other things or people. The important thing is to build a healthy relationship with yourself and to become the good friend to you that I touched on earlier.

How you do this involves not only the way you speak to yourself and treat yourself, but it also requires that you forgive yourself for all the poor choices that you may have been making as you blindly struggled to get your emotional needs met. You need to separate in your mind who you are from the things you have done.

You need to get to know yourself so that you can learn to base your self-image on an accurate understanding of who you are, rather than the understanding that has been skewed by all the false and warped perceptions that you have adopted in the past. You probably have also added to your self-definition the destructive behaviors that your emotional needs drove you to commit. You cannot base your self-esteem on certain behaviors alone.

As stated in an earlier chapter, many people become dependent upon doing good deeds for their validation. This leaves them only feeling good about who they are when they are performing these benevolent acts, and feeling disappointed in themselves when they are not. The reverse is also true. We all feel badly about ourselves when we're behaving badly, but too often we continue to feel badly about ourselves when we are behaving anything but badly. It is impossible to be a saint all the time, just as it is impossible to be sinning all the time.

Think about the person who only feels good about his or her self when he or she is doing good deeds. Imagine if all of your relationships were subject to these kinds of inconsistent restrictions. You like a person only when they are doing a certain type of activity and dislike them when they are busy doing anything else. Think about your friendships. You probably like your friends on a pretty consistent basis. This does not mean that you don't enjoy some aspects of their personalities more than others, but your feelings for them are not subject to fluctuations. You do not expect them to exhibit only one type of behavior in order to maintain your friendship. You make allowance for the fact that people are complex and have many different aspects of their personalities and probably engage in many different types of activities and behaviors.

We all have a great many passions within us that drive us to do different things. Perhaps you have a friend who loves to bake. Baking is not too likely to have a huge impact on the improvement of mankind. It is not likely to save an endangered species or bring world peace, but that does not make your friend an unkind person unworthy of love. We can be so irrational when it comes to ourselves, basing our self-love and sense of worthiness only on specific behaviors or activities.

You would surely feel the same about your friend whether she is baking or volunteering at the local hospital. Your feelings about her are consistent. You need to bring that same consistency into your relationship with yourself, and stop subjecting your feelings of self-worth to specific and unreasonable conditions. You are who you are, all day, everyday, no matter what activities require your attention at any given time. Your activities vary, but your character is constant and that is who you are and who you need to get to know and appreciate.

The first step you need to take in getting to know who you truly are is to recognize and let go of all the inaccurate notions of who you are, those self-visions warped by years of negative messages. One of the biggest obstacles in doing this is learning to forgive yourself. You may have some valid arguments with yourself because of some of the things you may have done as you tried to get your needs met. But if you are going to move into a new life with a bright future, you will not be able to drag the garbage from your past with you. This is where you empty your dumpster and cut your losses. The guilt stops here!

It is, of course, true that you are responsible for all of your choices and actions, but many of your poor choices were not made with all the facts. While you have been operating out of this damaged perception of yourself and with these desperate needs that you were not even aware of, it was like expecting a doctor to cure a patient of kidney disease, but only informing him of the patient's heart condition. Without all the facts and an accurate diagnosis of the health problem, he could not possibly be expected to administer the correct treatment.

This chapter is designed to help you to forgive yourself for making the wrong choices because you did not have the right information on which to base those choices. You have been operating blindly, and you need to realize this and forgive yourself for past mistakes, before you can move forward in your healing process.

As you know by now, I have been working in Oakland with women in a Christian-based recovery program for addicts for the past several years. I have been teaching the women there the same self-esteem building skills that I am attempting to teach you in this book.

These women have come from all walks of life, but many of them have come from the streets of Oakland and San Francisco where they have exhibited every kind of self-destructive behavior you can imagine, and probably some you can't.

If you could know some of the dozens of women I have been blessed to become involved with through this program you would be amazed at the depth of their compassion, the openness of their hearts, and the courage of their spirits, as they fight the battle of their lives that truly is the battle for their lives. Many of these women have suffered loss and abuse that I can not imagine bearing.

I have learned as much from these women as I have taught them, and I am grateful and honored to have been trusted with the privilege of being able to offer any help to them as they engage in battling the horrific cycle of their addicted lives.

Many have committed a wide variety of crimes, including prostitution, stealing, armed robbery, and other violent types of crime to support their drug addiction. These addictions have ranged from crack cocaine to heroin to crystal meth, as well as alcohol, and anything else they could get their hands on. They come into this rehabilitation home so filled with guilt and shame that they are emotionally devastated and spiritually paralyzed. The thought of ever forgiving themselves and learning to love themselves seems nearly impossible to them.

One of the first challenges they face is learning to accept that Christ forgives them, and loves them, even when they feel so unlovable. One of the toughest challenges they face is learning to do this for themselves.

One way I have tried to help them is to look at their pasts by using an analogy to illustrate how they could have been lovable people and still made some of the choices they made. In order to understand how this analogy applies to you as well as to these women recovering from addiction, you need to remember that feeling loved and appreciated is as much a basic need of the human condition as our physical needs like food, water, air and sleep. It is the way we are made.

If you are unable to produce that love and appreciation for yourself you will go about finding it with the same desperation of an addict in search of their drug fix. A drug addict may smoke crack to feel good and drown out any painful feelings where you may have shopped with money you could not afford to spend or overeaten when you were supposed to be on a weight loss plan. The drug of choice may differ, but the motivation and the desperation are pretty much the same.

I mentioned in chapter nine that my counselor had once told me that it was no minor miracle that I had not ended up a prostitute or addicted to drugs with the history I had. It would have certainly provided me with enough excuses had I gone about trying to get past my unmet emotional needs in such a manner. That may have had something to do with my immediate desire to connect with these women and my dedication to trying to help them in the only way I know how. I must have recognized on some level that, "There, but for the grace of God, go I."

I firmly believe that addiction, like other chronically poor choices, is not as much a disease as it is so often called, but a symptom of a disease. I believe that disease is actually pain. Often at the core of that pain there are feelings of self-loathing, shame and worthlessness. An addict uses drugs or alcohol to numb down and drown out pain as they seek the same relief we often find in a variety of other types of abuses (many of which I've already mentioned).

It matters little what you choose to use to avoid feeling your pain. The only long-term and truly effective tool for pain management is to deal with its cause. You must get to the core of the pain and treat the disease and not just medicate the symptoms as you've been doing. Most all of the poor choices you have made in the past have amounted to taking pain medication for cancer treatment. It may have made the cancer more bearable, but did nothing to eradicate the disease. Your choices have been part of a vicious cycle that has only served to perpetuate the shame and the pain. Every bad choice builds more shame, and shame increases your pain and drives you to try again to medicate that pain, usually with yet another bad choice. It is a vicious cycle of self-abuse. Poor self-esteem is like cancer for the spirit and you have been practicing that band-aid for a bullet hole medicine I spoke of earlier for too long now.

Let's try a little chemotherapy for the soul and kill off the bad to save the good. Part of the bad that we need to destroy is the guilt and shame that you have likely been punishing yourself with. In order to forgive yourself and end this cycle you need to truly understand that the feelings that led to your poor choices in the past are being healed on this journey and will no longer exist and be able to control your life.

You are already in the process of ending these behaviors. You must understand that while those desperate needs were controlling your life, they were more powerful than your resolve, than your will power, than your good sense. They were more powerful than all the tools you may have had available to you to resist making those poor choices.

I use this analogy to help to make this point to the women at the rehab house who clearly have a great deal to forgive themselves for, including behavior that has not only been destructive to themselves, but often to their children, their spouses, their parents, family, friends, and strangers as well. They have been operating out of a need that is so powerful it has left them feeling certain that they had no other options. This truth is equally applicable to you.

Imagine that you have been without food for four or five days. You were literally starving and weakened with hunger. You've been living on the streets and wander into a restaurant hoping to use the restroom and get a drink of water and perhaps clean up a bit. Of course you have no money so a meal is out of the question. On your way to the restroom you pass the counter which is quite close to the door. You see that the waitress has just placed a large cheeseburger and a hot order of French fries into a "to go" bag on the counter in anticipation of the arrival of the customer who called in the order.

She did not notice you enter and has turned away as she goes about her job. You have a clear shot at the door. Your desperate need for sustenance takes over and you grab the bag of food without a moment's hesitation and bolt out the door. You would probably not slow down until you are a safe distance away and can sit down and gobble your priceless treasure to quiet the voracious hunger pains that have plagued you and your thoughts for days.

Now let's look at this same restaurant, the same waitress, the same burger and fries on the counter and the same clear shot at the door. This time however, let's imagine that you stop to use the restroom because you need "to go" and you have a long drive ahead of you. Let us also imagine that you are on your way home from your parents' house where you have just eaten an enormous thanksgiving dinner topped off with two pieces of pie. You are stuffed. If you love cheeseburgers, under other circumstances you might be tempted to order one for yourself. Because you are full and satisfied though, the thought of ordering one, let alone stealing the one on the counter, never even crosses your mind.

You do not grab the burger and run. Why? Well, first of all, who can run after thanksgiving dinner? More importantly though, is that the desperate need for food did not exist. You were full and satisfied.

The poor choices that you have made were likely made out of that same level of desperation to have your emotional needs met that a starving person faces when trying to get their physical need for food met. You surely felt that you had no other options in satisfying your need to feel good instead of feeling pain. So you chose the drug, or T.V. or sex or whatever it is that you used to quiet your pain.

The most lonely people are those who have not learned to fill their empty hearts with their own love. Just as an empty stomach makes you desperate to fill it with food, an empty heart is also starved and desperate to be filled with love.

The problem is, just like the burger, the things you grabbed out of desperation only offered temporary respite from the real problem. In the case of the analogy I used the real problem or "disease" was homelessness. Hunger was just one of the "symptoms," one of the desperate needs created by that bigger problem. The burger is only a temporary solution to a permanent problem. After it is gone, you would still be penniless and would soon be hungry again. The burger was only a quick fix and another "band-aid for a bullet hole."

You must look at past mistakes from this perspective. You did not feel you had other options and did the only thing you knew to do at the time to quiet your aching heart. Remember that you were operating with the wrong diagnosis and were unaware of what the real problem was and how to cure it. You did what you thought you needed to do in order to find relief from the symptoms you were experiencing.

Let's take the "burger" analogy one step further. Imagine that just as you were finishing up the last of the fries, a police officer showed up. Just your luck, he was the one who had called in the order to go that you grabbed and he arrived just seconds after you rushed out the door with it. It didn't take him long to find you and he arrests you and takes you to jail. The next thing you know you are in front of a judge being arraigned.

So you explain to the judge that you are truly sorry and would not have stolen the burger if it were not for the fact that you lost your job and got evicted from your apartment and have been living on the streets for some weeks now. You have no money and cannot find a job in your disheveled condition, but cannot clean up because you have no place to do so. You had not eaten in days and were desperate for food.

The judge is not about to impose a life sentence on you for stealing this burger. He would probably understand the desperation with which you made the choice to commit this relatively minor infraction, and would probably not find it difficult to forgive you. In fact, he is likely to have compassion for you and direct you to services that can help to get you off the streets and back on your feet. He would in this way be attempting to treat the "disease" and not just the symptoms.

This is the way we need to treat ourselves; with compassion. If you were the judge and it was a stranger standing there in your courtroom under those very same circumstances, you too would surely have the compassion to forgive them and would also try to help them to get in touch with the resources that could enable them to fix the bigger problem of their homelessness.

We must use this same compassion we would feel for a stranger when dealing with ourselves and the mistakes we have made in the past out of our desperation. We must recognize that we deserve not only compassion, but forgiveness as well. We do not deserve a life sentence and yet that is what we often impose upon ourselves by punishing ourselves over and over with guilt and shame. We often spend years, decades even, torturing ourselves with every mistake we have made as proof of our unworthiness.

Remember, forgiveness is not a feeling. It is a choice and we need to choose it again and again as that guilt and shame for our past mistakes enters our minds screaming for our attention and hammering us with all the evidence of our lack of value. We must remind ourselves that we are doing the work to find the cure for our disease and are beginning to heal the bigger problems that have been creating the desperate needs that have driven us to make those mistakes, and that we are growing and healing and are deserving of forgiveness and love. We must do this every time we begin to beat ourselves up with the memories of our past shameful behavior, every time those memories rear their ugly heads and begin screaming insults at us. We have paid the price for our indiscretions and it was much too high to begin with.

Let those memories go! Dismiss them from your mind every time they pop up! Replace them with your positive affirmation and remind yourself over and over that you do deserve good things and love and forgiveness are two very good things.

It would be a gross injustice not to forgive yourself for mistakes and to base your relationship with yourself on your behavior, especially if you have incorrectly defined yourself by your behavior, particularly your poor behavior. I am not absolving you of the responsibility for your past actions. I am only trying to show you that there were mitigating circumstances that changed the way you behaved from the way you would have behaved had you been the whole, emotionally healthy person that God made you to be.

*Forgiveness is
forming a little
mental pearl
from an irritating
grain of thought.
It's turning pain
into strength
and anger
into love.
It's an exchange
of pride
for power.*

chapter eighteen

GETTING TO KNOW YOURSELF

It is true that your behavior is partly a product of who you are, but it is mostly a reflection of who you believe you are. It is vital to get accurate information and a correct, clear understanding of who you truly are, who God made you to be, before people and events combined to alter your way of seeing and dealing with yourself and the world around you.

If God planned you to be a truly kind person, but you were forced to steal to get the money for an operation that would save your child's life, that would be an unkind act, but it would not necessarily mean that you are an unkind person. As illustrated in the previous chapter, there may have been specific circumstances that drove you to behave in certain ways that were not really true to your nature. Your response was likely more the result of how your history affected you. You need to begin to separate your perception of who you are from your history and your behavior so that you can truly ascertain your character and your true nature and determine who you actually are. You must get to know yourself objectively, honestly, and intimately.

You cannot love what you do not know. If you had never seen the movie *Gone With The Wind* (my personal favorite) and only had someone else's account of that movie, how could you love that movie? Now imagine that their account was neither very accurate, nor very in depth. In fact, this person who described it to you really didn't even like the movie much. How could you feel that you know that movie? When it comes to your self-image, you have likely formed your opinions from a shallow, inaccurate account given to you by someone, maybe even you, who has never really seen the whole picture.

I've already established that you have probably spent countless years focused on every flaw and shortcoming that you believe you have. Now you should be focusing on all your attributes. Again I remind you, *what you choose to look at determines also what you do not see.*

Remember my friend Jackie who had so many obvious gifts and talents, but could not acknowledge a single one? I cannot be sure whether she truly did not believe any existed or whether she simply could not bring herself to outwardly acknowledge them. I fear you may not be all that different. I am not sure if she had the same intellectual awareness that I possessed in regard to my attributes, but it was certain that she did not feel she had any gifts that she should acknowledge. This is not uncommon among Christians. We sometimes have a slightly confused picture of what the Bible refers to as being humble. I assure you God does not mean He wants false humility, nor does He want you to disrespect His creation (you), or to live in misery. He specifically tells you to love all His children. Hello! That includes you. You, too, are one of His children. In Matthew 19:19 Jesus told us to "love your neighbor as yourself." He did not say "love your neighbor, but not yourself."

You need to take a serious and objective inventory of your positive characteristics, your gifts, talents, abilities and even your likes and dislikes. Every single human being is made up of a unique combination of these traits, so don't even think about copping out like Jackie did, and deciding that you are the one exception to this rule. You are not the one mistake our otherwise perfect God made.

If you have allowed your perception of yourself to be so skewed for so long that it has become too ingrained for you to even begin to change your focus and start to recognize and acknowledge your attributes, then you may need to speak to someone, or even a few people who know you and care about you and do not have an agenda that would lead them to do you any disservice. You don't need to divulge why you're asking. You can say you're taking part in a survey, or are just curious, or ran across a questionnaire and you need to get the opinions of a few people who know you. None of this is a lie. You really are doing just that. Ask them, "If you had to list my three or five (or whatever number you wish) best qualities, what would you say they are?"

It can be a good jumping off place that will at least help you to get started seeing a different perspective than the warped one you are used to. It may just help you to begin thinking of some of the things that you do well and some of the things that you have accomplished.

As you begin looking for these attributes, you may need to do a little archaeology. You may not have thought about yourself in an objective and positive way for a very long time, if ever. As you start really thinking of who you are and the abilities that you possess, you may notice that you already seem a little different than you were at the beginning of this book.

If you have been processing all those old, convoluted, and repressed feelings from your past, and have been retraining your brain to be more positive, and have begun to forgive yourself for past mistakes, you will have cleared away a lot of the debris that has been hiding your strengths from your mental line of vision. Processing all those bottled up feelings should have begun to free you from their negative effects and the power they have had over you. Now you should be able to see and get to know the real you, your core self.

When I was a little girl I danced
to well worn records in my room
with a makeshift, make believe
microphone in hand
and soundless words working their way
through my pale pink lips.
Something musical, something magical
would happen
that would cause my small, straight hips

to sway,
my tiny toes to tap,
small steps taken
in irregular rhythm.
Inevitably life dances with time
and little girls transcend childhood
and are miraculously and laboriously
transformed into women,
into wives,
into mothers.
Now that little girl of long ago
only dances to a silent song,
treading the edge
of my too busy mind.
She dances there
on the head of a pin,
the smallest of thoughts,
a tiny flicker of hope,
a minute spark that somehow withstands
the hurricane of my world.
She dances away from my grasp,
like a tigerswallow dances,
doing a wild waltz with the wind,
tango dips
and tiny twirls,
all of spring its' dance floor
as it crosses between blooms
and boughs.
While I dance with dizzying speed
and feet that lack any deftness,
that still move with irregular rhythm,
between income and output,
between mother and lover,
between professional and homemaker.
I dance with numbers and knowledge
and with words,
some thrown like stones,

some whispered like a cloud,
some that even have my power pink lips
curled around them,
but still will not come,
leaving silence to fill the space,
like untouched piano keys.
I dance with memories
flirting, but not touching,
leaving them unexamined,
always afraid to peel away their layers of bark
that serve as armor against the world,
afraid to expose my raw, unhusked soul.
No, I just square my shoulders
while the minutes unfold the hours,
unleash the days.
Now my own daughter dances
every Wednesday from 4:00 to 6:00,
plays soccer on weekends,
does homework each night
as though she too
were trying to outrun the stride of light,
driven for grades,
driven toward goals,
driven by me,
while I push her forth,
out into the world
like a prayer.
All the while a voice with wings dances
around me,
calling for me to seek out
the peace in the chaos,
to reach the eye of the storm,
to become submerged
in the dead calm there
that moves like the slow birth of a continent,
instead of being enveloped in the lie
that defines the high speed madness

that swarms and swirls about my life
as necessity.
The voice is my childhood dancing
far away, long ago,
freely
and without purpose, goals,
or deadlines,
whispering sweet winged reminders to me
to slow my racing life,
find the me that I was born to be,
the me that remains
still within motion,
quiet within commotion,
to find living in those things
that keep my atoms knitted together,
things like the padded greenery
of a grassy plain,
a poem, a song, a giggle,
a tigerswallow,
or dancing.

People with low self-esteem have been conditioned to behave differently than they might have, had they been better nurtured by life. You may have thought you were ill-tempered and mean spirited when in fact you may simply have been very angry. Unresolved anger can lead an otherwise calm, kind person to behave very aggressively and cynically. A person with a very kind nature can become very defensive and bitter as they attempt to protect themselves when they have been taught that the world is an unkind place and when the lessons they have learned have been filled with hate and hurt. Likewise someone who has been deeply hurt may have been behaving in a very timid and cowardly manner, when in actuality, they may truly be bold when their pain has been healed and their confidence has been restored.

There are countless ways your history and its resulting unresolved emotions may have altered your behavior, and thus your perception of yourself. How those feelings may have manifested themselves, and how they may have been expressed, are likely very different from the ways you would behave if the core of you had been nurtured instead of stunted. You could have loads of leadership qualities that you do not exhibit, perhaps because you suffered the pain of rejection and humiliation when you asserted yourself in the past. With your confidence deeply shaken you may have begun behaving in the meek manner of a follower rather than risk rejection again.

Do you see why you may need to get reacquainted with the real you? You cannot have a genuine, healthy relationship with someone you do not know. If you did not live with your father while you were growing up and did not have much contact with him on any regular basis, you could not exactly qualify that as a genuine relationship. By the same token, if he lived with you in the house, but you two never spoke, leaving you aware of each other's presence, but having no real interaction, that would not qualify as a relationship either. If you have been carrying on all your internal conversations with the false image of the person you thought you were, rather than the healthy, whole, fabulous person that you truly are, than that too has not been a genuine relationship.

Not only is it impossible to love someone whom you do not know, you also cannot have a real relationship with someone whom you do not know. I got over Rob when I realized that I had not seen him with objective accuracy, but rather with the warped perception that came from seeing only the carefully crafted illusion he had presented, the person I wanted him to be and he wanted me to see. I had fallen in love with a fictional person. Once I realized the inaccuracy of the facade he presented, I was then able to see the truth of who he truly was, and that was not a person I would have ever fallen in love with. He was, in actuality, a person I would pity, not a person I would love.

If you have simply made the assumption that you were the deeply flawed person that you were told you were, by yourself or others, this is the time to question that assumption and to hold it up to the light of reason. If you are still having a difficult time recognizing your attributes and are still stuck on your flaws, take each one out and check it for accuracy. For example, if you have always believed that you are stupid, think about something that you are interested in as a hobby. Let's say you like photography and find you have always loved taking pictures. You may have tried to improve your photographic skills by reading a book or two on the subject and experimenting with different techniques. Is this something that a stupid person is capable of doing? Of course not. Only a bright person pursuing a hobby reads up on it and tries pushing the envelope with new techniques.

Perhaps you like penguins. You may have read several books on them and watch nature shows whenever they feature penguins as the subject. Think about some of the information you have retained about penguins. A stupid person does not know the correct term for a baby penguin or how they get their food. What about your work? Most jobs require a certain amount of thought and reasoning. You probably have many skills that require intelligence that you use every day at work and at home. Do you see how easy it is to come up with a variety of facts about you that disprove your old notion that you are stupid? There are countless ways you use your intellect every day.

I barely graduated from high school and even then I was about twenty when I finally went back and applied my limited college credits toward my diploma in order to earn it. I discovered that I have a very high I.Q. when I was in my thirties. My level of education and many of the grades I had received were certainly not an accurate reflection of such a high I.Q. It would have been easy to convince myself based only on this inaccurate information that I was stupid. This is a clear example of why it is important to stop accepting your old negative beliefs about yourself without question. You have to challenge the insulting statements you have made to and about yourself for so long.

Perhaps you have often told yourself that you can't do anything right. This is a ridiculous statement. It is not even mathematically possible to never have done anything right. When you logically analyze all the negative statements you have been making all this time that assert your inadequacy, you will find that nearly all of them are simply not reasonable, accurate, or true. Use this type of technique for questioning and disproving all your stubbornly held beliefs about your perceived inadequacy.

This does not mean that you will be able to dispel every single statement that reflects an area that you wish was improved. Though you will find that many are completely false or too generalized and absolute, a few may be fairly close to the truth. I still have a short fuse and can too often display that rotten temper. The older I get and the more I work on self-control, the better my temper gets, but it is still there and one of my shortcomings nonetheless.

You do, of course, have some shortcomings. We all do. You must understand that's ok. Do not impose those ridiculous standards of perfection upon yourself that I used to impose upon myself. You have to understand that your weaknesses are part of being human and it is the specific combination of your strengths and weaknesses, and your likes and dislikes, which make you unique. It will be much easier for you to accept and allow for those shortcomings when you have realized all your strengths.

Once you have taken a more positive and more realistic look at yourself, you should be able to recognize abilities and talents that you have. Grab your notebook and pen and retreat to a place where you can be alone to think and to write. Begin by thinking of all the things you have accomplished that you deserve to give yourself credit for. List each one and if you do this exercise quickly, then you are cheating yourself yet again. It should be a very long list if you are doing it correctly. You should be able to fill many pages with this information. I want you to list every small accomplishment as well as the larger ones. List that drawing your teacher complimented you on when you were in the third grade, that test you got a B on in the fifth grade, the time you made everyone laugh at a funny quip or story, the diploma you earned, making the band in high school, the degree you earned, potty training your toddler, saving money on your home loan, that beautiful cake you baked, the promotion you got at work, the girl scout badges you earned, etc...

This may feel silly and self-serving, but it really changes your mindset to get you focused on the positive. This list will give you some insight into yourself. Looking back at the list you will find it begins not only to paint a picture of your value, but also of who you are. It will even show you some of the things that you are interested in and can serve as a reference list that will help point out some of the things you do well. These things provide more of the blueprint for who you truly are and the life you will begin to build.

You may even notice some attributes that you have never thought about or acknowledged before. Now that you are seeing yourself more positively and more clearly, you might discover that gifts you have, but have only thought of as barely above average, are actually quite superior. You may also discover wonderful character traits that are just beginning to emerge now that you are in the process of healing. Just as I reclaimed that part of me that embraced my fiery nature and strong sense of justice and the courage to stand up for what's right, you may begin to notice other aspects of your own personality that have been repressed by the weight of pain and the damage done to you in the past.

In addition to getting to know your positive attributes, you must also get to know your true likes and dislikes. You may find some surprises here as well. You might have been doing certain things because you were accustomed to them, because they were familiar or had been expected of you. There are many things that simply have to be done for practical reasons that you have never even questioned, never even explored whether or not you like doing them or whether there might be a different, more enjoyable way of accomplishing those things.

We all have bills to pay and for most of us that means we have to work. You may have never really spent much time thinking about what type of job you would really like doing. You may have based your decision on where to work on your warped perception of yourself. Perhaps you believed you had limitations that held you back that didn't really exist, limitations that you had actually imposed upon yourself. I never even considered doing anything outside of selling jewelry because I was certain that I was not qualified to do anything else. This, of course, was not true as I later proved. You might be imposing those same types of limitations on yourself.

Maybe you were pressured by your family into getting a certain type of degree and are in a line of work or a field that is not fulfilling to you. There may be financial pressures keeping you feeling unhappily trapped in your career. You may have never considered changing fields though because you are afraid of that risk, not to mention a possible cut in pay.

Since I was a teenager I have always dreamed of being a counselor. I certainly do not have the time with a full time career, a family, hobbies, a ministry, and a social life, to go to college to earn a bachelors degree, let alone a master's degree. There are types of counseling jobs that require far less education and training than six years of college, but the pay is far below what I earn in sales. I might pursue the necessary training in a few years when my girls are out of college and no longer require as much of my time and money. This way, when my husband and I move to the country as we dream, and are able to be free of a mortgage payment, I may be able to pursue this line of work. You may also find a compromise that will allow you to pursue your desired career change that may or may not include reducing your financial obligations, but will certainly include some risk. I remind you that risk requires courage and courage comes from confidence.

The point is that you may have never really explored the inner you and there may be many things you would love to be doing that you have never pursued. You may find new avenues of interest or you may finally decide to pursue your passions. There may be a hobby that you have always wanted to indulge in, but until now have lacked the courage to get started and the commitment to your own happiness that would have justified your devoting any time to a self-interested pursuit.

You may discover you have many interests, some that if pursued will turn into lasting passions, some that will be quickly satisfied. There might be one thing that you find on the list you are exceptional at or many things that you do pretty well. Some things you might enjoy, you may not even be good at, but who cares as long as you enjoy them. Occasionally I like to play tennis and once in awhile I might even indulge in a game of pool or bowling. I am decidedly bad at all of those, but they are fun for me so who cares? I'm not trying to go pro. I'm just having a little fun.

Getting to know the things that you are good at and have accomplished will not only give you information that will help you to know yourself better, but it will also provide you with knowledge that can help you to treat yourself better. You can begin to make changes that will allow you to pursue some of your talents and may help you to become aware of and make changes in regard to the aspects of your life that you don't like.

> *I hear you*
> *speak in silences,*
> *crying out*
> *in the empty spaces*
> *of arms that do not hold you,*
> *as you lament,*
> *"know me,*
> *please know me."*
> *I try to draw you near to me,*
> *for if I see you,*
> *really see you,*
> *then surely*
> *I will hear you,*
> *and if I hear you,*
> *truly hear you,*
> *then certainly*
> *I will know you,*
> *and if I know you,*
> *even just a little,*
> *then surely*
> *I will love you.*

Things that you like and love and hate are all pieces of the puzzle that makes you who you are. They fit together with that unique combination of gifts, talents, attributes, abilities, and weaknesses that make up the other pieces of that puzzle. As you begin to gain an understanding of who you truly are, you can begin to have a healthy relationship with your true self and within the framework of that relationship you can learn to love yourself. As you care more and more for yourself, you will improve the way you treat yourself and that will include building for yourself a life that you deserve, a life that you will also be able to love.

To help you to gain this insight, here are a couple more exercises to help you with this process. As with the other written exercises, set aside some quiet time when you can do this undisturbed.

- Write the words "I am" at the beginning of every other line on at least two pages.
- Go back and finish each of those sentences with a positive statement about yourself such as "I am smart," "I am kind," "I am interesting," "I am curious," "I am passionate," etc...
- Next write "I like" at the beginning of every other line on at least two pages.
- Go back and finish those sentences also with things you like or love.
- Now write "I am not" at the beginning of every other line on at least one page.
- Go back and finish each sentence with any derogatory statement, name or adjective you used to label yourself with.
- Last: write "I do not like" at the beginning of every other line for at least two pages.
- Go back and finish each sentence with specific things, people, places and most of all ways you have been treated that you do not like.

This information is a wonderful way to get a more concise and accurate picture of who you truly are. Add to the lists as often as you feel inspired to do so and don't be surprised if some of the statements change a bit as you grow.

As I was growing and had begun getting to know myself I was learning that one of my positive traits was that I possessed good instincts about people. Hard to imagine after that whole "Rob" fiasco, but in looking back with the wonder of twenty/twenty hindsight, I realized that my instincts were on fire about him. Remember that I asked to see his driver's license because I knew in my gut he was too good to be true, but I justified his behavior and rationalized away my doubts and convinced myself of what I wanted so desperately to believe.

I asked my counselor in one of our earlier sessions, "How on earth will I ever learn to trust another man after Rob?" She told me that I didn't need to learn to trust each man that came along. What I needed to learn was to trust my own instincts. They had been good and would always be good. I really needed to realize that. The experience with Rob had changed the way I felt about my ability to judge people. I needed to be convinced again that the ability was still there. A slice of my life had caused me to doubt it, but that did not mean it did not exist.

Learning that about my ability to judge people reinforced what I was discovering about how easily events and people can alter the way we see ourselves. I could easily have never opened up to another man for fear that they would turn out to be like Rob and that I would blindly fall for another fictional person who would end up hurting me. Because I was shown that I had possessed, and still did possess, those good instincts, I found the courage instead to begin a new relationship.

I know what you're thinking. Here we go again. It was different though. He was a young, handsome dentist just beginning his practice. He was six years younger than I was so looking at things realistically, I knew from the beginning that he was not ready to get serious with anyone, and that he would most definitely never get seriously involved with an older woman with two kids. I even knew that it was not because I was not good enough, it was just that he was far too young and freewheeling (a.k.a. immature and selfish) to be ready for the responsibility of a ready-made family, and when he did become ready for a family, I knew he would want his own, not Steve's.

I debated getting involved under the circumstances, but decided to risk it and just enjoy his company in a casually romantic relationship for as long as things felt good. Had I not grown in my confidence, I would have never had the courage to take that risk. Had I not begun to truly heal, I would not have seen the situation to clearly assess it and gauge that risk. I would have likely believed he was my new knight in shining armor, ready to rescue me. I would have probably just set myself up for yet another soon to be "damsel in distress" tragedy. I would have missed out on a really fun relationship that ended easily and on good terms. Because the end was more his idea than mine, I would have been heartbroken had it occurred even just a year earlier. I would have convinced myself that he was "the one" and I also would have convinced myself when it ended that I deserved it, that it was all my fault, that I had been somehow lacking and that's why he left.

Instead I listened to my instincts and they protected me. I did not take the end as a personal rejection, but as a change of paths. I knew it was not that I was unlovable that kept us from some eternal, fairytale romance, but that we were just suited for a brief, but enjoyable romance. It did not indicate anything lacking in me. It did not lessen any of my gifts in their value. It was just the way life and timing, circumstances and differences, came together and played things out.

A failed romance does not mean rejection and rejection does not negate your wonderful traits and talents. Those traits are indisputable regardless of who recognizes them or doesn't. They do not go away when a relationship, or a job, or anything else fails. Rejection is all about a bad fit between two parties and not at all about being undeserving or unlovable.

Those were a couple of pretty valuable lessons I had learned in my growth. Soon after that break-up I was able to purchase a small two bedroom condominium in a security building in a lovely setting. I was so very proud of this accomplishment and thrilled at the example I was setting for my daughters, as it is no easy feat for a single woman to own a home in the San Francisco Bay Area.

This was to be a truly life changing event, as my future husband was also a homeowner in that complex. I'll never forget the first moment I saw him. I had not quite moved in yet and was showing a friend the complex when I caught a glimpse of him while I was driving out. I became dangerously distracted by his good looks. I remember that the song by Randy Travis, "Forever And Ever, Amen" was playing on my car radio quite prophetically as it turned out. Though it would be some months before we actually met, we began dating immediately after we did and a healthy, loving relationship quickly began to develop.

Just prior to my actually meeting him, I had gone to visit my mother, just as I did every few weeks. This visit however turned out to be different from any before. Completely unexpectedly, a dialogue began between us that soon found me able to explain to her how her constant criticism and backhanded compliments had made me feel so hurt, as though she was always deeply disappointed in me. For once she didn't get defensive, but actually listened and then explained how proud she really was of me, and that she only meant to help me to see and reach my fullest potential, certainly not to hurt me.

I was even able to share with her that I had been angry since the rape because I had felt the need to protect her, rather than having her take care of me. I had learned enough not to use accusatory words and to explain how I felt without blaming her for making me feel that way.

She explained to me how deeply she truly loved me and vowed to stop criticizing me. We healed our relationship that day and she kept that vow almost all of the time after that. Our relationship as mother and daughter was forever changed, and when she died a little over seven years later, we were at peace with each other, both of us knowing how much we loved, and were loved by, one another.

chapter nineteen

EMOTIONAL MATURITY

I wrote earlier about the ridiculous way I believed that I had to be absolutely perfect or it meant that I was utter garbage. I did not hold others to those insane standards, only myself. I never even considered the absurdity of that type of thinking. I never challenged myself on it or subjected it to the light of cold, hard reason.

I simply did not apply logic to my self-image. I never questioned the fact that what I knew about myself did not match how I felt about myself. I just accepted that I was unlovable and sub-standard no matter how many facts in my life were proof of the contrary.

We develop all kinds of opinions and feelings and make numerous assumptions that have no real basis in reality. We will blindly accept that we are stupid because some inept teacher told us that we were when we were in the fourth grade. Why? Being told we were stupid did not make it true. That unkind remark did not have magical powers that all of a sudden robbed us of our ability to gain and recall knowledge.

We have unquestioningly believed numerous things that would never stand up to analytical reason. Just as we needed to apply reason to our perceptions of ourselves, so do we need to apply reason to the feelings that were generated by the people and events that have had such a profound effect on our lives. That is how we remove the power from those negative attacks, by disproving them. Just because something or someone was able to have an enormous impact on our vulnerable six year old self, does not mean that it would have had the same impact on our empowered, adult self, nor should we continue to allow it to impact us. Now that you have begun the healing process, those things in our personal histories should no longer have power over us. It is time to drag the rest of our garbage out into the light where we can examine it closely and with the capacity for reason that a healthy adult has, and with the ability to see things more clearly and objectively than we were able to when the event first occurred.

Go back to the first writing exercises you did that enabled you to get in touch with all those unresolved emotions that you had been carrying around with you. Were you hurt, angry, afraid, or happy? Those are the four main feelings that we experience as human beings. You have likely defined the specific or recurring events and people that significantly and negatively impacted you by now.

You need to look at those situations and relationships with a more logical and objective approach now. You may discover emotions associated with situations that, in retrospect, no longer seem appropriate. For instance, it is perfectly normal and appropriate to feel frightened when you are driving and experience a near miss that brought you dangerously close to being in an accident. It is also normal to feel anger towards another driver if it was their fault that you came so close to a collision. It would not however be an appropriate response after such an incident to feel too afraid to drive ever again, or to begin plotting the murder of the offending driver. This is what I mean by looking at your emotional responses first to see if they are even appropriate.

Are the emotions associated with a given situation within the realm of normalcy given the circumstances and your age and mindset at the time? Are they far too intense for the actual event? It was appropriate for me to be angry at my mother when she took my pennies when I was five. It would not have been appropriate for me to have wanted to kill her for it. It would not be appropriate for me to still be angry at her for it now that I am in my forties. Check your emotional responses to those people and events that have greatly affected you. Hold them up to the light of objective reason. Sometimes we hold grudges and intense anger that is far greater than the situation should have produced. Those over-emotional responses that would be inappropriate now that you're an adult need to be examined and recognized as such. You need to let them go.

You also need to let go of all the feelings that you had buried and have now processed. Holding onto anger and pain from the past after you have faced it only continues to punish you and to act as an anchor that holds you back as you attempt to drag that garbage around. Letting go of the past is part of healing and growing emotionally. This means when the memories of those events pop into your head you toss them back out of your head. You do not dwell on them and anguish over them. You keep them in proper perspective by dismissing them. This is not the same thing as burying them because now you have faced them, processed them, and dealt with them. It is more that you have acknowledged the event and then released it in order to move on with your life, your present life, the life you have here and now.

Occasionally you may have a difficult time accurately identifying your feelings. As I stated in a previous chapter, hurt and fear are often disguised as anger. It is not always easy to determine exactly what you are feeling in the present, let alone what you may have been feeling years or even decades ago.

I had to learn to identify feelings that had become so ingrained that they had become more habits than anything else. Many people raised in chaos and instability spend their whole lives "waiting for the other shoe to drop." I was no exception. I often went through periods of what I learned was nameless anxiety; periods with a permeating feeling of disquiet, of concern, of worry, over something or some things I could not even identify. I would simply have this sense of dread as though there was something wrong or about to go wrong.

It made me unable to relax and fully enjoy it when things were going great. I was certain good times would not last, for when I was growing up they never did. When I was married to Steve they never did.

This dread of bad replacing the good was compounded by my overwhelming certainty that I did not deserve the good times. So I spent energy searching for the flaw, the crack in the dam, which would soon allow the wall to crumble and send raging waters to flood my joyful situation and sweep me away upon a tide of disappointment, of failure, of frustration, pain, and anger.

I lived in fear of all those negative feelings washing away my moments of joy. So instead of focusing on that joy, I focused on everything that could take it away. Again: *What you choose to look at determines also what you do not see.*

My counselor helped me to recognize this unhealthy, destructive pattern and to learn to determine if this anxiety had any basis in reality or if it was just a product of my emotional habits, those things you feel only because you have been so conditioned to feel that way. She taught me to recognize the feeling and then to subject it to reason. This meant looking at things objectively to determine if there was an actual problem that needed to be addressed and solved, something that I could take some concrete steps to remedy, or if the anxiety was uncalled for and had no basis in reality and needed only to be dismissed. This helped me a great deal to learn to relax and enjoy the current moment, to live in the "now", and was an important part of my learning process in identifying my feelings.

It is necessary to apply logic to those feelings that have been leftover from our pasts, those feelings we are so used to feeling (like much of my anxiety), but that may now have no real reason to exist. We all drag our past into our present, but we do not need to carry our past into our future. If we are to affect any positive change we must not only understand how we felt about certain events, but also how those feelings are affecting us now.

Often we need to try to see those events from a different perspective in order to diffuse them. If we have only seen things from the viewpoint of our childish reasoning then we have not seen the complete picture. A vital part of our growth is maturing emotionally. This means being able to see situations from viewpoints other than our own. This ability can help to heal our old wounds by placing them in a more accurate and comprehensible framework, one that allows us to see from a more mature and emotionally healthy perspective. It can also open our hearts to forgiveness and healing relationships as well as help us to learn from other people.

Let me use an incident in my childhood that had a lasting effect on me as an example of how I responded emotionally then, compared to the way I am able to see the situation now. I was six years old and very, very ill. My father had come in to my room at night to give me my medicine. It was in the form of a tiny pill that I was completely unable to swallow. The next thing I knew, I was being bundled up and taken to the car for yet another trip to the hospital. I remember crying and pleading with him and my mother not to take me. I promised to be good and take my medicine. I was convinced that I was being punished for being bad and not taking my pill. I'd had plenty of experience with hospitals and they always involved shots and they often involved lengthy stays in cold, wet oxygen tents. If that was not a form of punishment, it should have been. It would have proven very effective I'm sure.

My pleading was unsuccessful. Shortly I was in a cold, sterile, steel, crib-like bed that looked more like a cage with only a single blanket that was too small. I remember being so cold that it hurt. I probably had a pretty good fever raging. I begged my mother not to go, but she left me there crying in near hysterics. I cried for what seemed like an eternity after she left even though I had been repeatedly scolded for it by the nurse on duty.

I don't know if I slept that night, but I do remember staring out my window well before sunrise watching for my parents to drive up to the hospital. They had assured me that they would come to visit me the next day and as far as I was concerned that was way too long to wait.

Up until only recently I did not understand how my mother could have possibly left me there like that. I was scared, sad, and certain I had done something terrible to deserve being abandoned in that austere and lonely place. For years I was hurt and angry about that. When one of my own daughters was about two and was facing the possibility of being hospitalized, I immediately began making plans to stay there all night in a chair by her bed. I would have endured anything to keep my little girl from feeling scared and alone. I could not comprehend why my mother had not done the same. With both my father and my grandmother living at home and able to care for my sisters, I simply did not understand why she left me like that.

The way I viewed this situation changed over time. At six, I thought I was taken to the hospital, not as a life saving measure, but as punishment for failing to swallow my pill. This was the extent of my childhood reasoning skills. Obviously I knew better as I got older. I understood as a young adult that I had not been punished, but rather I had been saved. I still held fiercely to the conviction that my mother had not loved me enough to stay there with me though, that she had casually abandoned me there. I figured she had selfishly valued a night's sleep over the desperate emotional needs of her six year old little girl.

As I have become more emotionally mature, I have tried to look at this situation with more objectivity. I have attempted to see it through the eyes of my mother, from her perspective. Although I can't confirm this now that both of my parents are gone, I believe there were likely regulations in hospitals back in 1966 that would have prevented my mother from staying there with me overnight. I know there were far stricter regulations regarding visiting hours back then. They even went so far as to prohibit children under the age of twelve from visiting their own relatives. I think that my mother may have even had to make special arrangements for me to see my father before he died. Hospitals have come a very long way in relaxing regulations since then.

I now figure that it had to have been heart wrenching for her. It was probably just as hard on my mother to leave me there like that, as it was for me to be left. Imagine having to leave your very ill, and emotionally traumatized little girl hysterical in the hospital. How cruel that back then parents had no choice but to sacrifice the emotional health of their child in order to protect the physical health.

This is a great illustration of how we can see things differently as we become more emotionally mature. It clearly shows how having more information, the information that the other party involved has, can enable you to see things from a completely different perspective, a perspective that is often far less painful than the initial assumptions we made based on our limited knowledge and reasoning capacity. Applying logic to this situation that was so emotionally charged for me as a six year old completely disarmed it for me as an adult.

We need to be able to do this with all the emotionally charged situations from our pasts, those situations that have continued to have power over us and have continued to haunt our hearts. I, of course, cannot promise that all those situations of yours will be diffused in the same manner or to the same degree that had occurred in the example I used from my life. Not all of the situations that contributed to the erosion of my self-esteem looked that different to me as an adult. There may be many situations that are painful no matter how you look at them, especially if there was any kind of malicious intent involved, or physical or sexual abuse, but you will likely find that there are many situations that are far less painful when you are able to apply the additional knowledge that comes with knowing all the circumstances and understanding the other persons perspective.

Every situation is comprised of many components. The reality is that every interaction between people contains all of the baggage each of the people bring with them. Many of us have had humiliating experiences at the hands of some schoolyard bully. The schoolyard bully probably brought a lot of anger to that schoolyard. Perhaps he (or she) was bullied at home, either physically or emotionally or both. He may not have wanted to beat you up at all. He probably would have much rather taken his rage out on the actual target of all that anger, but was helpless to do that. Instead he did what seemed to be the only thing he could do with all that rage, and unfortunately, that meant it was directed at you. The bully may have been desperate for the feeling of power his bullying gave him, perhaps because he felt so helpless everywhere else. Maybe you presented not only an available target, but a safer target, one whom he could easily take, perhaps because of a size advantage he had or maybe just because you were not likely to offer much resistance. You may have been an easygoing kid, or maybe you were a loner without the safety of a network of friends to protect you.

Either way, the bully probably had issues that he brought to school, and his attacks on you probably had far more to do with his flaws and the defects caused by whatever he had been subjected to, than any flaws you may have had. This does not excuse his behavior, but it should help you to see that the situation was more a reflection of his shortcomings than yours. I hope that you will not overpersonalize the situation by accepting the blame for being bullied due to your size or the courage you possessed as a small child or any other reason you have used as justification for accepting blame for his actions. There was nothing wrong with you that justified his bad behavior anymore than it was my fault that I was raped. There may have been plenty wrong with that bully however, and a lot of that may have been more due to his being victimized somehow than you could have possibly known at the time.

The truth is he may have been already getting worse than he was giving, so all those thoughts of revenge you may have been entertaining all this time have likely been played out in the sad course of his life. Happy, emotionally healthy children do not bully those that are smaller and less able to defend themselves than they are. You may have had to deal with the pain and fear and humiliation of that bullying and I do not mean to trivialize that, but I want you to be aware that his life could have been just as bad, if not much worse than yours. I only want you to realize that there are always two sides when there is interaction between people and they are not always as black and white as one victim and one victor.

Does this mean you should feel sorry for him? Maybe, maybe not. He certainly had choices to make about how to handle his feelings and he obviously made very poor ones. Forgiving him is entirely up to you. It does mean that you should be able to let it go however. That is the true crux of forgiveness, letting the anger over things go, rather than continuing to hang on to it. Sometimes all you really need so that you can do that is to be able to see the other side.

I can look back at my mother now and understand her side of things far better than I could understand it when I was a kid or a teenager. She had been so mistreated as she was growing up and in her first two marriages, she had simply developed a self-defense mechanism that prevented her from forming the emotionally intimate relationships that my sisters and I longed for growing up. At the time we felt neglected and rejected and unimportant, but our limited relationships with our mother had nothing to do with our lovability and everything to do with her inability to form the kind of bonds we needed.

She had brought the baggage of her past into the home where she raised her children. Factor into that home the instability of an unavailable, alcoholic father who was incapable of consistently providing for us and often unfaithful to my mother, and her already limited resources were stretched way too thin. She simply was not capable under all those circumstances of giving that much of herself when she had continually had so much taken from her.

Sometimes what seems to be emotional abuse or mistreatment comes in the form of neglect. There are circumstances under which a parent may not be available and that is not always avoidable. A child however may not have the reasoning capacity to understand why their parents may not spend an ideally healthy amount of time with them. Perhaps they have to work a great deal just to make ends meet. Children are far more likely to respond to the absence of their parents emotionally, rather than logically. Young children are generally not that capable of being stoic and pragmatic. They have real emotional needs and limited resources with which to handle them.

Though most parents need to work for the basic necessities, there is an epidemic among many in this nation that has them nearly obsessed with acquiring material wealth and social and corporate ladder climbing. This often leads to selfish career pursuits at the expense of family time and values. Unfortunately the well being of children is all too often sacrificed because both parents are placing their careers higher on their list of priorities than their own children.

But the reality is we now live in a society that often requires two incomes to secure even the most basic necessities, especially here in California. If a child's parents are often absent from the home and are distracted by all of their daily pressures when they are there, they simply seem unavailable to the child. If a child's needs are not being met it will seem to the child that their needs are not important. If their needs are not important, the child automatically draws the conclusion that they are not important. In a child's heart they misinterpret facts because of their limited knowledge and reasoning powers. They can feel the absence of their parent is a direct reflection of their value. If these feelings are left undealt with, they can settle into the psyche of a child where they take up residency and color the way that child grows up and reacts to the world.

Children are naturally self-absorbed and are only able to see things through their own perspective. They cannot be expected to understand the reasons that adults do all the things that they do.

They automatically respond to every situation with "How does this affect me?" I know plenty of emotionally immature adults who have never quite developed beyond this stage. They don't get along with others too well and rarely have very successful marriages. Most of their relationships are turbulent and yet they fail to see that they are the common denominator in all the turmoil that occurs in their lives. Because they are so focused on how everything affects them and are only able to see things from their own perspective, they are usually challenged at being considerate and reasonable, and are often emotionally impulsive and self-absorbed.

They may have been raised by emotionally immature people who never taught them by example how to be open-minded and reasonable when dealing with others, and how to constructively deal with their emotions. Perhaps they simply suffered as a child and their emotional development was stunted and they were forced to become overly protective of themselves. They may have had to become very forceful in demanding their needs be recognized and met, learning that they would have to always be vigilant and aggressive when it came to their needs. I also don't believe it is unusual to find a child that has suffered a sudden and severe emotional trauma to have ceased their emotional development directly at the point in their lives when the trauma took place. This is one of the ways a trauma can become a life altering experience.

Here is another way: Not long after I had begun dating my husband, Mike, we had spoken the night before and had discussed having dinner together the next night. I had a perfect view from my living room of all the traffic that came down into our complex and often would see his truck as he came home. I hadn't seen his truck and so I did not start dinner. I had begun to convince myself that he had changed his mind or something and was not coming. It was one of the most unreasonable things I had felt in a long time, but you already know that feelings have nothing to do with reason. I was so used to being abandoned by undependable people that I just reverted right back to that place in my life where I did not believe I could count on him showing up until I saw his truck.

He arrived at my door promptly at six as agreed. I guess he had gotten home while I was not paying attention. I told him I wasn't sure if he was coming so I hadn't prepared anything and he asked me incredulously, "What on earth have I ever done to make you think that I would not show up when I said I would?" I realized that he had never done anything to make me come to that unreasonable conclusion, but my father and Steve had done plenty to create that emotional habit in me. I had not taken that emotional anxiety I was feeling and held it up to the light of reason. Mike did not (and still doesn't) drink or engage in any other type of behavior that would cause him to be unreliable. In fact, to this day he is the most reliable person I know. I should have known better, but I relied on my feelings and they were just residue from old emotional habits that had absolutely no place in my current situation.

As an adult we must hold our emotions up to examine them for signs of our own unreasonable history encroaching upon them and changing them from the appropriate emotional response of an emotionally healthy person into the warped emotional responses we had become conditioned to experiencing. Even as we grow we are still subject to emotional relapses that are completely unreasonable and no more than old habit, yet can continue to affect our lives adversely if we are not vigilant.

Emotional maturity also gives us the ability to see things, both past and present, from the perspective of another person. Mike and I rarely argue because we both try to see one another's side in issues that we disagree on. He never has hurtful intentions. I know that about him to be absolute fact. So if we are disagreeing about something it generally means that he has a valid point. An emotionally mature person will try to see what that point is and will remain open to hearing it to see if it makes sense to them also, and can help them to come to a mutually agreeable compromise.

There are usually two sides to every contentious issue. It just so happens that I am writing this book a few months after President George W. Bush has declared the major combat in Iraq to be over. You would have had to have lived with your head in the sand not to have been aware of the huge controversy that has raged in this nation over the necessity of this war, especially here in the politically liberal Bay Area.

My older daughter, Katie, had already adamantly decided that we should go to war. This was not a surprise to me, as my husband, my ex-husband, and I are all moderately conservative republicans. I am passionate about my politics because I am passionate about my country and am a bit of a news junkie also so both my daughters are pretty aware of politics and current events. Katie was in her sophomore year of high school and a couple of months before the war began she had been given an assignment by her current events teacher to write an essay defending or condemning the impending war with Iraq. The class was presented with papers that outlined the main issues on both sides of the argument.

She did not even want to read the pages that spoke of the reasons we should not go to war. She believed it would be a waste of time as her mind was already made up. I made her read all the pages, including those that made the argument against the war. I explained to her that you never learn anything if you are not open minded when it comes to hearing an opinion that differs from your own. There are valid points on both sides of almost every issue and if you are not willing to hear the other side, you will become very, very stagnant. You do not grow if you do not learn and you do not learn if you are already convinced that you know it all.

We all initially respond to, and form opinions based on, what appears to be a logical argument for or against a given issue. However if we make up our minds immediately and then refuse to look at any other possibilities regarding that issue we may never learn of an even more logical and compelling argument that represents the other side of it. Katie did not change her mind about the war, but she learned a very valuable lesson that day nonetheless. She learned that even if you have formed an opinion, never refuse more information about the subject. This is one of the vital facets of emotional maturity.

Here is another example: for most of my life, I have been pro-choice when it comes to the abortion issue. I would have never believed I could be swayed from that stand, but I have learned a lot in the past few years that has made me reconsider my opinion on that subject. I can certainly no longer say that I am still pro-choice, but I don't necessarily believe that the government should be legislating the issue either. I just truly thank God that I have never had to face making that decision because as I have gotten older and have been presented with more information about the pro-life side of the issue that I so long opposed, I have come to change my opinion on it. We need to remain open to learning more information about issues, personal and otherwise, even after we believe our minds are made up.

Many of us, especially those of us with fragile self-esteem, are so afraid we will look stupid, or worse; be proven to actually be stupid if we turn out to be wrong about something that we refuse to look at the other side of an issue, so we often do not hear, really hear, the other person's point of view regarding a situation. An intelligent, emotionally mature person with healthy self-esteem is not afraid to explore both sides of an issue, even if it means ending up saying, "I'm sorry, I was wrong." It is the only way to be able to make an intelligent, informed decision that is reasonable and rational, rather than purely emotional.

Of course, it is more difficult to objectively look at both sides of an issue when we are examining a situation that has a personal impact on us, than it is regarding something that is simply political, philosophical, or intellectual. The ability to do this however, is key to having and sustaining healthy relationships. Of course, you cannot choose your initial feelings in regards to a given situation, but you can and *must* choose how you respond to and behave based upon those feelings. For example, you may not be able to help getting angry at someone who launches some type of verbal attack on you, but you have to choose what to do with those feelings. You may let loose with a verbal assault of your own sure to out do theirs. You may haul off and hit the offender with knee-buckling force. You may just turn and walk away. The point is you need to make choices every day about how you handle your feelings.

Another way you need to introduce logic into your emotional responses is to learn to have reasonable expectations. No two people can agree and get along all the time. I'm not sure it would even be healthy to try. Disagreements will arise. Expect them. Make the effort to try to handle them with emotional maturity, looking at both sides of the issue and remaining calm enough to clearly communicate your own side.

Keep your expectations realistic and reasonable when it comes to all aspects of your life. As I've said before, it is human nature to stubbornly resist change, even when it will be for the better. Change, however, is one of the only things you can realistically expect. Though change can be frightening, it does not mean it will be a bad thing. Every time I have lost a job, I have found a better one. Most of us tend to subscribe to the theory that "if it's not broken, don't fix it." The problem is that we often don't recognize when something is broken. What if I had resisted change so much that I stayed with Steve? When I married him I was pretty sure I would be with him forever, but his relationship issues escalated as did my intolerance, and things changed. Try not to panic or expect the worst when change is suddenly thrust upon you and don't be afraid to initiate change in your own life in order to make positive strides. Try to look at change as an expected part of life that often brings about positive surprises that you may not have sought, but can surely benefit from.

Perhaps you have unrealistic expectations in the way you figure your life to be. You may see your life quite different from the actuality of it. Perhaps you have convinced yourself that it is always hard and miserable, when you have many reasons to find pleasure and fulfillment in it. Remember: *what you choose to look at...*You may believe it is filled with only pain, when logically speaking, your life, like most people's, is comprised of both good and bad, hard and easy, joy and pain. I am a prime example of someone who has certainly had their share of hardships, but I have also had my share of blessings. I do not expect my life to be constant calamity, nor do I have unrealistic expectations that lean to the other extreme, expecting it to be all love and lollipops.

I generally see the world with a reasonable balance of "hope for the best, and plan for the worst." I do not look at my life with dread, nor do I see it through rose colored glasses. We often define the world and our lives in the same absolute terms we were in the habit of defining ourselves with, terms like; always, never, completely, and totally. It is this same black and white thinking that I unreasonably indulged in when I believed I could only be "perfection or garbage." If you have unrealistic expectations in life and are expectant of only smooth sailing you will be absolutely devastated when an inconvenience, let alone a crisis comes along. If your expectations lean to expecting only disaster you will not recognize and enjoy your blessings.

Try to begin tempering your emotions with reason. Examine them, especially the extreme ones and those that do not seem appropriate. As you emotionally mature, you will be able to recognize when you are succumbing to old habits and having an emotional relapse. You should also begin to see much of your past and the damage inflicted from a different perspective.

It was emotional reasoning that allowed me to heal my relationship with my mother. Healing that relationship was a little like having the last piece of the puzzle of my past put into place, sort of clearing the deck for me to soar into my future.

About four months into Mike's and my relationship, we both realized that we had fallen in love. Everything he had claimed to be, he was. This was not difficult for him, because unlike Rob, he had made no claims, certainly no grandiose claims anyway. He had never said anything to try to impress me. In fact, he had said many things that were so refreshingly honest that they definitely reflected someone who had not spent much time considering whether it was wise to have divulged so much. Had he been a bit more deliberate and skilled at dating, he might have withheld some things in order to create an even better impression. The very fact that this never occurred to him was possibly the most endearing thing about him. After having watched Rob painstakingly spin every detail of his life for maximum effect, Mike's candor could not have been more needed or more appreciated. He was (and still is) genuine and kind, and possesses one of the most important qualities a human being can have; integrity.

> *You are host to a noble soul.*
> *I float away upon the ocean*
> *of your turquoise eyes.*
> *I can see*
> *the sunset red of your love*
> *as if it glowed*
> *in the western sky.*
> *I know you somewhere deep within.*

I recognize you with that part of me
that remains unfinished.
I can feel your silver fingers
touch me where I'm incomplete.
My face is stained
with the pink of your kisses,
as you sweep the gray dust
from my pale moon heart.
The ardent angels awing
have somehow found us worthy,
bestowed this starry love upon us
and have tied our helpless hearts together
in a purple lovers knot.
Yes love, like a green ivy vine
has snaked its way around us.
Though we are still brushed
by the fainthearted haunting
of lost loves,
I find that I never stopped tasting
the tiny, pearl white feathers
of the dream of rediscovering love.
I see droplets of that dream
were still afloat in your eyes too.
Now you have burst in my heart,
loves golden flash and flare ignited
to dislodge all the love lies
that came before.

With so much going right in my life, suddenly I had the courage to furiously and seriously pursue my deepest passion; poetry. I had written poetry since I was in my early teens, but always sporadically. I had always vacillated between the extremes of feast or famine in terms of my writing, sometimes going as long as two years without having written a single piece, other times prolifically producing thirty or forty pieces in a two week span. It was inconsistent to say the least.

But something had been let loose inside me, like a dam had broken in my head and the water of words rushed the pages as poetry flowed like blood through my veins. I can almost believe there was a connection between my renewed commitment to writing and that fact that I had also begun seeking spiritually.

My constant desire for wisdom and my dedication to understanding people and life had early on created in me a curiosity regarding the spiritual side of me and of others, of God, and of truth. I had explored a bit of philosophy and religion before and had even considered myself a Christian since having given God a whirl back in my teens. It was different now though. I was somehow hungrier spiritually. Perhaps having settled so many of my mental and emotional issues I had been freed to feel the urgings from my soul which was clearly longing to be satisfied at last. Until I had quieted the chaos in my mind and heart I was simply unable to hear the gentle call of Christ.

One day, being a book addict, I purchased a book on religions of the world and began studying bits and pieces of various religions, especially the eastern religions. While I found great philosophical truths among them, I did not feel as though I had connected to those truths on any kind of a spiritual level, an intellectual level sure, but not deep down in my soul.

I read the *Celestine Prophecy* by James Redfield one weekend and bits of that did seem to resonate within me. It seemed to inspire more questions than answers though. God wasn't concerned. He had planted His seed deep in my heart decades before and He had arranged a deep and steady supply of people He had prepared to parade through my life to give me those answers. It would be a lengthy and complicated process to be sure, but the outcome was never in doubt, at least not to God.

Anyway, during this time I had become confident enough and serious enough about the poetry I had already written to take an even more courageous step than making a mid-life career change. It took even more courage than confronting my mother, than seeking the spiritual truth, or digging my past out of the deepest recesses of my head. I bought a computer.

It was nineteen-ninety-four. The girls were seven and eight and would certainly be coming to the age where they would need one, but I'd be lying if I claimed that as my sole motivation, my best justification maybe, but not my only motivation. It was to be a glorified word processor for my writing. I had decided it was time to type my poems onto disks so that they could be printed at will and readied for submission for possible publication one day. With over two hundred poems and the typing skills of a developmentally disabled chicken, it would take a good, long time to get them typed, but I had no hopes of ever having my life long dream of publication realized if I didn't do it.

I had also discovered around then that the cancer that killed my father had started in his lungs at the age of thirty-seven. I was thirty-five. I could not take the chance of leaving my daughters the way he had left me. After having been smoking by then for another couple of years, I decided I had been rebellious, independent, and foolish long enough. Besides, I no longer required their comfort the way I had back on that summer afternoon when I first indulged again with my sister.

I sat down and came up with a plan to quit. I addressed all the emotional reasons that I smoked and listed plenty of alternatives to deal with those needs as they arose. It takes seventy-two hours to rid your system of nicotine, so if I kept going back to smoking after having been nicotine free for months and even years I knew the addiction had to be more emotional than physical. I discovered that my true need was not a cigarette, but comfort; not a cigarette, but independence; not a cigarette, but to rebel. Cigarettes had become my reward, my escape, and my excuse to relax.

One thing that helped me quit was that I did not allow myself to indulge in the fantasy of smoking a cigarette the way I had all the other times in my life I had tried and failed to quit. That would have been fatal to my efforts. Getting an automatic cue to smoke a cigarette was uncontrollable, but how I responded to those cravings was not. When they arose I did not begin imagining how good that cigarette would taste and how satisfying it would feel to deeply fill my lungs with the smoke. I did not dream of rewarding myself with that five or ten minute break that would allow me to indulge in relaxing with that cigarette. Instead, when those cues for a cigarette popped into my brain, I told myself, "Smoking is not an option" and forced myself to think of something else. I thought of alternatives to smoking and listed them in the plan I had made to help me quit. One of those alternatives was to keep my hands very, very busy and if that happened to engage my mind as well, so much the better.

I began various writing projects that were a great and constructive distraction and, as if in answer to prayer, all of a sudden I had discovered, or developed, or been granted like a wish, a way to constantly remain in the process of writing poetry. It was a creative formula that enabled me to write poetry pretty much at will as opposed to being at the mercy of having to wait for the inspiration to hit me. I even began keeping a micro-cassette recorder with me in the car as I had suddenly become able to glean poetry from everywhere I looked and everything I heard. I found lines of poetry being inspired in me by lyrics in songs, lines from movies, words in a thesaurus, dialogue overheard in restaurants and in the reading of poetry itself.

It was like a switch had been flipped inside me and as I began keeping notebooks filled with all this material I had been gathering, I began to categorize it in terms of the type of poem it would most likely fit in, and suddenly I found it easier than ever to create poems. It had taken me twenty years to create that first volume of two-hundred plus poems and only six months to create the second volume of an equal amount.

What a glorious time in my life! I had grown so much, accomplished so much, was succeeding beyond my wildest dreams at work, was healed and happy in my heart, and I was in love. Both Mike and I were enjoying the healthiest, happiest relationship of our lives. For the first time for either one of us, we each had the emotional maturity necessary for a healthy relationship.

chapter twenty

RISK TAKING AND BOUNDARIES

Physically, I'm a self professed wimp. I am not now, and never have been, athletic. A childhood filled with asthma, illness and an overprotective mother rarely adds up to an athlete. Factor in the unmistakable lack of any athletic talent, except for a moderate ability to shoot baskets, and you do not have the makings of a prime specimen of physical prowess, let alone any kind of a daredevil.

It's okay. I may not race downhill on packed powder in the winter or climb the sides of mountains in the spring, but I have never broken, fractured, or sprained anything either. Heck, I've never even had stitches except the ones the obstetrician put in after my two C-sections. All my trips to the emergency room have always involved breathing treatments. You see, not being athletic, I am also not a physical risk taker, so I have never put my body (such as it is) in dangerous situations. No extreme sports for me. No way.

I don't snow ski, although I tried it once and actually survived the day, making it all the way back down to the lodge on rubber legs. Would it surprise you to learn I did this only because some guy I was dating at the time skied and it was a way to spend the whole weekend with him in the snow? God knows, he never treated me very well, but that had never stopped me from dating anybody before.

I don't water ski, even though John taught me when I was a young teenager and I did go with him again so he could teach my daughters and Mike. I don't ride bicycles, unicycles, or motorcycles, nor do I ride snowboards, wakeboards, skateboards or any other type of board. Boards are for building, not for riding, although I don't build things either. Power tools are also not my friends. I did ride a horse a couple of times, though the second time I am convinced the horse was seriously considering throwing me off the side of the cliff he had stopped on and was staring down from intently. Those horse incidents were the results of other outings I had with John as he tried to remain connected to me during my turbulent teen years. What kind of a nut wants to be connected to a troubled teen? The most loving kind.

Anyway, you get the picture. I truly am a wimp. This does not mean I don't like sports. I love them, as a spectator. There is little that I like better than junk food in front of a Raiders game, but you won't find me out there on a soccer field using my head to block a goal, let alone another soccer player.

This however does not mean I don't take risks. I am a great risk taker, just not with my body. I am an emotional risk taker. It is probably just part of the way I responded to a chaotic upbringing. I moved so often as a kid and attended so many different schools, I am not afraid to move as an adult. I don't like it, but I don't fear it either. Change is never welcome, but it is also not that scary to me. I've changed jobs numerous times and even changed careers. I've rushed into countless men's arms in the hopes of finding that lasting healing and ended those relationships just as rashly when I suspected no such healing existed there. I've gone through divorce and eventually a remarriage in true "happily ever after" fashion.

I'm just saying that I am not afraid of emotional risk. Okay, maybe I'm a little afraid, but I am still willing to take those risks in the pursuit of happiness. Though change is scary to most of us humans, I have always been able to overcome my fear of change and move forward into the new day when necessary. It is why I am happy now and not stuck in an abusive marriage and a dead-end job.

Julie, however, is quite the thrill seeker, well at least compared to me. She rides jet skis and motorcycles and is quite athletic. There have been a few broken body parts over the years and she has suffered a concussion or two besides, but she is not afraid to run with the big dogs. She is very petite, but she has no fear physically, although she is a bit of an emotional wimp. She has held the same job since she was in high school twenty five years ago. It is only the slightest bit fulfilling to her, and she has entertained the thought of leaving it on several occasions, or furthering her education to advance, but she has never quite made the jump.

I have another friend who has been married to the same man for nearly thirty years and has been unhappy much of the time. He is not abusive or unfaithful and is not a drug abuser or a mass murderer or anything, but he is often a self-absorbed, whiney, emotionally black-mailing child who is actually many years her senior and treats her more like his child than his equal. Oh she loves him alright, but it is not the happily ever after, passionate, best friends kind of love that I am fortunate enough to share with Mike.

I almost wish he was worse to her, because at least then it might force her to make a change. Of course I don't actually wish divorce, let alone any form of abuse, upon her or anyone else, but it is frustrating to see someone I love remain in a life of mediocrity that does not fulfill her because she is afraid to make a change. I do not even advocate that she leave him. Personally I like him just fine. He's not a bad guy overall, but I do wish she would at least insist upon being treated with the love and respect she deserves. I have often recommended that they see a marriage counselor who might be able to offer them some objective and professional advice to create a more intimate and enriching marriage, but she is so uncomfortable with risk, that she is also very non-confrontational and is not much good at making demands. So she takes no risks and makes no strides and just goes along for the ride even though she doesn't much care for the view. It breaks my heart.

Please, if you're going to be a wimp, protect your body, but fight like mad for your life! There are no do-overs when you leave here, no second chances to get it right. Don't be so paralyzed with fear that you imprison yourself within a cell that you have constructed or allowed someone else to construct for you.

Dare to believe me when I tell you that you deserve to be happy, but you may need to take some risk in order to get there. You deserve a life that's fulfilling and you deserve to embark upon your own journey to joy. Does this journey involve risk? Of course it does, but what is mostly at risk is the familiarity of doing things the same way you have always done them, which the very fact that you are this far in this book ought to tell you is probably not working out all that great for you. Your journey will only risk making changes to that which is mediocre or worse in your life.

As you begin to heal and to change the way you look at, treat, and feel about yourself, you will also begin to change the way you allow others to treat you and that may put some of those less healthy relationships at risk. Those relationships could involve family members, friendships, and quite possibly your romantic relationship or marriage.

As you begin to establish new boundaries based on your newly grown unwillingness to accept bad treatment, you may find some people unwilling to accept those new boundaries. They may not want to play by the new ground rules that you, as an emotionally healthy person will set, particularly if the lack of those healthy rules had given them all the advantages in the power struggle before. If the relationship was one based more on your willingness to accept their unfair ground rules than it was based on an honest concern for you and your happiness, then you may meet some real resistance from them that truly jeopardizes the chance of the relationship surviving and becoming a healthy, happy one.

Thank God my mother was willing to accept the new boundaries I had set. It enabled us to turn a previously not so healthy relationship into a new and emotionally fulfilling one. This was a gift for both of us as it made me want to be around her much more and it taught her how to be more clear and gentle in expressing her love and good wishes for me. It is a gift I will always be grateful for as we were able to enjoy a loving closeness based on true unconditional love as never before.

It could have turned out differently however. There was a risk in engaging her in the dialogue I began that day. She could have easily become defensive and turned the conversation into an argument that would have solved nothing and may have even escalated the existing discord between us into something even worse, but it was a risk I had to take.

You may have this kind of success in changing the dynamics of all the unhealthy relationships in your life. It may not even require you to have specific conversations with the people involved in those relationships. It could be that just the changes in your behavior and your responses to their "business as usual" behavior begins to teach, or to re-teach, them how to treat you.

Some perpetrators of offending behavior may alter that behavior when they realize they no longer get the desired response from you. Just as a child usually stops throwing temper tantrums when the parent finally gets tough and learns to ignore them rather than to submit to them, adults can often learn the same way. For example, let's say your spouse often uses guilt as a weapon to coerce you into acquiescing to their requests (or demands). As you gain self-esteem, you realize that you have nothing to feel guilty about for saying no. After you begin resisting the guilt tactic and stop giving in, your spouse will probably figure out eventually that this approach no longer works.

People do what works for them to get the results they desire, so if something stops working they are forced to try something else. This means your spouse will either find an honest way to try to convince you to meet their need, and then respect your decision, or they may not get it, in which case the relationship may deteriorate even further. If this is the case the relationship may require some outside help such as a marriage counselor.

This happens a lot with those friendships that are not healthy, mutually respectful relationships. You may have a friend whom you have allowed to take advantage of you. Perhaps it was because you were afraid of losing that friend if you refused their many requests, or maybe you just figured you were obligated to do much more for them than they did for you because you believed your friendship was not very valuable. You may just not have had the self-respect to stand up for yourself and people instinctively pick up on that and those that are self-absorbed are often quick to take advantage of it.

You may find changing the rules on this type of friend will take care of the problem. As you begin setting boundaries and learning to say "no" to their incessant or unreasonable requests and demands, they may get more reasonable. If however, they have been predominantly interested in your friendship because of your willingness to do for them, rather than because of who you are, they may just go find someone else to take advantage of, someone who will blindly accommodate them. Either way, with a friend like this, there is no huge risk because you've got nothing to lose.

Sometimes the person you have just changed the ground rules on will require an explanation as to why the "same-old, same-old" is not working. They may not even be aware that their behavior is hurtful to you in some way. Often hurting you is the furthest thing from their mind and is definitely not their intent. Try to be as tactful as possible and explain things in a non-accusatory manner that does not emphasize blame and reflects your responsibility for your own feelings. In other words, explain how you feel when certain things take place in the relationship without making statements like "You make me feel," "You are," "You never," or "You always." This will help to keep the person from becoming defensive and will help to ensure a clear and constructive dialogue between you.

If the other person in the relationship still does not understand, you may require the help of a professional counselor, especially if it is your spouse you are attempting to get through to. If your spouse is vehemently against making these changes and accepting your new boundaries an expert can help both parties understand the adjustments necessary to recreate the relationship into a happy, healthy one, and can offer helpful, objective ways to communicate and to facilitate changes.

Any hope of salvaging and healing an unhealthy relationship requires that both parties be willing participants. There is always the risk that the other party may not be willing to work at it. If the person loves you enough and values the relationship enough and truly understands that the changes are absolutely necessary and non-negotiable (this does not mean there can be no compromise), they should be willing to work to save it. If they do not love you and are involved with you for some other reason or reward, they may not be willing. Even if they do love you, but do not value the relationship greatly, they may not be willing. If they sense that you are not serious and that you will not do anything different if they do not change, they definitely will not be willing.

There is nothing you can do to alter the first two reasons listed as to why they may not be willing. You cannot control the way another person feels and by now you had better understand that their willingness has nothing to do with your lovability and who you are, and everything to do with their ability to love and who they are. You may just be in one of those mismatched relationships. Perhaps you settled for it way back when, and now find there is little hope of becoming well suited for each other. You two may have simply remained together out of habit. Maybe you are with a person who has never been willing to invest too much of themselves in the relationship.

Though you will of course want to exhaust all avenues before giving up on a marriage, if it is a physically abusive relationship in any way, and your partner is not actively participating in a professionally guided program for change, you may have no choice. You may have to take action to remove your spouse or yourself and your children from the home in order to protect yourselves physically and emotionally.

Sometimes the relationship may involve someone who, for any number of reasons, may not be willing to work things through now that your demands are a bit greater. There is little you can do sometimes except to remember not to settle for an unhappy, and destructive relationship and not to take it personally if it ends.

The only control you have when it comes to persuading the other person to make the necessary adjustments, is to not be wishy-washy about them and to firmly and consistently assert your needs without making empty threats that you will not follow through with. You must be strong and you must not vacillate. This does not mean becoming mean and nasty about it. You will still catch more flies with honey than you will with vinegar. It means you will need to be clear and visibly determined. Remember, human nature resists change and no one is likely to change familiar behavior unless they know unequivocally they have no choice and they truly want to save the relationship. You have to be fully committed to your well being. If you're not committed, why would you expect them to be?

There are two people in every relationship and they both come to it with their own needs and histories. Emotionally healthy people are secure and generally treat others well because they do not have all those desperate and convoluted needs that alter and distort the way they treat people as they attempt to get their own needs met. You may be dealing with a person who has brought a little baggage, or a lot of baggage, into the relationship. If they are not too emotionally healthy it may require a bit more work on their part and that means a bit more willingness as well. The beauty of it is that they may be giving themselves the greater of the gifts by seeking the growth and the changes in their own behavior that will rescue the relationship.

These are the people though that present the greatest risk of blowing up the relationship, rather than doing the inner work that will enable them to grow and create a "new and improved" version of your former relationship. Steve was one of those people. If they not only refuse to treat you well, but are still truly destructive to you, then good riddance to them. Grieve the passing of the relationship, and the death of that dream, and move on.

You must be prepared for the possibility of this, not the probability, but the possibility. You may need to end a deeply unhealthy relationship with someone who refuses to change their behavior and will only continue to mistreat you. It is not enough for them to promise to change the bad behavior. Rob promised not to cheat on me anymore, but refused to get the counseling that I was sure he would need in order to change the core reason for his constant infidelity. I insisted that he treat the disease and not just the symptom of the disease. It would have been no more effective for him to have had a bad cold, but promise not to cough. No matter how much he may not have wanted to cough, without taking the proper medicine and curing the cold, he was going to cough; and in somebody else's bed.

As you know, I eventually grew to the point where I found his lies and selective truth to be too disgusting to endure. Sadly enough, after I had moved on he eventually married another woman with whom he had two more children. (He already had two children from an ex-wife when we met.) He called me a couple years ago, while he was married to this poor woman and I just blew him off. He called again a couple of months ago and told me how sorry he was for having blown the great love that we had, and having lost the family we had become. He also went on to tell me that his wife had left him six months earlier. I didn't have to ask why. I told him I was happily married and blew him off again. He clearly never got the help to treat his disease.

I strongly recommend that you do not accept a promise to change a chronic bad behavior without seeing proof that they are taking whatever medicine is necessary to cure the disease. A promise of fidelity is not fidelity. If they are a substance abuser, they need to be in treatment and working a program. A promise of sobriety is not sobriety. In my opinion if they are physically abusive, they need to be living apart from you, have completed anger management and be in intensive psychotherapy before you should even entertain the thought of resuming the relationship in any form.

This can feel like a huge risk if you have been in a long term relationship and are naturally afraid of the unknown and of being alone. As I stated a few pages back, you may be risking those friendships that have always felt one-sided in their give and take. You know the ones, you give, they take. There is also a risk when it comes to those family relationships that have been unhealthy. There is the chance that they will not only never get better, but they may even become worse. If this is the case, I have to assume that there was not much of a relationship to begin with. The greater resistance you meet when taking steps to protect and to heal yourself, the less vested interest that person probably has in your well being. I have already described true love as having the recipient's best interest at heart. If this person does not love you enough to truly desire your happiness, then their reasons for being in the relationship may be more closely related to their own needs than they are to love. There are a lot of emotionally unhealthy and otherwise self-absorbed people in the world, and when you were emotionally unhealthy you probably allowed and even invited many of them into your world.

Sometimes it is not that the other person has no interest in your well being, but is emotionally immature and maybe emotionally damaged themselves. They may be unable to see the situation from any other perspective but their own. I have another friend whose father continually made hurtful and insulting comments to him. He could not get his father to recognize this pattern he had that had always been painful for him to endure. Fortunately when my friend sought help for his marriage, he also gained a great deal of understanding of himself and the governing dynamics of his past. This verbal abuse his father had continually subjected him to had done considerable emotional damage, but as he made progress in his counseling he began to heal his self-esteem and the damage his father had inflicted.

Though he was unable to convince his father to acknowledge and change the behavior, his self-esteem had grown to the point that he could apply logic to his father's hurtful comments and was able to understand clearly that there was no basis in reality for the comments. They had failed the litmus test of accurately reflecting the truth. No matter how much his father criticized him, it didn't make the criticism true and my friend knew it. He stopped taking the criticism personally and his father lost the power to hurt him as he had done for so long. The criticism could not inflict the damage on a confident man that it had inflicted on a vulnerable little boy who, like every little boy, was constantly seeking his father's approval.

Of course, every child seeks the approval of his or her parents and those that do not feel that they have it often have lower self-esteem. They can grow up to spend immeasurable amounts of energy trying to gain that parental approval. I was very fortunate that my mother did at last verbalize her approval of me and my life, but many are not so lucky. My friend is such an example.

He had three choices under the circumstances. He could have severed the relationship with his father to avoid the pain. He could have healed the relationship by changing the rules if his father had been willing to admit any culpability and/or to make the necessary adjustments. Finding that his father was unwilling to recognize his role in the dysfunction that existed in the relationship, he was left with the third choice. He set a boundary by testing the criticism to see if it was valid, which of course it wasn't, and so decided to ignore it and dismiss it, thereby removing all the power to hurt him his father's criticism once had.

Only you can decide which of these options fits best in each of your unhealthy relationships. Some may be so destructive that you have to sever them. Others may be salvageable if the other party is willing to work on it. Some you may want to keep, but if the other person is not willing to play by the new rules your self-respect demands, you may have to change the way you respond to the offensive behavior. My friend found that he had become able to just let the insults roll off his back, rendering them completely impotent.

You need to determine if the tactic my friend employed is a viable option for you, and that largely depends on how much your self-esteem has grown, how much you value the relationship, and how destructive or offensive the behavior is. If there is physical or sexual abuse for example, without the offender engaging in intense therapy as suggested earlier, the only logical option is to end the relationship altogether.

Whatever option you choose, remember that the other person will have to make a decision also. Every relationship you find you need to change in order to make it a healthy, constructive one brings up risks to the relationship. You must be willing to take the risks that come with change when change is necessary for your emotional health.

There clearly, was not going to be any change in my marriage to Steve. Eventually he lost me because of his stubbornness and refusal to change the way he treated me and it nearly destroyed him when he did. By the time he realized it might be worth changing, and I emphasize the word *might*, it was way too little, it was way too late, and I was way too gone.

We are all stumbling around,
foraging in the great forest
of loneliness,
scavenging for small snippets of love,
fumbling for fragments of joy.
For some of us
this forest is in our own home,
in our own marriage,
where pale stains of ghostly pall
are cast across our future.
Today I reach red-eyed for the coffee
with uncertain hands,
the Monday morning elixir
a desperately necessary evil

to pull me up
and into my day.
I close my swollen eyes;
a bride glides down the aisle
in pale clouds of chiffon
and remains strung across
my memory grid.
This grid is filled
with cells in my brain
that remain dead to the future,
fully committed to the past,
wholly cemented in yesterday,
cells in which
our marriage still lives,
still breathes that sense of certainty
into my day,
cells where your honeyed smile
still beams,
cells in which
you still glorify me.
I open my eyes;
there is no covenant here,
not since you fell into the habit
of objectifying me,
somehow transforming me in your heart
from the woman you dreamed of finding
into the wife object
you acquired way back.
There is no glory
in this grief.
Here I sit,
trapped in the wreckage of a dream
we once called marriage,
weighed down beneath the burden
of memory.
I am raw and unhealed,
constantly reeling

from the shock
of love undone.
Habit binds us
like roots intertwined,
bound here together
in the same soil,
both reaching for light,
longing for wet,
aching to see the world
through undamaged eyes.
Some days I'm reduced to
no more than
a gelatinous substance
inside a skull,
fear running through my veins
like blood
and down into the soil bed
of my heart
like those roots.
This is one of those days.
The coffee tastes like dark music,
like the color of death,
as bitter as our marriage,
which has taken on
a life of its own.
We have shut each other out
and locked ourselves in,
become victims of our own isolation,
our self-imposed exile,
banished to our solitude,
each of us vilified
in the other's downcast eyes.
I have chased the lies of marriage
until I have caught the truth.
I stir it into my coffee,
wrap my cold hands around the cup
and drink it down.

I risked that relationship, but look at the tradeoffs. I gave up being trapped in the fear and the anger that had come to be the basis of our marriage, and ultimately received my emotional health, my happiness, a new career, and a truly wonderful husband. Heck, if I hadn't left him I would have never written this book. I might not have ever even realized that I needed to read a book like this, let alone write one. It didn't happen overnight as you know. In fact it took about the same amount of time that I had spent married to Steve to realize all my dreams after my divorce. As if that alone wasn't worth the risk, I also gave Katie and Laura a much greater chance at a happy future as well, instead of the preordained dysfunctional future my remaining with Steve would have guaranteed us all. Not a bad trade off at all.

Was it scary to take that risk? Oh yeah! Was it worth it? You decide. Ironically enough, Steve and I were eventually able to salvage the friendship that had once been the real basis for our relationship. Julie now describes our relationship more as that of a brother and sister than anything else. It's a pretty accurate assessment.

chapter twenty-one

EMOTIONAL INTIMACY

Another of the many ways my marriage to Mike differs from my first marriage is the level of emotional intimacy or closeness we share. True emotional intimacy cannot take place if both people are not in touch with their feelings and do not understand them. You cannot express what you do not know, and you cannot be truly close to someone you cannot share your innermost world with, the world that exists inside your heart.

A healthy relationship is an honest relationship and that requires not only your willingness to really communicate, but the ability to really communicate. You also must be able to identify what you are feeling and what your true needs are. Furthermore, you need to be secure with who you are, and believe that your innermost thoughts and feelings are valid if you are to be brave enough to really open up with someone.

Maybe even more importantly, you need to be secure in the relationship, and certain that you can trust the person you are with. It is a truly vulnerable position you put yourself in when you are emotionally intimate with someone. I know for a fact that when I share my deepest feelings with Mike, even if he doesn't quite understand them at first, he would never make light of them or make fun of them. He will always try to understand and to support me in my effort to deal with my emotions, and he will always try to help me to get my needs met. Does this mean that he is perfect and that he always succeeds in his efforts? Of course not. In fact, some days he is better equipped to handle the challenges of our relationship than others, just like I am. He is only human after all, but at least I know I can trust him to try to be worthy of the great trust I place in him each day.

How many of us have experienced humiliation from trusting a deep secret to a person we thought was a close friend who then told someone else? How many of us have then discovered the horrifying reality that our secret had ended up public knowledge? When a person we confide in indulges in the tiny thrill of revealing our secret as a little juicy gossip, it can be devastating. Instead of showing us the value of our trust by keeping our confidence, he or she betrays us. We need to know deep down that we are not risking that horror again, that we are not revealing something that can come back to haunt us. It is like being the first one to say "I love you" and getting a blank stare or hearing "Thank you" as a response. We have taken a risk in giving that person the power to hurt us by the way they handle the information with which we trust them. It is vital that we know that they would not do anything to hurt us before we can feel safe to be that vulnerable with them.

> *With my eyes closed*
> *and my hands open,*
> *with my arms spread*
> *and my heart extended,*
> *with my soul naked*
> *and my mind receptive,*
> *I can truly be touched,*
> *for I know,*
> *only when I am exposed*
> *can I be loved.*
> *So here I am*
> *beside you,*

> *vulnerable*
> *to the point*
> *of near rawness.*
> *I allow you*
> *total penetration*
> *of my heart.*
> *It is like*
> *letting you stroke*
> *the soft underbelly*
> *of my soul.*

You cannot solve differences if you are not able to share your deepest thoughts and feelings with one another. That is the only way you will both able to understand each others needs and how to help meet them. Neither one of you is psychic and you cannot read minds. So often we expect our partner to somehow magically know what we need and then we become angry with them when they do not give that to us. Our needs have to be expressed clearly if our partners are to have a chance at meeting them. This requires an emotional atmosphere that allows both people to feel safe from being judged or criticized. People who are concerned that their feelings or needs will be twisted into a weapon to be used against them in a future disagreement are not likely to open up and share them. (Just as a side note, let me caution you here. It is important to understand that it is not your partner's responsibility to meet your every need. Never forget your own responsibility to meet your own needs, emotional and otherwise.)

A safe, healthy relationship is one in which a partner does not trivialize, dismiss, or degrade that which the other partner feels, but rather acknowledges, respects, and accepts those feelings while trying to find a way to accommodate their partner's needs. They can express their needs to one another because they both know that they will be treated with loving care. This is a reflection of having a partner who has the other person's best interest at heart. It takes time to gain this deep and intimate level of trust. It is vital that you know not only that your partner desires to meet your real needs, but also that your partner would not ask something of you that would be detrimental to you in some way. I know in my heart of hearts that I can trust Mike not to request something of me that would be harmful to me.

Emotional intimacy is an integral part of a healthy relationship. Clearly it was not present in my relationships with either Steve or Rob. Steve was never any good at being able to identify his feelings, let alone express them. He was decidedly old fashioned and unenlightened when it came to those mushy, girlie things like feelings, and was not about to learn how to recognize, express and deal with them. We had both gone into what I call protection mode anyway as we did not trust one another to keep the other one's best interest at heart. We were in a constant power struggle, both of us trying to keep the other one from taking what we were afraid or unable to give.

Let me illustrate an example of how protection mode alters the way two people treat each other and deteriorates relationships by pointing to Steve and me again. Steve never gave me cards to commemorate special occasions. He was pretty bad at gift giving as well. He forgot our first three anniversaries, not to mention Valentine's days, and often gave me cash for my birthday. I even got cash for Christmas one year along with a stocking filled with junk food from the Seven Eleven. Mother's days were no better. One year not only did I not receive a card or gift, I got screamed at for having bought a card for his stepmother that had two African-American children on the front and being that he was more than a bit racist, he found that insulting. I had always been the one to purchase the cards for his family members since he was bad at doing that for everyone, not just me.

Anyway, even though I had always loved the challenge of finding special gifts for those I loved and cards that truly expressed how I felt, I began to only resent doing that for Steve. Eventually I stopped buying cards for him altogether. I stopped giving something because it was not valued. We do this with things that are not material as well. We withhold praise, support, encouragement, sex, affection, and love. We will often close up and build emotional walls that will not allow the other person in. We stop communicating and sharing our deeper thoughts and feelings when those things are not reciprocated, or worse, when they are unappreciated, devalued or degraded. When it gets to the point where we feel unsafe to give our love and begin holding that back (choosing not to love), it indicates that the two people are not really partners at all and are, in fact, no longer even on the same team. A healthy relationship requires that both people be on the same side, fighting together against the world, not fighting against each other. When they have become opponents rather than each other's proponents the relationship disintegrates.

Obviously I was also unable to have this intimacy with Rob as well. It requires honesty to be emotionally intimate, not fiction. He was incapable of real honesty as he was busy trying to maintain the illusion of the man he had presented himself to be, rather than sharing the truth of what was really going on within him. It is likely that he faced fears of his own inadequacy and fears of yet another failure. Furthermore, honesty was certainly not an option for someone who was chronically unfaithful. It took time for me to learn this about him though and that is a prime example of why emotional intimacy cannot be achieved quickly and should not be rushed.

It cannot exist in all romantic relationships, but it should develop in a healthy, long term one. It is not strictly limited to romantic relationships though. Emotional intimacy exists in any relationship where you feel completely safe to divulge the deeper parts of yourself and can trust the other person to support you and not to condemn you for your true thoughts and emotions. You may be fortunate enough to have one or two friends close enough to share that kind of intimate trust with and perhaps you are lucky enough to have a parent or a sibling that you can enjoy that kind of relationship with. It is the greatest fruit of any relationship, especially a marriage.

Some people, particularly those who have suffered abandonment or betrayal, especially if it is what they learned when they were young, go into protection mode and stay there. This protection mode is not limited to obstructing their romantic relationships, but can interfere with the healthy development of their friendships and family relationships as well, just as it did with my mother. She was unable to trust after having been hurt so deeply and so often by people who were supposed to care for her, and it damaged her ability to be truly emotionally intimate. My stepfather was able to help her to rebuild her ability to trust, but I'm sure it took a great deal of time and consistent love and dependability.

People who have suffered abandonment, as we did in my family, often struggle with allowing people to get truly close to them. They have their ability to trust people and to rely on people damaged by all the issues that naturally surround abandonment. They tend to keep most relationships on a very superficial level and rob themselves of the joy available within the deep bonds of trust and love. They become so certain that people will let them down that they often even sabotage relationships just to avoid being left.

Often when they do allow someone to get really close, they pick people wholly undeserving of that trust who will end up betraying them and deeply hurt them, confirming their belief that they should not trust anyone or get close to anyone. It is amazing how often we sub-consciously invite people into our lives that will validate our worst feelings and fears. I felt I was worthless so I married a man (at least the first time) who confirmed that by telling me that I was worthless and by treating me as though I was.

Having achieved true emotional intimacy in my relationship with Mike, we were both certain that our romantic relationship was the right one to become our final romantic relationship. We had discussed our future and had both verbalized our willingness to walk the whole road should it lead us into marriage as we had come to believe it likely would.

So when the time came that I would no longer be able to live in my condo in Hayward and continue to transfer my girls into the much better school district nearby in Castro Valley, we began to explore our options. Having been neighbors had been kind of like having the best of both worlds and we had been spoiled by it. We had sort of fallen into a routine of spending certain nights together as most couples would, but we were also used to having our *phone conversations* on the nights he would not be staying over, *in person,* due to the convenience of our close proximity. Our unique arrangement as both neighbors and lovers offered the advantages of living together along with the personal space and independence of living apart.

But the priority I placed on my daughters' education threatened to put an end to that situation. Their needs came first and a first rate education was definitely one of their greatest needs. Mike not only understood that, but being such a quality person, he explained to me that he wouldn't be in love with me if I wasn't the type of person who would put their children's needs first. This propensity to put them first I would love to say comes from some great nobility or selflessness, but it is surely more because of my innate sense of responsibility.

Anyway, I told him I had to move. He was welcome to come with me, but with or without him, I had to move to Castro Valley to keep my girls in their school. I was not only determined to give them the best education that I could, but I was also not about to have them start over as I had done so many times throughout my school years. Without hesitation he decided to come with me, so we both put our places up for sale and began looking for a home to purchase together in Castro Valley.

This turned out to be a much more stressful endeavor than we could have imagined. It was vitally important to get both places sold and another bought before the new school year began and it would end up requiring three escrows to be started on my place before one would finally hold together and close. Each of the two preceding escrows that collapsed felt like huge and disappointing blows, further prolonging my already overwhelming level of anxiety, an anxiety that actually was based in reality.

As I wrote earlier, I had begun seeking answers to my spiritual questions and God had chosen to provide the answers to them through various people, the most vital one being Matthew, that first new client I had landed at work. He was enrolled in Bible college and was able to explain some of the more confusing issues in regard to Christianity that had kept me from faith and establishing a relationship with Christ.

One of those questions was "If God is so loving, how can He sentence all those good people who don't believe in Him to hell?" His answer made sense to me. He told me "God doesn't sentence anyone to hell. That's why He sent His son, Jesus Christ, so that all would be able to get to heaven. Few, if any, of us would have qualified for heaven based on the old legalistic requirements set forth in the Old Testament. He sent Christ so that all we needed to do was believe in

Jesus as our savior and the son of God and believe that He had paid the price for our sins through His crucifixion so that we may have forgiveness and be saved. God gave us free will so that the choice would be ours, not His, so that we could truly love Him of our own volition rather than just be zombie like in some pre-programmed devotion."

I also asked Matthew "How then, could God allow children in remote places like Ethiopia to die of disease and starvation only to end up in hell because they have never heard of Jesus?" Matthew explained that no children ever go to hell. They are not held responsible for their faith or lack thereof until they are old enough to make that choice. "What about the adults in those far away places that have no knowledge of Jesus Christ?" I asked.

He answered, "Those who truly have not heard will be judged on their hearts, while those who have heard and have chosen to reject Christ have willingly chosen to accept not only a life apart from God, but a death apart from God as well. This is a choice for man to make, not a sentence that God imposes. It is God's most fervent desire that none of His children should perish, but that all should have everlasting life."

These answers made enough sense to me that I felt satisfied in my budding faith. At the same time God was using Matthew to answer my questions, He sent a minister to buy Mike's townhouse. Mike and he had numerous conversations that had opened Mike's mind and heart also to the voice of God. I guess since God had surely brought us together, He knew we would be a package deal, and in His infinite wisdom He had clearly been working on us simultaneously.

As the second escrow on my condo broke down I began to pray that God would help me to make this all work out for the sake of my daughters. Before long a woman came to see my condo. It turned out that she had lost her husband to cancer a couple of weeks before, just prior to the closing of an escrow they had begun on the purchase of a mobile home in a senior citizens park. Her husband had been the one in the couple who was old enough to qualify them for the senior park, and without him the park would not allow her to move in. She was about to be homeless as a result of the cruel rules of the park. What a heart wrenching situation. She needed a safe place to live as she had never lived alone in her life and my condo was in a security building. She also needed a short escrow and I was willing to close the escrow quickly for her.

I realized then that the sale of my condo was never in doubt. God had allowed the first two escrows to fall apart because he knew she would need my place to be available. He had answered her prayers as well as mine in one fell swoop. (What the heck is a fell swoop anyway?)

My greatest challenge then became finding a place to buy or at least rent before the accelerated escrow on my condo closed and left us all homeless. We were scheduled to begin looking that Friday afternoon. I had been talking with another client of mine that day and had described my situation. He explained to me that having faith in God meant that sometimes you had to step out on that faith, not just in faith, but on that faith. He compared it to that scene in the third *Indiana Jones* movie where the character had to cross a great chasm without a bridge. Indiana was told to step out on faith though the ravine was deep and wide and there appeared no way on earth that it could be crossed, but he did as instructed and just as he took that first step of faith off that cliff, something solid, but basically invisible, was suddenly there beneath his feet allowing him to cross. Without that faith he would have stayed where he was, frozen and seemingly without options. My client told me, "Step out on your faith, and I promise God will not let you fall."

I did. The last house we looked at that afternoon turned out to be the one we wanted to purchase. It was, however, also the one another couple wanted to purchase. As we were working out the details of the offer we were about to make on it, something (or someone) told me to increase the amount by a thousand dollars.

I trusted my instinct, or God's little inaudible voice, and told our agent to increase our offer by that amount. We beat out the other couple by exactly one thousand dollars. It also turned out that the house was vacant and that enabled us to move in quickly, and our next door neighbors happen to be wonderful people and devout Christians to whom we have become close.

I learned through what should have been a routine process that God is the Master of all plans and will use any situation to reveal

Himself to us if we will only open our hearts up to look. I also discovered that if you will trust Him you will see that He has everything well in hand, in His hands.

chapter twenty-two

HEALING RELATIONSHIPS

A wise man once said, "I'd rather be happy than right." It was the life philosophy that he credited with the success of his twenty year marriage. This is sage advice indeed. I know I've spoken of forgiveness in previous chapters, but it is such an integral part of healing relationships, and healing the relationships that you value is such an integral part of a journey to joy, that I feel it deserves a bit more attention. You see, it is not just about healing the relationships that gives forgiveness its value, but about turning the poison of anger into peace of mind. As long as you choose not to forgive you are in essence choosing to hold onto anger. Holding onto anger is much like holding onto a porcupine. It is painful and punishing, but mainly to yourself.

Anger is slow, bitter, and acidic, whether it's justified or not. It permeates all your relationships, not just the ones you have with those that have incited that anger. As I discussed earlier, it affects the way you feel, live, behave, and interact with everyone you meet. This became painfully evident in my own life right after my divorce in the way I behaved toward my own daughters. I freely confess to having numerous challenges in my personality, two of which are very little patience and a quick, explosive temper. Not good when combined with excess anger stuffed like gunpowder in the chamber of my mind. Factor in the enormous amount of stress on a full time working mother of two young children going through an ugly divorce, and you get a very volatile situation that can be quite dangerous.

As I progressed in my therapy and began to process all that unresolved anger, my relationship with Katie and Laura improved in leaps and bounds. Having exorcised the demons did not suddenly bestow upon me great quantities of patience, nor did it cure me of my lousy temper, but it did however infuse me with so much more inner peace than I had known previously that I became much calmer and more in control. I became a little slower to anger and a little longer on patience. It made a great difference in my life and the lives of my daughters.

I am incredibly grateful for that personal growth because now that Katie and Laura are teenagers we are unbelievably close. It frightens me to think that had I not expelled that anger I might have continued to spew my poison at them and could have done severe damage to them and their self-esteem and psyches, as well as to our relationships, damage that might not have ever been repaired. Instead they are very happy, well adjusted young ladies that are nowhere near the trouble I was already in at their ages. Believe me, they are not perfect kids and I am certainly not a perfect mother. I face constant challenges with them like every parent does with every kid

I was very concerned when they were young that they might not turn out to be well adjusted due to the often traumatic psychological effects of divorce on children. I had taken them several times to my counselor for evaluations and any necessary therapy to help them to cope with the situation and to avoid any lasting damage that the divorce might cause. My counselor assured me that they were doing well and adjusting nicely.

Initially upon our decision to divorce, Steve and I had agreed to be careful not to blame and bad mouth one another in front of the girls. I had read something that explained how young children gain a great deal of their identities and self-worth from the image they have of their parents, and that they are not capable of distinguishing the difference between who their parents are and who they are. Therefore if you insult the other parent in front of them, the child takes it as personally as if you had insulted the child directly. Remember a young child's capacity for reasoning is quite limited.

It was easy enough the first few weeks to refrain from playing the blame game around the girls, but once Steve changed his mind and began to want me to come back it became very difficult for him to keep his promise. When this happened he often broke down in front of the girls and then was quick to blame me for the divorce and tell them all about how he wanted us to be a family again, but that I refused to come back.

As indicated back in part one, that was the beginning of the scariest year of my life. Steve simply did not have the emotional maturity to handle the magnitude of his loss. He was just unable to cope with the hurt, the anger, and the helplessness. He had always been a macho control freak who suddenly found himself completely unable to control the situation, and unable to control me. There was nothing he could do to get me to come back or even give him another chance and he did not respond well to that sudden loss of power over me.

Steve could be an incredibly charming man (believe it or not) and every time we had broken up in the past he had been able to somehow persuade me to try again, but this time I understood how much courage it had taken me to leave. I was certain if I went back I would never again find that much courage and would only end up suicidal as before. As hard as it was for me to see him so hurt I knew if I gave even an inch I would be lost forever and I mean that in the most literal sense. I wanted to make everything alright for him, but going back to him would have only succeeded in trading my happiness for his. I was no longer willing to make that deal.

I wanted to hold you
during that storm
but I was the wind
and not at all warm.
I drew that pain
across your sweet face
as I slammed the door
again and again.

> *I'm weary of war.*
> *The one between us,*
> *the one inside me,*
> *as I fight to be yours*
> *and I fight to be free.*
> *And there's a war inside you;*
> *first you fight*
> *then you weep,*
> *long to rock me to sleep*
> *like a mother that loves*
> *and a child that fears.*
> *I speak, then you scream.*
> *neither one of us hears.*
> *You love then you hate*
> *'cause it's easier alone.*
> *You chase, but I wait.*
> *I'm fire, then I'm stone.*
> *How many times*
> *must we tear, must we shred,*
> *and rebuild and relove?*
> *We have given and taken,*
> *blessed and cursed*
> *this doomed love.*

He finally did begin to adjust, largely because he finally got involved with another woman. The problem was that it was the friend we had met back in our Lamaze class who had been babysitting the girls and was my source of daycare after the divorce. Occasionally he would be the one to pick up the girls from her. I guess one night he picked up more than the girls there. She had become separated from her husband not too long before we separated, and Steve and she ended up staying together for a few years. (This was before he began dating the bleached blonde alcoholic with the duffle bag that he met in a bar.) They always enjoyed it when people asked how they met and they answered "in Lamaze class."

Unfortunately it turned out to be a very destructive relationship for Steve. She was a pathological liar. Her own mother had called me up to warn me of this after the two of them had gotten together. To make matters worse, she was keenly aware of the Herculean efforts Steve had gone to in trying to win me back. She knew that at least for awhile after our split, he had remained in love with me. She perceived this as a great threat. I guess it never occurred to her that I had no interest in him when I left, and had even less interest by the time they had hooked up. In fact, When Steve first told me he was sleeping with her, I responded by saying "I don't care if you're sleeping with her, in fact there's only one woman in the whole world that I would be upset if you slept with, and that's me." For me to have gone back to him would have been like escaping from a burning building only to run back in and chain myself down.

Still blind to this deep resolve of mine to stay away from him, she engaged in a fervent campaign to keep us at odds with one another. She told him lovely stories about me, such as I was sleeping with everyone in sight. She even added that I refused to use protection. I guess she hoped to add a little fear of sleeping with me to the fury he was already engulfed in. Talk about throwing gasoline on a fire. She even threw in a little tidbit about me abusing the girls for good measure.

Then she began to work on me, convincing me that he was abusing her and had sort of lost it even beyond anything I had already seen, and was leaving his loaded handguns and marijuana within easy reach of the girls. Talk about drama! She should have been the writer. This was the same time period during which I was involved with Rob. The irony is not lost on me that all the while he was lying to me, so was she.

Needless to say, Steve and I were not getting along too well during that time. She had worked hard to ensure that, but we were not trying to destroy each other either. As I stated earlier, once Steve had moved on with his life and had gotten involved with a new love (such as it was) he had come to the conclusion that I should perhaps be allowed to live. What a guy! So our battles were far fewer and far less intense when they did arise, and we were both making an effort to keep them away from the girls.

They broke up not too long after Rob and I did. At that time Steve and I began putting two and two together and discovered all the lies she had perpetrated in order to keep enough tension between us to remove any risk of a reconciliation. Once we realized all the deceptions, we actually began to resurrect the friendship that had actually been the fabric of our relationship. This was something that had once seemed impossible.

Once two people have passed the point of retaining basic courtesy and respect for one another in a relationship, it is very difficult to re-establish those necessary, healthy boundaries. This must be done though to heal a relationship. Too many people try to remain in relationships where this courtesy has been breached without repairing this boundary. Think about all the relationships in your life where you get along. The respect is in place and you do not call each other names, attack each other, or seek to cause any harm to one another. In marriages and close family relationships, these boundaries are easily broken through, because we take for granted that the person will always stick around. This can make for an extremely ugly relationship. Steve and I had to relearn how to treat each other without resorting to the nasty fighting tactics we had become so used to. Furthermore, we had to forgive each other for all the damage we had done to each other in the past.

This required a huge amount of forgiveness on both of our parts. Steve needed to be able to forgive me for leaving him, and I needed to be able to forgive him for all the ways he had been abusive, both before and after our divorce. It was not easy for me, but I believed my daughters were worth it, besides, he had been such a huge part of my life since I was barely nineteen, it would have been sad to think that we could have never gotten past old hurts and allowed the only roles we played in one another's lives to be antagonistic roles like villains.

Katie and Laura were the big winners in all of this. They have the best case scenario when it comes to divorce. Once forgiveness took place, they have had two parents who get along very well and were able to simultaneously attend all of the important functions of their lives as well as all the social events that involve our mutual friends.

We try to remain on the same page when it comes to discipline and to back each other up when it comes to the rules. This does not mean that the girls are never able to manipulate one of us (usually Steve) to get their way. They have played us against each other as often as they thought they could get away with it, just like most kids.

Steve has grown a lot over the years. Let's just say he was a late bloomer. He and I have been able to count on one another in many instances where we may not have been able to count on other friends. He even gets along well with my husband Mike. We have often gotten together to watch a football game or take the kids to dinner. Steve refers to Mike as his husband-in-law, and even offered to give me away at our wedding.

Was it worth it to forgive him? You bet! Does he ever make me mad now? You bet! He still has some real problems and is not always dependable when it comes to his responsibilities or his drinking, but at least I am not trapped in a marriage with those problems anymore, nor am I subjected to his past forms of abuse.

The other relationships that I have been able to heal have also been hugely rewarding. Had I not forgiven my mother and healed that relationship I would be left now, just a few months after her death, with mountains of regrets and a hole in my heart where precious memories of loving moments we shared during the last seven years of her life reside instead. The pain of her passing would have been even further compounded by the anger I would have still held towards her, along with the guilt of not having made peace with her. What a waste and a shame that would have been.

Instead I was able to see my mother with complete acceptance of who she truly was, and how all that she had endured in her life had affected her and her ability to build close and healthy relationships. The emotional maturity I had gained as I grew had enabled me to understand her and her intentions and her limitations. Because of this, I was able to fully forgive her for the mistakes she had made while raising me.

A couple of years before she died I felt that the Lord was leading me to do more for her. I had been doing volunteer work in an attempt to bless the lives of strangers, and nothing for my own mother. So I offered to come up weekly and fix her hair for her. At fifty-five she had suffered a stroke that had rendered her only partially able to use her left hand and that made doing her hair difficult for her.

One day while we were chatting as I worked on her hair, the conversation turned to me and my life and the changes that had taken place in it. My mom then told me how proud she was of me and every aspect of my life. She even listed them for me, telling me she was proud of the job I'd done raising my girls and how wonderful they'd turned out. She said she was proud of all that I'd accomplished in my career, my choice in a husband (the second one anyway), the volunteer work I did, my Christian walk, and who I had become. Wow!

That is what every child seeks, their parent's approval. I was forty years old, but I finally knew I did indeed have it. Those words will warm me all of my days. Those words are the fruit of forgiveness, a priceless treasure that was a blessed reward for having made the effort to heal that relationship, and for having rid myself of the poison of anger that had infected me for far too long. It truly is better to be happy than right. Of course, I realize this is a best case scenario, but even if all forgiving does is replace anger with peace, I say it's a win-win.

Forgiveness is more a gift you give to yourself than anyone else. It is not saying to a person who hurt you that they did not hurt you, nor is it saying that what they did was right, or that they are somehow absolved of the responsibility for their actions. It is simply a choice you must make to let go of the anger that has done nothing but punish you. Even if your anger has been perfectly justified, it wields its power to rob you of your joy and does little or nothing to the recipient of that anger. It does not ease your hurt. It does not give you peace. It does not even grant you revenge, which by the way, does not accomplish any of these things either.

Forgiveness does not mean you are forgetting the infraction. You are simply moving on. This also does not mean you continue to allow the other person to hurt you. We dealt with that a couple of chapters back.

What forgiveness does mean is that you often have to be the bigger person. This is not the same as allowing others to walk all over you as you may have done in the past because of low self-esteem. This means that as you become more confident and more emotionally mature, you are able to allow people to believe you have made a mistake without it devastating your fragile ego. You can withstand being the one to apologize even when you may not truly feel you owe that apology, because you understand that it doesn't matter so much who is right and who is wrong as long as a better relationship can be begun, and that often requires a clean slate.

I have described some of the things that my sister Danni has done and said to me that were deeply hurtful. I could have listed other examples of such things but what's the use? I'm sure I have said things to her that were horribly inappropriate and left her deserving of an apology. I am also certain that I have been justified in my anger toward her.

Sure, it would have been nice for her to have apologized, but that was also probably not going to happen. Our relationship had been strained for many years when I felt the Lord urging me to apologize to her. I did not quite understand why He would ask that of me when I was certain I was much less guilty of hurting her. In fact, I didn't even believe I had the power to hurt her, as I was pretty sure she did not care too much what I thought of her.

I was obedient though and I called her up and apologized for having held ill feelings towards her for so long. I was able to do this because the Lord had pointed out that she had never meant to hurt me. She is not a mean or cruel person by any stretch. She is anything but. In fact, she is a very kind and generous person who has only good intentions. She had likely only wanted to help me all those times when she said things that cut me deeply, but her application was often lacking. Danni often thought that her criticism might be helpful to me. My mother also did this often. For example, my mother somehow believed that if she pointed out the weight I had gained, I would be enlightened and inspired to lose it, thereby becoming happier. Danni believed that pointing out what she saw as my errors in judgment might help me to see how better to accomplish my objectives.

Needless to say, her approach didn't work very well. I wondered if this propensity for "constructive criticism" is hereditary since it seems to run in my family. In order to be able to forgive Danni, I had to realize that, like my mother, she only truly wanted for me to have the best, be the best, and do the best. Also, like my mother, she was just not too terribly effective in helping me to achieve it.

Once I recognized this fact, I felt compelled to forgive her and, just as importantly, to ask her to forgive me. It was necessary to do both to heal this relationship, and it was one worth saving even if it meant I ate a small meal of crow. She had hurt me yes, but had certainly not abused me in some horrible fashion that would prove nearly impossible to change. Had I come out demanding her forgiveness, instead of offering mine, she likely would have only gotten defensive and that would not have healed anything.

When I realized that her words may have felt unkind, but her heart was not, I obeyed the Lord's leading and called her, apologizing for all the ill will and negative feelings I had long held for her. She was stunned and overwhelmed, and truly receptive to my overture. She confessed that I was right, that she had only wanted to help, and she realized that she had probably too often not gone about it in the best way.

That was a few years ago and to this day we are far closer than we had been since we were little girls who were totally dependent upon one another for our entertainment. Our relationship is not all of a sudden perfect. She still occasionally says things, as do I, that are more hurtful than helpful, but armed with the knowledge that she loves me and the wisdom I have gained that allows me to better understand her, I am far more able to let things slide, rather than take them as a personal attack that will go into my memory and be added to the scorecard I hold against her. When I forgave her I ripped up that scorecard I had long been keeping, the scorecard I added to with each new infraction I perceived. I still continue to make a conscious effort not to make a new one.

> *I gave what seemed to be*
> *a precious gift,*
> *a great sacrifice.*
> *It was a bit of my pride*

> *in the form*
> *of an apology.*
> *What I truly gave up*
> *was an enemy.*
> *What I received*
> *was a friend.*
> *I know now*
> *I'd rather be happy*
> *than right.*

Healing this relationship was different from healing my relationship with my mother, because I did not feel compelled to apologize to my mother, although I probably should have. Apologizing to Danni was well worth a swallow of pride. I told Danni not long ago while our two families shared a vacation house in the Sierra's that she had been the best part of my childhood. How heartbreaking it would have been to have lost that precious connection to my family and my history. This is even more true now that both our father and mother are gone. The relationships I have with my two sisters are now more valuable than ever.

There was a bonus for being a big person and extending my humble hand to her. It built character in me and brought a feeling of pride and peace knowing that I had come so far and had become enough of a person, that I could take my obnoxious ego out of the situation and do the right thing. I was proud that I had the confidence to remove my ego from such an emotionally charged situation and be obedient to the Lord and reap the great reward that lay in store for me by doing so.

We should never miss an opportunity to build our character. It is like a muscle. The more you exercise it, the more it grows and the stronger it gets. The less you exercise it, the more it atrophies and the weaker it gets. When your character is strong it is easier to manage those difficult situations that call it into use, but when it is weak, it becomes harder and harder to lift yourself above those tough situations in life that require it. Apologizing is one of those situations that definitely requires character, and forgiveness is a great way to exercise that muscle.

How many relationships are there in your life that might only require you to be the bigger person and forgive and offer an apology? Just as I have asked you to hold your own feelings up to the light of reason, I also urge you to search the hearts of the people that you may share some of these relationships with. So often their intentions are good while their applications are not. Judge the person based on their heart and their intentions. You will find more often than not that the person's intentions are harmless, even if their actions have not been. This new perspective allows you to take your ego out of the situation so that you can build a bridge and cross the chasm that has existed between the two of you.

We tend to automatically assume that people will respond in any given situation the same way that we would. This is just part of our human nature. We expect people to behave based on the same set of values and principles and with the same level of emotional health that we base our behavior on. All of our life experiences are different however, and so often our values and emotional health differ too, not to mention our personalities. These things naturally affect the way people behave. This sometimes will lead people to do things that we cannot understand, because they are things that we would not do. These basic differences often lead to disagreements and misunderstandings. It is important to take that into consideration when deciding whether their intentions are basically good and worth focusing on, and whether that makes their actions forgivable.

Once you have decided to forgive, even if it means that you need to be the one to apologize, the relationship can be healed as long as the other person is receptive and willing. If that is the case and the relationship has been salvaged, with the new boundaries set in place that come with healthy self-esteem, you should see the relationship begin to improve. If you do not, refer back to chapter twenty and determine how best to handle the relationship, if at all. Even if it does not become a healthy relationship, you will have worked the muscle of your character and will have grown a little more.

It is important to be objective and recognize your part in the dysfunction of a relationship as well. When my poor stepfather married my mother he was quite young (twenty-five) to be having to deal with two monstrous teenagers of twelve and fourteen. I see now that sometimes I was pretty darn cruel. I have too many memories of me teasing him and making fun of him. I even ridiculed him for his weight, something that he had struggled with his whole life. I can only imagine how hurtful it must have been for him to endure the cutting remarks I made.

I really faced this not long after Mike and I had moved in together and I watched the kind and nearly reverent way Katie and Laura treated him. I felt horrible when I thought back to what those first years living with me must have been like for my stepfather, Bill. I wrote him a long letter apologizing to him and asking for his forgiveness. He gave it freely and probably long before it occurred to me to ask.

He is a wonderful man and I hurt myself as much as him, because when he married my mother I at last had a chance to have a dad, a stable, loving dad, but I rejected him. I was a kid with the emotional maturity of a kid, and a damaged kid at that, who could not possibly believe a man could be a good and stable father figure just because he had married a woman with kids. I am relieved to say that at least as an adult I have treated him well and have deeply appreciated him. As my mother got sick we became very close and now that she is gone we are even closer. I told him a few weeks after my mother passed that sometime after her death it crossed my mind that I was now an orphan, albeit an old one, but that then I realized that even though my mother and father were both gone, my dad was still here. I am forty two years old and for maybe the first time in my life, I have a dad. That was the unexpected blessing hidden in my mother's passing. If you look hard in any tragedy you will always find a gift to extract. It's the way God works.

So sometimes it is not you that is the bigger person when an apology is made. Sometimes it is an apology long overdue, one you owe and need to be completely responsible for. When this is the case, face it, admit it, and do it, and you will likely find a burden lifted, a valuable relationship healed, and your character growing. This not only feels like something you can, and should, be proud of, but it is proof of your growing emotional health. Confident people are big enough to admit when they are wrong, not only because being happy is better than being right, but especially because being forgiven is better than appearing to be right.

So I grew as a person and salvaged precious and irreplaceable relationships. I had also been growing spiritually during this time. While Mike and I and the girls were settling into our new home and our new life as a four member family, I was beginning to recognize the way God works. He had been pursuing me, for all the years of my life, as any father would go after his beloved runaway child. He had left no stone unturned in His efforts to bring me home to Him, despite my rejection of Him and the fact that I never even noticed, let alone responded to, His overtures.

He had even been using my daughters to get to me. A friend of theirs had invited them to accompany her to the children's program offered every Wednesday night at her church. Just because I had no relationship with God at the time this invitation came, did not mean I did not recognize the value of introducing God into the lives of two impressionable girls in public school. Heck, I had after all, always included a nativity scene in our Christmas decorations and had explained its significance to the girls. Anyway, I had been bringing the girls to this church on Wednesday nights for several years prior to my rediscovery of God as an active, living, and loving being.

I however, had no intention of going to church. In fact, as a fiercely devoted football fan I would never have considered sacrificing watching a Raiders game filled with thrills for the boredom of church. I figured church was for funerals and weddings, not for Sundays. When I was still working in retail and employment applications asked if there were any days I would not be available to work for religious reasons, I used to write in "Sundays, because I worship the NFL." It was a flippant and extremely irreverent remark I know, but I meant it at the time.

I had asked my friend Matthew in one of our many religious discussions, if having a relationship with God mandated that you attend church, and was hugely relieved when he said no. So armed with that reprieve, as I was in the grocery store one Sunday (the Raiders were playing on Monday night that week), I was even able to ignore the guy who "just happened" to be standing there near the checkout. At the exact moment I was having my groceries rung up, he was shouting that we all needed to get back to church. He added that we shouldn't be there in the grocery store, and that we needed to be in the house of The Lord becoming reunited with Christ. I just chalked that one up to a crazy guy who had probably gone off his meds.

The manager of the grocery store was not exactly appreciative of this guy's message to leave the store and instead go to a church, so the guy was quickly ushered out the door. It was not before he had delivered a message though that I'm sure I was meant to hear, but was determined at the time to ignore. Matthew had told me I did not have to go, right? Right. So that was not really a message for me. That guy was just one of those fundamental lunatics who needed his medication and/or his psychiatrist. Yeah, that's it, that's the ticket.

I hadn't actually thought much about that little episode that had occurred just a couple of weeks earlier when I learned I would have to bring Katie to church one Sunday evening for some awards ceremony for the kids in that children's program in which the girls had been participating. I had every intention of sneaking out with her as soon as she returned to the pew we were sitting in with whatever award it was she would be receiving. It didn't quite work out that way. Instead of returning to my pew, she was ushered to the front pew with all of the other children. Darn! It was a conspiracy! I was trapped. Having been taught excellent manners and social graces, I was pretty sure it would be impolite and a little disruptive to walk to the front of the church and take her out while the pastor was preaching.

So I tried to make the best of this great inconvenience and began to listen to the sermon. I figured, what the heck? It couldn't hurt and might help pass the time until my release. Much to my shock and dismay, the sermon was kind of interesting. Actually, it was really interesting, and the pastor possessed something I never dreamed a pastor could have; a sense of humor. In fact, he was pretty darn funny and informative, and dynamic, and pert near exciting. (What the heck is "pert near" anyway?) But here's the real shocker; he was brief.

I would never have believed a pastor could preach that way. I looked at Katie and found her enrapt and even saw her hush the girl next to her who was trying to talk to her. Who'd have thunk it?

When we returned home that night we described the experience to Mike and Laura and asked them if they wanted to check it out some time? They both said "yes" and a couple of weeks later we all went to church on a Sunday evening, and the next thing I knew, we were attending regularly. Months later I learned that the grandparents of the girl who had first invited Katie and Laura had been praying for me to come to God and to church for years. I guess you could say, He answered those prayers. He always does.

As we began showing up weekly, the pastor came to our home to get acquainted with us. He discovered my passion for writing poetry. (I'm guessing you might have picked up on it too by now) Before long it was coming up on Easter and he asked me to write and recite a poem for the occasion.

I did so and found it to be very well received. This was the first time I had ever shared any of my work with an audience greater than one, and the one usually had to be hogtied to get them to listen. Having so many compliment me on the poem helped to give me the confidence to begin actively submitting my work to potential publishers. After receiving eight or nine rejection notices I submitted several pieces to a magazine called (ironically enough) *Our Journey*.

I literally jumped up and down with excitement and joy after reading the response letter that told me they wished to publish all of the work. My lifelong dream was coming true! I was getting published! I was indeed a poet after all and had been validated as such in a very tangible way.

I would go on to be published many more times and even to win several awards for my work. I was unwittingly taking a few more steps toward writing this book, that God had clearly planned for me to write. The most important steps I took however, were the ones I took way back when I walked into the office of the psychologist who taught me these skills and enabled me to begin this journey.

chapter twenty-three

WHO WE ARE IS NOT
HOW WE LOOK

The following Christmas Mike proposed marriage to me. I had fervently hoped he would. It was not that there was ever any doubt about whether or not we would marry. I believe we both knew that we would early on, but I have always loved Christmas with a passion and could not imagine a better present than Mike's eternal pledge and formal proposal. The diamond ring was not too shabby either.

It is not so much Christmas that I love as it is the whole season. I have always found it brings out the best in people. A sense of hope and expectancy permeates the air. Even in all its secular meanings there lies the promise of magic and miracles. Now that we both knew it in biblical terms, there could have been no better day on which to propose formally and to make our instinctive beliefs that we belonged together for all time official. My entire family celebrated the good news when we arrived at my mother's later that Christmas day.

The following Sunday at church we asked the pastor to marry us there that summer. Yeah, I know, but better late than never. It was a beautiful celebration that not only served to pledge our eternal love and commitment in front of our friends and family, but also included many of them. My daughters gave me away. I believed it was their duty since they were the ones who would now have to share my life. Julie was of course my maid of honor. The pastor's wife sang and my sister Katrina catered the reception at our house. I compiled this poem from some of the poems I had written for Mike during our relationship and had the pastor recite it during the ceremony.

> *Today we stand*
> *at the very epicenter*
> *of our universe,*
> *sprinkling starlight*
> *in an otherwise ebony sky.*
> *It is both moon and sun*
> *fairly bursting in our kisses*
> *that have caused our edges*
> *to begin to blur*
> *and fade into one another.*
> *For we have left our fingerprints*
> *upon each others souls*
> *and we have found our homes*
> *in one another's hearts.*
> *And so today we marry*
> *the one who holds our hand,*
> *the one who holds our heart,*
> *the one who holds our life.*

I would love to tell you that since marrying Mike everything's perfect. It isn't. I would love to tell you that since my counseling I have become perfect. I did not (but then, you probably already figured that out). I would love to tell you that since I entered into a relationship with Christ my life is perfect. It is not. (I bet you guessed that one too.) I would love to tell you I am never plagued by self-doubts. I am. I would also love to tell you that I never criticize or berate myself. I do.

The truth is while my life is immeasurably better since I began doing my inner work and since finding the truth spiritually, I still face challenges continually. Some are new and some are the same old ones I have always had to do battle with. The difference is that now I possess the tools to handle them better, especially the old ones.

I confess that sometimes I don't handle them as quickly as I should, allowing the self-criticism to go on far longer than I should before reminding myself that I don't deserve all that inaccurate garbage my brain is spewing out from an old and crummy emotional habit. I'm not making excuses for myself (alright, maybe I am), but I still live in the same world that you live in, the same world that has largely controlled the image we are constantly shown as the standard to meet and I still fall hopelessly short of that ideal image. I still occasionally wrestle with the idiocy of paying even the slightest bit of attention to all the junk the media spits out. I have to remain a diligent caretaker of my self-esteem and emotional health and that requires me to resist subscribing to the ridiculous standards that society as a whole has bought into.

The media is continually shoving a barrage of air-brushed perfection and otherwise impossible standards down our throats. Those of us who make up the baby-boomer generation (which is the largest living generation in our country) have grown up on T.V. and the images it has always projected as the minimum standard of beauty; the standard necessary for gaining just acceptance, let alone accolades in our society.

It was hard enough to compete as a mother with the likes of June Cleaver and Donna Reed, but now that we live in a society where the demands imposed by a basic standard of living nearly force most of the mothers of this upcoming generation to produce income as well, we are faced with standards of being a beautiful, nurturing, Betty Crocker with a high powered career. We are now expected to be able to match up to Claire Huxtable of the Cosby Show, with her career as a highly paid attorney, who is thin and beautiful (even in her forties after having had three kids), is a perfect parent, and has married a doctor who is equally perfect. Sure, no problem, unless of course you view a minor detail like reality as a problem. Heck, how many of us could live up to those standards even for the twenty-two minutes a day Claire Huxtable did on that sitcom, let alone for the twenty-four hour days we face, seven times a week, fifty-two weeks a year?

These are the standards we, as mothers, have been handed over and over again, courtesy of American television. We are often so vulnerable when it comes to our self-esteem that we buy into these standards and hold ourselves accountable to them in some sick and impossible to win mind game.

It's not enough that we have grown up in the mirror of this media bombardment that demands that we all be flawless Barbie look-alikes as women and that men be perfect like Ken dolls. Now we all have to incorporate those impossible standards into every aspect of our lives; our careers, our homes, and our parenting. The media bombardment is only getting worse. Our kids are now growing up with more media than ever. It is louder, comes more often, and has more outlets (not to mention less values) than we ever could have imagined when the baby-boomer generation was still in its infancy.

What effect has this had on us? Plenty and little of it good. How many of us even have a winning lottery tickets chance of achieving those lofty standards set forth for us? How many of us still feel as though we are supposed to and have therefore fallen grotesquely short of those standards? How many of us punish ourselves with feelings of failure and worthlessness because we do not look like supermodels, we do not earn like supermodels, and we do not enjoy glamorous lifestyles like supermodels? Again I say, "plenty."

How many of us believe we would be happy and deserving of love if only we were prettier? Too many. So many of us misplace our admiration, looking up to those who possess physical beauty with little regard for, let alone knowledge of, their true character. We admire Madonna more than Mother Teresa when God knows Mother Teresa contributed more to society than any media star ever will. Think of those who have contributed the most to our society and you will likely think of people like Albert Einstein who was not exactly drop-dead gorgeous. I have read the New Testament many times and have never come across a physical description of Jesus Christ. Why? Because how he looked didn't matter. It had nothing to do with who He was and could not have added anything to the enormous gift that He gave us. The sad truth is too few of us value the huge contributions made by those who have true character and great ability, and get caught up instead in admiring the pretty people the media spoon feeds us.

Most of us do not believe we must be as smart as Albert Einstein or as selfless as Mother Teresa to be valuable, and yet we easily subscribe to the idea that we must look like Britney Spears or we have no value at all. Worst of all, there are those of us who subscribe to the insane notion that we must be as smart as Einstein, as giving as Mother Teresa and look like Britney Spears to be valuable.

These are not reasonable standards to hold ourselves to. In fact, they are absolutely ridiculous expectations. We should all know this by now after the chapter on holding our negative thoughts and emotions to the light of reason. Remember though: what you know does not always translate into what you feel.

Those unrealistic expectations had an interesting effect on me in regard to my dress size. When I was thirty-five and still smoking I was a lovely little size eight. At forty two and not smoking I am a far less lovely size twelve. I am twenty pounds heavier than I was back then, and though I am quick to remind myself that at least it is healthy fat rather than the easily diseased tissue of a smoker, I still do not like to see it in the mirror. I vacillate between bowing to my overgrown vanity and waging all out war on those twenty pounds or just reminding myself of what an unimportant detail like dress size is and that I should just relax about this change and accept it as part of the aging process.

I don't care much for all the little wrinkles that seem intent upon multiplying upon my face either, but apart from taking a little longer on my morning make-up, in a slightly less than valiant attempt to disguise what time has done on the playground of my face, I pretty much accept them as unpleasant, but inevitable. Perhaps that is because, short of surgery, there is little one can do to reverse those lines, but weight, that's a different story. There is a multi-billion dollar industry devoted solely to convincing us that we can and must reverse weight gain.

The ironic thing is that when I was still married to Steve, and likely at the all time low of my self-worth, I was that same size eight, but found my body utterly repulsive. I had expressed this to the marriage counselor that we had seen and was told by her that I suffered from what she referred to as a distorted body image. Though my body looked great to others, I saw it as horrible because even when I looked beautiful, I didn't feel beautiful. I expected myself to be the same size I had been when I married in my twenties, rather than the size I would naturally be in my thirties as a non-smoker who'd had two kids. My expectations were unrealistic and yet I despised myself for not being able to meet them. It was unreasonable not to feel beautiful then, but I didn't.

Feeling beautiful is actually more important and more valuable than being beautiful. I know a very large African-American woman who does not fit the supermodel image of beauty that we are continually being told is the standard we must meet. She will tell you she is beautiful though, because she feels beautiful and does not need some marketing expert to make that decision for her. The best part is, when you are around her you believe she is beautiful also.

This is because happy, confident people are so much more attractive than people who are cursed with low self-esteem. Often people who feel that they are lacking are only able to see their flaws, and they are certain that everyone else only sees their flaws. They may even draw attention to their flaws. How comfortable is that to be around? Confident people are not focused on their flaws and therefore those around them do not notice them either. When a person likes him or herself they are happier, and happy people draw others to them, like honey draws flies, because happy people are pleasant to be around. They are more uplifting and inspiring and optimistic and upbeat. Perhaps this is because, being aware of their gifts, they are able to keep their shortcomings in perspective and remain positive instead of negative like many people with poor self-esteem are so prone to being.

A couple of years ago I had gained enough weight to have made size fourteen dresses tight and yet I barely noticed. You see, I had separated my self-image from my body image when I healed my self-esteem and had come to understand that my flaws were just a small detail about me. They were not me and could not eclipse all the positive traits that contributed to the whole of me. My dress size, like my lousy temper, is not who I am, but rather just one of the many, many parts that make up who I am. Who you are, just as who I am, is always greater than the sum of those parts.

I realized one day that even my temper has its place in me. It is just another way, certainly a less positive way, that my intense passion manifests itself in me. This same passion enables me to write, to love deeply, to fight for underdogs, to protect my children, to create artistically, to keep learning, and to serve The Lord. Though I try to control my temper I have come to accept that it, like my extra padding, is just one part of me and certainly does not make me unlovable.

As women age
our thighs become
a sweet, soft place to land.
Even the tops of them
become larger, more lavish,
a lap for children, our children,
and our children's children,
a warm, inviting place
where the hard discomfort of bones
and the world
cannot be felt by the small,
where the small can sink down
and settle into our love.
Yes, so often as we get older
we expand,
fill our bodies
with the blessing of wisdom,
are recreated, reinvented,
turned from the long, lean lines of youth
into those who bear the lines of having lived
and learned,
not only to love,

but to love well.
Our hips bloom
beneath the sunshine of years,
become full blossoms
under our skirts.
We morph into mothers
and grandmothers,
gain more and more
of those golden cells
that live as laps.
We gain more of those life lessons
that enable us to grasp life and living
with cerebral clarity
and passionate wisdom
unreachable in youth,
as we are finally fed
those unknowable truths.
We become endowed with experience,
become better lovers,
better livers,
better humans,
better givers,
able to bear the depths
and reach the heights,
become slow of step,
but quick of mind,
designed for comfort, for holding,
for light and for love
and for those things that matter,
those things that will last.

Perhaps you struggle with your weight, maybe it's a personality trait that stubbornly remains to taunt you into feeling like a failure, or maybe it's something as permanent as your height that you are unhappy with. I refer you back to the Serenity Prayer. If it is some-thing unalterable that you perceive as a flaw and feel badly about, you need to learn to accept it and to keep it in the proper perspective as just a small part of you. It is not you.

I would like to be taller than five foot two, but have long accepted that I cannot do a thing about that except buy a step-stool. I can assure you that I do not waste any mental or emotional energy lamenting over my height. I would like to say only kind, witty, and intelligent things, but that is also impossible. The difference is, I can consciously make an effort to think before I speak, thereby minimiz-ing the chances of saying things that would be unkind or stupid.

I have the wisdom to realize that I cannot change my height, but can attempt to improve myself as a person and to try to grow as a human being, as long as I never lose sight of the fact that I am already a priceless and perfectly made (notice I did not say perfect, but perfectly made) human being who is inherently deserving of love. I am not now, and have never been, expected to be perfect.

It's fine to try to keep a handle on those shortcomings that you can improve. For example, I don't allow myself the amount of food I would really like to consume. (I really love to eat!) I don't lose my temper at my boss, whom, I might add, is mightily deserving of a good tongue lashing, if not a beating. I could list plenty more examples of flaws I possess, but try to minimize, as well as flaws that I cannot do anything about, but I think you get the picture. The important thing is not to become obsessive about your shortcomings or to allow them to define you or to rob you of your belief in your self-worth.

I do not compare myself to others for that is another complete waste of time and energy. There will always be someone who has or is more of something you desire to have or be, and someone who has or is less of that something. There will always be someone who is pret-tier, smarter, kinder, etc…and someone who is not as pretty, as smart, or as kind. How we compare to others is completely inconsequential to who we are or how valuable we are.

For example, my friend Julie is almost always able to keep from losing her temper, even though she has two kids, while I struggle to keep a lid on mine, or to at least keep it confined to the nasty little names I call other drivers. My friend Patty is able to maintain her ideal body weight with little or no effort. She is a lovely, tall blonde over forty with two kids. I know, I know. It isn't fair.

I would have to survive on twelve-hundred calories a day, or maybe even just twelve, with several hours a week devoted to exercise to have even the slightest chance at getting rid of all my extra padding, let alone keeping it off. This does not make Patty better than me, luckier yes, different; yes, thinner; definitely yes, but not better. That extra weight does not make me a bad person. Maybe it means that I am just a bit more lazy than I am vain, but even so, there is no amount of extra weight that means I'm a bad person. I am one of those people who absolutely hates exercise. To make weight loss more difficult, given my passion for creativity, most of my hobbies and interests are sedentary pursuits. It requires an enormous amount of effort and discipline on my part to get me to exercise. This can make us less healthy and can subject us to a lot of heartless and cruel judgment, but it cannot make a good person, innately deserving of love, into a bad person who does not deserve love.

A person who is lucky enough to meet the media's standard of beauty is not automatically good any more than the person who is not lucky enough to meet that ridiculous standard is automatically bad. I have always told my daughters that the fact that they are very pretty is just luck, but the content of their character, those things that they have control over, are the things that matter, the things that define them. They cannot choose their genetics and therefore their looks, but they can choose to be kind and compassionate and to exercise integrity in their words and their actions. Those are the things that we should all be striving to maintain a high standard for. These are the only things that truly matter, the only legacy that will not only remain here, but even follow us to heaven.

I also have a friend who weighs roughly double what she should ideally weigh based on those strict media standards. She is one of the kindest, brightest, warmest people I have ever met. Do I love her any less than my friend who easily maintains her ideal weight? Of course not. So why should I deny myself any love based on my weight? How shallow and absurd would that be? Why should I expect myself to be perfect in order to be able to love myself, when I would never demand perfection from my friends in order for them to gain my love?

Just as I have repeatedly written in this book, *"What you choose to look at determines also what you do not see."* I do not focus on the body size of my friends or on any of their shortcomings. I look at their gifts and find them easy to love. Again I remind you; love is a choice.

One of the women at the rehab house asked me to stay after group one evening so we could talk. She is one of the sweetest women I have ever known, but she is very overweight and was really struggling with her self-esteem because of it. I tried to help her to separate her self-image from her dress size. I used an analogy that I hoped would put it in perspective for her, just as I had hoped the analogy involving the homeless hamburger thief, would help put past behaviors into perspective.

I explained that our bodies are simply vehicles for our souls which are the very essence of who we really are. Our bodies will end up in the ground one day while our spirits will enter heaven to be with God. We must do the necessary upkeep on our bodies and preventive maintenance that we can to keep them running well for as long as possible. This is mandatory because unlike a car, we will never be able to go out and buy a new body when this one becomes inefficient, or beyond repair.

If our car breaks down we cannot get around. The same is true for our bodies and our quality of life is inextricably linked to the condition (health) of our bodies. We need to remember however, that whether our vehicle (body) is a sixty-six Nash Rambler or a two-thousand-six Mercedes SL, the real value lies in the cargo; the person within it. No one would give up their life for either car. What would be the point? If every person disappeared from the face of the earth tomorrow, what value would there be in any car?

Sure, some of us are lucky enough to be able to drive a Mercedes and are cruising around with the body of a movie star, while others are not quite as lucky and may be driving a Ford Taurus or an old Volkswagen bus instead (relatively speaking, of course), but the true purpose of that car/body remains the same; to transport us (who we really are) down here on earth. I can't deny the ride may sometimes be better in a Mercedes than in that Rambler, but we absolutely have to understand that we are far more valuable than any vehicle we could ever occupy.

Let me attempt to put it in perspective in yet another way. Let's look at the average life expectancy of say seventy or eighty years. Even beautiful women are lucky if they are not gawky in high school and can reach their peak beauty in their late teens. Often it is closer to their early twenties when they hit their peak. Once they hit their thirties, or have children (whichever comes first), their beauty begins to descend that slippery slope we call aging. By their mid thirties the aging process begins attacking even the most flawless of faces with an endless supply of lines and wrinkles, not to mention the likelihood of additional weight.

So there you have it. If you're lucky enough to be born with the genes that create societies standard of beauty at all, you've got maybe twenty years at best to enjoy it. You can devote gads (whatever gads are) of time and money and energy trying to maintain that beauty, but it will be a fruitless battle, for even if you temporarily win the battle, you are guaranteed to lose the war.

What this really means is that even if you are in the minute percentage of people born beautiful, you will be so only for about a quarter of your life, and that is only if you're lucky. What will you base your self-esteem on for the other three quarters of your life? Do you see now why it is so important that you base your self-image on who you are and not on what kind of body you "drive" and your physical beauty?

Whether or not you are beautiful in society's classic sense is no bigger detail of who you are than whether you are right or left handed or whether or not you can hit a fastball, which you've probably guessed, I can't. The greatest challenge is that how we look is the first thing anyone sees about us and that is why we place so much importance on that small aspect of ourselves. We assume we are being judged based on our looks and it's sad to say, but very often we are. That is also why it is so important that we build our self-esteem to a healthy level and base it on the things that are truly important and are constant parts of us, the things we know are there even if they are not readily obvious to others when we first meet them. It is vital to know our true worth so that we don't leave our feelings of value subject to what others see.

If we all had to be beautiful in order to have high self-esteem, then the huge majority of us would have no chance at happiness. Only the pretty people would have a shot at the most basic and inalienable right we have as human beings. Sadly enough, I know first hand that even being pretty is no guarantee of happiness, let alone healthy self-esteem. How sad would it be to make being physically attractive the main criteria for self-esteem? How ridiculous it is that we rarely understand how trivial the true value of beauty is and how invaluable true character is. It should be taught along with math and reading if you ask me, right along with the skills for building self-esteem. After all, happier people are more productive people in every aspect of their lives.

Even understanding all of this, I still wrestle with what society says I should look like and I freely admit to wishing I were taller, slimmer, and bustier, but I do try to always keep it in perspective. At a size eight while married to Steve I looked in the mirror and hated what I saw. I thought it was because of how I looked, but at a size fourteen after healing my self-esteem I looked in the mirror and loved myself. I may not have loved my figure, but the important thing is that the value of my figure was in proper perspective. I loved myself and it had nothing to do with how I looked.

These skills you have hopefully learned by now are a lot like a program to lose weight. Once you have changed your eating habits and lost the weight you do not automatically become someone who is never hungry and tempted by favorite, familiar, fattening foods again. If you begin indulging in those foods occasionally you will probably be just fine, but if you begin giving in to those temptations all the time you will soon regain all the weight you lost and be right back where you started.

I continue to have to knock back my old demons and emotional habits that try to make me feel worthless. I face them often on some days and rarely on others, but they never win for long because I understand so much more now and I now possess the skills to keep them from making any real inroads in my life. I no longer allow them to snowball and to grow and gain momentum until they change the way I feel about myself. Yes, sometimes I put myself down, but the difference is that now when I do it, I no longer believe it, not even as I say it.

You must remain vigilant and continue in your new and healthier habits or you will begin to lose the ground you have gained. You must continue to exercise the skills you have acquired to remain emotionally healthy, just as you would need to exercise your body and continue with the healthier eating habits you would have acquired during weight loss to remain physically healthy.

I often have to remind myself that I am a good and lovable person deserving of all good things. There are still times I even question whether I could have possibly accomplished all that I have. Sometimes I still hear that nagging little voice that wonders and worries that perhaps I am really not capable of handling all these responsibilities. That voice whispers that I am somehow still a little girl, helplessly caught in the chaos of a dysfunctional family and that my new life is but a house of cards that will soon fall down, and all the world will know that I am a big fraud. This is that old emotional habit of nameless anxiety that occasionally pops up and is only too happy to hook up with some of those other old emotional habits like self-criticism and feelings of failure.

When these old ghosts come haunting, I need to remain in control and stay reasonable in identifying them for what they truly are, rather than giving in to them and subjecting myself to their cruel and absurd insults. I can now laugh at these demons and I no longer allow them power in my life. I try to dismiss them the moment they rear their ugly heads. I share this with you to show you that it is an ongoing process that you must remain committed to. Remember, life is a journey, not a destination, and I am still on my journey to joy, but thankfully, I am much farther down the road than I once was.

So you see, I have never been, and am not now, and never will be, perfect. Big deal! And as they say in many a cheesy T.V. commercial, "but wait, there's more." My life is not perfect either, and I never expect it will be. I am just grateful that it is so much better than I could have imagined ten years ago it would be.

Actually my life is somewhat boring now compared to the vicious cycle of drama it used to be caught in. Yeah! I find the richness of joy and fulfillment to be far superior and infinitely more thrilling than the exciting and dramatic chaos living crisis to crisis brought. I now have a calm, predictable life filled with good, healthy people and relationships, a pretty constant sense of joy, occasionally interrupted by life's challenges. That along with the confidence to handle challenges and pursue my dreams and indulge in my passions, is an immeasurable reward for having done the inner work to trade my life of drama for my life of peace.

I no longer create or attract crises, chaos, and drama in my life, either consciously or sub-consciously. I no longer perpetuate my own victimization in this way in a sad and desperate cry for attention and rescuing and distraction from my deeper pain and the emotional habits that have come with it.

Now I do not need the attention of others as some warped way of feeling important. I matter to myself and in my emotional health the attention that I do receive comes because of my strengths and not my weaknesses. I have become far more valuable to those around me as well. There are no more roller coaster rides in my life except at amusement parks. There are no more sky high peaks and hell deep valleys.

My life is a fairly smooth ride and one that is welcome. My joy does not fluctuate wildly. It is not dependent upon the number on the scale. It is no longer subject to the vicious mental attacks I used to perpetrate upon myself, nor is it dependent upon my latest triumph or my latest setback. It is not dependent on a man, not even my husband. The joy and peace that I feel is stable because it comes from a good and healthy self-image and a life I have built out of people and pursuits that I love as well as a saving knowledge of, and a loving relationship with, Jesus Christ.

chapter twenty-four

BUILDING THE LIFE
YOU DESERVE

There was a sort of natural progression in my journey to joy. I had hit that proverbial "bottom" inciting me at last to commit to making the changes that were necessary if I were to ever become happy in a lasting way. I entered into counseling and began digging through the trash heap of my past searching for, finding, and examining, the events and the people that had damaged me and had forced me to deviate from the person God had created me to be.

I processed all the unresolved hurt and anger that I had been unable to cope with as a child and as a damaged adult. Doing that enabled me to purge myself of all the poison that had been motivating me to make poor choices that were destined to only cause repeat failures as I tried in vain to treat the symptoms of my unhappiness while ignoring the disease.

I began to recognize the destructive ways I spoke to and treated myself and to replace that negative behavior toward myself with positive, constructive behavior. I started feeling better about myself and began recognizing all of the attributes, talents, and gifts I had been blessed with and learned that they occupy far more of who I am than my shortcomings do. As I changed my focus from my weaknesses to my strengths, and the unique combination of traits that make me who I am meant to be, I found my self-worth and learned to value myself and to love myself for who I am, and to stop berating myself for who I am not.

I set new boundaries in my relationships by refusing to tolerate disrespectful and hurtful behavior. I became more adept at identifying my feelings and became more comfortable with processing and communicating them.

I learned to become more reasonable and logical as I gained emotional maturity in assessing situations and relationships, both past and present, helping me to see from other perspectives and freeing me from personalizing all the behavior of others. These new abilities enabled me to stop feeling responsible for the bad behavior of other people and to stop believing that I deserved that bad behavior.

I grew the confidence and courage to make changes and improvements in my life. Having healed myself and having grown as a person, I was able to heal those relationships that had been less than healthy, but were salvageable and valuable to me. I had even sought and found the answers to my spiritual questions.

After achieving all of those important milestones of growth I was free to transform my life even more. I recognized that though I was at last happy with who I was and even where I was, my life could be even more fulfilling and a source of even greater joy.

My greatest dreams had been realized; I had found and married my true soul mate, bought a lovely home in a great suburb of the San Francisco Bay Area, had wonderful, close and loving relationships with my daughters who were on track for success in every aspect of their lives, and I had been published as a poet.

I had indeed traveled very far on my journey to joy. Then it became clear that it was my turn to help others to achieve the joy in their lives that I had begun to enjoy.

By this time Mike and I had both become quite active in our new church. Mike, Laura, and I all enjoyed a love of drama (the theatrical kind, not the psychological kind) and had joined the drama ministry at our church. As adults, Mike and I had long since dismissed any interest in drama because we were certain no opportunity to indulge in it would ever arise, but surprise, here in our church there were plenty of opportunities. We thoroughly enjoyed the creative outlet the drama ministry provided for us and were grateful that we could bless others through it in some small way besides.

I explored other avenues of creativity as well, like drawing and painting, and was glad to be good enough to at least be pleased, though certainly not thrilled, with the finished results of these endeavors.

I felt compelled to do more for others though and began volunteering at the local homeless shelter for families. Mike had always done a great deal of volunteer work and that had inspired me to do more of it. So I began doing "story time" for the kids at the shelter. It was great fun and combined my passion for drama with my love of reading which I hoped might be passed on to some of the kids through my efforts. I tried to infuse a little drama into the stories by delivering the stories with different voices and appropriate inflections that I felt would make the characters more alive and the plots more interesting. I hoped the effort would lend authenticity and imagination to the readings.

I have to confess, however, to some great frustrations arising some nights at the shelter, because many of the kids there had been through a lot and were not all that well adjusted or well behaved. There were times when I couldn't persuade any one of them, let alone all of them, to calm down and listen quietly and respectfully. On one or two occasions I simply could not overcome the chaos caused by the more rambunctious kids so that I could be heard by the few attentive ones.

I gave up in despair one evening and left the shelter well before the designated ending time. As I drove home that night in complete frustration I considered not returning and was questioning whether I was doing any good at all. Suddenly a Scripture entered my mind. I had no idea when I had ever read it or heard it, but it was there as clear as if I had a passenger sitting beside me reading it aloud to me. It turned out to be Matthew chapter twenty-five, verse forty and said, "That which you do for the least of my brothers, this you do for me." I did indeed return to the shelter.

About that time my church had a vacancy in leadership for directing women's ministries. Truthfully, I had never really cared all that much for women as a gender. I had always related better to men and had lived determined to enjoy all the freedoms they had. I had often been accused of "thinking like a man" in fact, and I assume that helped me to succeed in my career in such a heavily male dominated industry.

Now I don't mean to imply that I don't love my women friends, but I have often found that many women are extremely insecure and can behave in jealous, petty ways, especially toward other women. If those other women happen to be more attractive or more successful, those shaky, insecure behaviors and comments can quickly multiply. It seemed to me that when I was younger I often had to work harder at my relationships with other women in order to convince them that I was actually a nice person, while I have rarely found this to be true with men. I have always been more comfortable around men and have enjoyed many male friends because of that. I just believe that women may be more susceptible than men are to having low self-esteem and being insecure, perhaps because they are more emotional by nature and more likely to express their feelings in one manner or another. So to say I was slightly apprehensive about becoming a glorified (or un-glorified) social director for women would have been an understatement.

Anyway, I felt as though the Lord was nagging me (by nagging me I mean relentlessly urging me) to volunteer for the position of Director of Women's Ministries. I could not quite bring myself to do this however. Though my self-esteem had risen considerably, I had very little experience as a Christian and none as a Christian leader, so I did not believe I had much to bring to the position. I hinted a couple of times, that I would be willing to help someone do it, but the hints were not picked up on, so I kept the leadership qualities that I did innately possess to myself and allowed the position to go unfilled for another nine months.

God did not give up though. He continued to nag me about it until His relentless reminding became so loud and persistent that I was finally nearly forced to acquiesce to His incessant calling. I approached the pastor, who by this time had, along with his wife, become very good friends of ours. If it had not been for that friendship, I don't know that I would have been able to make the offer and risk the rejection of putting myself out there. Rejection did not come.

My offer was met instead with warm enthusiasm and I was immediately placed officially in the position.

My first task as director of women's ministries was to put together a women's retreat. This event was traditionally meant to encourage fellowship and bonding among the women of the church as well as to help impart a bit of enlightenment and growth as Christians. The retreat was to be led by a knowledgeable speaker over the course of a hopefully fun filled weekend away together. Having become aware of the poor self-esteem in many of the women, I felt compelled to teach one of the sessions myself on building their self-esteem using some of the skills I have written about here, the same skills that I had learned to use to build my own. When I brought this idea up to the pastor and his wife, they both thought it was a great idea and should be done.

So one Saturday morning (my precious, designated writing time), I began to write the outline as well as the content I would cover in the session. It turned out to be a true "God moment" as the words came to me faster than I could even write them. Normally, even for a passionate writer, words are labored over in pursuit of quality. There was no labor in this endeavor, only flow, and incredibly quickly, I had five typewritten pages of text material to teach. It turned out to be a very worthwhile session that weekend, touching some of the women who were deeply in need of it. It would also turn out to be the first seed God would plant in me as He led me to give back in this manner.

This was not the only seed planted during that retreat. A woman accepted Christ as her savior that weekend and last I heard she was being actively used by God to spread His love and share the truth with many people in the state of Iowa where she now lives.

One thing I was not blessed with is a long attention span. Once a challenge is met by me I am easily bored and can lose interest. This was certainly the case with the women's ministry. My attention had soon turned outside the church toward all the people in my community who are in need financially, emotionally, and spiritually, like those children at the homeless shelter.

Both Mike and I felt (and still feel) the true purpose of a church should be about showing God's love in the community, especially to those who do not know The Lord, but desperately need to. Too many churches fall into the complacent habit of being a religious social club, where God's love is limited to the pews and the potlucks rather than being generously and consistently proven outside the building where it is needed most.

This time I was not uncomfortable about approaching the pastor. I nagged him to allow me to start an outreach ministry, almost as much as God was nagging me about it. After awhile, he agreed and Mike and I formed a committee with others in our church who shared our desire to reach out. We all felt compelled to do kind deeds for the needy in our area and to give God the credit for those deeds, so that those who do not have a relationship with Christ would come to see, feel, and experience His love, rather than just hear about it.

We encouraged the congregation to get involved and to do the same in a variety of ways. One of the ways in which Mike had been led to minister was to give out free coffee and donuts on the streets of Oakland along with simple business cards that I'd had printed up that read only "Because Jesus Loves You." There he ministered to the homeless and to addicts and to immigrants and struggling families.

I accompanied him one morning and ended up meeting three women from a newly established Christian rehabilitation house for drug and alcohol addicted women. They were on their way to a nearby Narcotics Anonymous meeting. I instantly felt compelled to help them in any way I could and returned to my church and requested donations of clothing and toiletries that they desperately needed.

As I began to get to know the leadership over my many visits with these requested items, on impulse I offered to teach that same session on building self-esteem to the women in the rehab house. The house counselor loved the idea and she and the pastor in charge of the facility immediately arranged it.

My job had forced me to get used to public speaking as I often had to do in-service training sessions for the end users of my products, and that experience combined with an outgoing personality and decent speaking skills honed sharp by years of sales work, made this an easy transition for me.

The group session went over very well with the women and left me feeling as though I had been able to make a small difference in their lives. I had only intended to teach that one session though I assumed that I might be asked to repeat it every so often as new women came into the house. They had other ideas however. Much to my surprise they asked me to come back every week to teach this group session. I knew I didn't have the time to commit to a weekly session, but I offered to come every other week, even though I had no idea how I would have enough material to cover other sessions.

As it turns out, there was plenty of material, and I have been teaching these sessions for five years now as I mentioned earlier in this book. I have learned as much as I have taught by doing this, enough in fact to help fill this book.

I cannot express all that I gain from giving back like this. I deeply love this work and feel as though in doing this I have found one of my true and anointed callings in life. It is as though it is something I was born to do. I was. In fact God had this planned for me long before I was born.

He endowed me with certain gifts and abilities that when combined with my life experiences and my passions have enabled me to do this well. Romans chapter eight, verse twenty-eight says that "All things work together for good for those who love God and are called according to His purpose."

> *It is only now that I recognize*
> *those memories that stand clear,*
> *shining as defining moments*
> *in my life,*
> *moments that reinvented*
> *who I am*
> *and where I would go;*
> *pivotal, directional moments,*
> *moments that carried an epiphany*
> *in on their wings.*
> *For now I see God's handiwork,*
> *how He'd been moving in my life*

all along,
pushing, prodding, giving, loving,
until He forced me
to stand up and take notice.
It was as though an angel
had come down
and pulled me from
the wreckage of my life,
leaving behind
a mass of twisted choices
and shattered priorities
that lay scattered
about the damage.
It is well beyond a healing,
for He has given me
the desire to heal others.
My heart is deep in the process
of transformation,
for when God touches you,
you are never, ever the same.

Nothing feels as good as helping others and making a difference in their lives. I believe we are all hardwired by God this way and that when we are helping others we are truly right with God.

Once your self-esteem has risen to a level of health you can begin really enjoying giving. You come to know and respect your boundaries, just as I knew not to over commit my time by agreeing to teach every week at the rehab house instead of every other week. You learn to recognize the difference between giving and having things taken from you. You become able to say "no" when necessary because a request may be too imposing or demanding and "yes" to those that feel right and are valued by those making the request. When granting a request is right, it becomes as much a blessing to you as it does to those who have requested it.

Using my gifts and the benefit of my experiences, even the painful ones, had given meaning and purpose to my life. I have positive outlets for my passions now and this makes my life so much more wonderful. I feel even better about myself by using what God has equipped me with to help others. It is another example of how your behavior can enhance your self-esteem.

It is time for one last exercise for you. Go back to your notebook where I asked you to list your abilities and to where I asked you to list your passions. Use this information you gathered about yourself to explore ways to add more meaning and purpose to your life. As you get to know yourself, you should also begin to have a better understanding of the things that you would like to pursue in your life and those things that would give your life greater meaning, joy, and purpose. If you need more detailed help in further shaping your new life into one that you would be passionately happy about and deeply fulfilled by, there are several books that can help you to do this. One is called *Living The Life You Were Meant To Live* by Tom Paterson. I read it and diligently did the exercises and prayer work and was led to write this book as a result. Another great book on the subject is Dr. Phil McGraw's *Self Matters*. There is also a book by Barbara Sher called *Live The Life You Love*. I strongly advise you to read one, if not all, of them.

As you examine all that you are and all that you have to bring to life's party, keep an eye toward not only what this world has to offer you, but also what you have to offer the world. The world has been robbed long enough of being blessed with all that you truly are and all that you really have to offer. A rich and fulfilling life consists of a symbiotic relationship between you and the world. This world is filled with unlimited opportunities to discover and pursue new and old interests. Explore yours and determine which ones you may want to incorporate into your life. This is why it is so important for you to not only know who you are, but also what you love. This information is vital to building a life you will love. I wrote this next poem well before I ever thought of writing this book, with no ulterior motive other than as a personal statement.

I love
my daughters
and husband
and the family
from whom I came.
I love my friends
and good conversation
and selling
and music
and books.
I love writing,
especially poetry,
and reading,
playing games
that are mentally challenging
and acting
and movies.
I love mountains
and trees
especially redwoods,
waterfalls and rivers,
the ocean
and sunsets.
I love roses
especially red ones,
clouds and rainbows,
thunder and lightening,
and animals;
dogs and cats
and those seen as exotic
in my suburban life,
but common in wild Africa
or the Amazon.
I love alligators
and crocodiles,
sharks and birds,
especially birds of prey.

*I love National Geographic
and the Smithsonian,
humor and sarcasm,
kaleidoscopes,
crystal and porcelain,
antiques
and tiny, fancy boxes.
I love perfume and lingerie,
flowers and ruffles,
lace and small perfume bottles,
and football,
especially the Raiders
and playing basketball and tennis.
I love colors,
especially bright ones
like scarlet and emerald,
amethyst and sapphire
and pastels
like lavender and aqua,
coral and sea foam green.
I love encyclopedias
and Roget's Thesaurus,
learning and growing,
gaining knowledge
and spirituality.
I love encouraging people
and giving genuine warmth
and small fragments
and whole bunches
of love.
I love wisdom,
acquiring it and sharing it.
I love church
and Sunday school
and mostly
I love God
from whom all this came.*

While the preceding is certainly not one of my better poems, it aptly expresses who I am through revealing what I love. If your lists from the earlier chapter are not as thorough as you now wish, use my poem as a formula and rewrite it replacing my passions with yours. Your finished product will help you to get a more detailed understanding of some of the things you may wish to include in your life, and those that you may choose to build your life around.

My sister Danni is a stay-at-home mom. If my home looked as lovely as hers I might want to stay home too. She is very creative and artistic, though not in the arts and crafts kind of way. Her canvas is her house and she has a true gift for decorating. She has a bold eye for color and style and instinctively seems to know what works together. She has done a magnificent job in creating a beautiful and unique style in her home and has tried things she was able to envision that would never have occurred to me. Frankly, even if I had thought of many of them, I would never have had the courage to try them. Yet she is able to produce breath-taking results in her decorating and I often seek her advice on my own decorating dilemmas. Thanks to her, I even have some walls with color on them now.

My other sister, Katrina, also has great flare, but her passion is cooking and entertaining rather than decorating. She sells home furnishings and manages a furniture store for a living, and her home is lovely also, but she really adores cooking. She brings the same bold and daring to her cooking that Danni brings to her decorating. Katrina is a gourmet cook and has such a gift for the presentation of her food that her ability to entertain surpasses many a professional. She may however fall just a tad short of Martha Stewart, but then again, she has no full time staff, nor a multi-million dollar company, but hey, she didn't have to do any jail time either, so it's a trade off.

At one time she was hired as the executive chef of a catering company even though she had no formal schooling for it. She received rave reviews from the clients she worked for. She also ran a small kitchen/snack bar at a private swim club for awhile as an outlet for her cooking passion. Her creativity combined with the knowledge she has gained and her instincts for how to combine, cook, and present foods, has brought her (as well as me and countless others she has fed) a great deal of joy.

There are unlimited ways to engage our world and to add pleasure to our lives and even the lives of others as we cultivate our interests, abilities, and passions. Sometimes the most difficult part is realizing what those specific interests are and how you may incorporate them into your life and use them to bless others. It is well worth the effort it may take to not only pursue them, but to share them. It really will maximize the blessings you receive from them. Who knows, you may even find a way to profit from your talents.

We are all given the task
with our lives
to paint what is not there,
what could never be
if not for us.
We are all born to something,
called to something,
even those of us
who are endlessly taunted
by all those flawless faces,
those genetically blessed faces
that buy for those,
fortunate enough to have them,
lives unobtainable
for the merely ordinary,
those of us who are
mocked by the mirror,
not graced
by the light of loveliness,
but rocked
by the randomness of fate.
We must listen closely,
hear our own art calling,
step into life
even when armed

with little more
than a pocketful of words.
It may seem as though
there are others able
to eat there whole lives
in one great delicious bite,
while we,
unremarkable, unrenowned,
do not flow through fluid days,
but must live instead with heroism,
both ordinary
and extraordinary.

EPILOGUE

As in many areas of this overly politically correct society we now live in, common sense seems to have deserted the arena of self-esteem. There is this ridiculous movement by some self-esteem fundamentalist fanatics toward removing competition and even many grades on school performance from children's lives.

There is concern from these people who are clearly overly enthusiastic about protecting children from feeling badly about themselves, that competition produces some winners and many "losers." Of course competition produces winners, but keep it in perspective people. Winners and losers in a game are just that, winners or losers of a game, not life.

Grades are a measurement of a child's grasp of certain academic material. This information is a necessary component of an effective educational system and helps students to avoid being unwittingly left behind. Of course it feels better to receive a high grade than a low grade, and it feels better to win a game than to lose a game.

But this does not mean there should not be competition or grades. Life will always be filled with successes and failures and children need to learn to handle both and feel good about themselves, regardless. It is all about perspective and helping children to understand, just as we adults need to, that each person is perfectly planned by God to be exactly who they are, and that a poor grade is not indicative of the quality of that person. Remember, every one of us equals more than the sum of our parts, and a lost game or a low grade are mere specks of sand on the beach that makes up a person.

Children need to truly understand that they are innately deserving of love because of who they are, and that love should never be subjected to conditions such as their grades or athletic prowess. If that were not true, only those children (and adults) who are fortunate enough to master everything would be deserving of love, and if by now you don't understand the absurdity of that idea, then you need to reread this book, maybe a few times.

We must not avoid measuring children's levels of achievement because we are afraid to hurt their feelings. The world does not work that way and we are responsible for preparing the future generations of this world to live happily in it. I am a firm believer in giving children roots and wings. This means we need to help them to understand their inherent value and we must also help them to grow up to be independent, and that includes being able to bounce back from disappointments and struggles and failures, so that they do not come to define themselves by those unavoidable situations in life. We cannot depend on schools to do this. It is up to us as parents to teach our children that their value is constant and permanent and no failure or success in life can alter that. This is a responsibility we must take seriously.

Children must learn that when they compare themselves to others they can always find those who do better and those who do worse. A comparison is not an accurate measurement of their own value; it is just an illustration of the fact that each one of us is unique. If God did not intend for a child to be an academic scholar or a star athlete, that in no way indicates that they have not been perfectly planned to be exactly who they are. He is infinitely wise and has planned for every one of us to excel in some ways and not in others. Our gifts may not become evident at the exact moment that we wish them to, but that does not mean that they are not there, or that we have any less value than someone else whose gifts are very visible.

Just as God does not decide who will go to heaven based on their "good works," He does not decide who deserves to be loved based on what their particular talents are. He made us all deserving of love,

His and ours. He created us in His image and made each one of us precious and absolutely irreplaceable.

No matter how smart you are, you are not smarter than God, and you do not know better than He does. For you to say your are worthless is to fly in the face of God, the one true Father, the only perfect parent there has ever been. It is to tell Him that He was wrong and that He screwed up when He made you, for you are certain that you are some kind of a mistake He made. He does not make mistakes and you are not the only exception to this unalterable truth.

If you have even an inkling
of wonder,
learn to listen
to the stillness in your soul.
That silence is
the absence of God.
What you do not hear
is your hearts longing
and God calling for you.
For no matter who you are
or what you've done,
there are no small souls,
no spindly spirits,
only those who are yet unreached,
hidden and cloaked
behind a thin veil of disbelief,
waiting for someone to become
that angel God would send
for their healing,
armed with blessed words,
loving hands
and a faithful heart.
Yes, if you have wondered,
then you are waiting,

*even if you have not only been
driven to sin,
but driven by sin,
and even if the sin is so great
that it would have
all the dead eyes weeping,
God is still calling you.
For there is a commingling
of good and evil
that stirs within us all.
There are demonic tendencies
flirting inside all of us,
but they are no match
for the enormity of
God's mercy.
So though Satan draws his weapon
of temptation upon you,
be assured
that God will be there
to wield His love,
and it is not so much
that you need to call Him
as it is that you need
to answer His call.*

I hope and I pray that the wisdom I have gained from all the pain I have endured and all the work I undertook to heal my heart, my soul, and my life will inspire you and help you to do the same. May the end of this book find you somewhere down the road, having already embarked upon your own journey to joy.

I don't believe in auras,
but at times I swear
I can see the colors
of people's lives.
I see some are paled
by their timidity,
their unassuredness.
They are barely brushed
with colors designed
to blend in with the throngs
of conforming spectators
on the sidelines,
in the grandstands
and bleachers of this world.
Oh to be sure,
some have fifty yard line seats
way down in front,
close enough to smell
what they see,
though still out of reach,
while other's colors are so muted,
such dull earth tones
and meek grays,
they are indistinguishable,
way off in the cheap seats.
But me,
I want to live a life of crimson.
I want to be right there
on the field of life,
even when it's a battlefield.
I want to slash my scarlet scent
boldly across the play,
to gleam vermilion
in the center of it all.
I want to wash my color
over the world,
to let it run beneath the surface

of everything,
the passion of my living
flowing like a river
cut deep into the landscape
of the mob.
I want to be bold.
I demand to be bright.
I refuse to submerge
into the background
or to skulk among the crowd
of bound and envious onlookers.
I will not be taupe
or charcoal,
not beige or even mauve.
No, I will live life
blood red!

Victoria O'Kane can be reached by e-mail at *okaneabc123@aol.com*. She may also be available for teaching workshops and seminars or doing other speaking engagements on the content of this book.

CPSIA information can be obtained
at www.ICGtesting.com
Printed in the USA
LVHW052216131118
596831LV00007B/669/P

9 780692 993248